Perennials

TIME
LIFE
BOOKS

THE TIME-LIFE ENCYCLOPAEDIA OF GARDENING

Perennials

by

James Underwood Crockett

and

the Editors of TIME-LIFE BOOKS

Watercolour Illustrations by

Allianora Rosse

TIME-LIFE INTERNATIONAL (NEDERLAND) B.V.

THE TIME-LIFE ENCYCLOPAEDIA OF GARDENING

SERIES EDITOR: Robert M. Jones
EDITORIAL STAFF FOR PERENNIALS:
Text Editor: Jay Brennan
Picture Editor: Sheila Osmundsen
Designer: Leonard Wolfe
Staff Writers: Helen Barer, Marian Gordon Goldman, Lee Greene, Gerry Schremp
Chief Researcher: David L. Harrison
Researchers: Edward Albert, Gail Cruikshank, Helen Fennell, Bea Hsia, Catherine Ireys, Shirley Miller, Mary Kay Moran, Sandra Streepey
Design Assistant: Anne B. Landry

EUROPEAN EDITION
Editor: Kit van Tulleken
Picture Editor: Pamela Marke
Assistant Picture Editor: Anne Angus
Design Consultant: Louis Klein
Text Editor: Simon Rigge
Text Researcher: Jasmine Taylor
Picture Researchers: Judy Aspinall, Milly Trowbridge
Designer: Joyce Mason
Design Assistant: Shirin Patel
Copy Staff: Ingrid Larssen

ISBN 7054 0551 6

THE AUTHOR: **James Underwood Crockett** is an eminent American horticulturist and writer on gardening subjects. A graduate of the University of Massachusetts' Stockbridge School of Agriculture, he has lived in—and cultivated a wide variety of plants in—California, New York, Texas and New England and has served as a consultant to many nurseries and landscapers.

CONSULTANT, EUROPEAN EDITION: **Frances Perry** is a well known gardening authority whose books and broadcasts have gained her an international reputation. She is a member of the Linnean Society, and was the first woman to be elected to the Council of the Royal Horticultural Society, whose coveted Victoria medal of Honour she holds. She has lectured in Australia, New Zealand and America and has collected plants in such diverse areas as Lapland, Africa and South America.

GENERAL EUROPEAN CONSULTANTS **Roy Hay** is a horticulturist well known for his articles in English publications, including a weekly column in *The Times* newspaper, and for his monthly contribution to the French magazine *L'Ami des Jardins*. He carries on a family gardening tradition—his father, Thomas Hay was Superintendent of the Central Royal Parks in London (1922-1940). Mr. Hay is an Officer of L'Ordre du Merite Agricole of Belgium and France. **André Leroy** is the emeritus chief engineer for the Paris parks and gardens. Since 1958 he has been technical consultant for the magazine *Mon Jardin et Ma Maison*. **Dieneke van Raalte** studied horticulture and landscape gardening at the college of gardening in Fredrikscord in The Netherlands. She is a regular contributor to European gardening magazines and is the author of many Dutch gardening books. **Hans-Dieter Ihlenfeldt** is Professor of Botany at the Institute of General Botany and Botanical Gardening in Hamburg. He is the co-editor of several botanical handbooks and has published in scientific journals. **Heinrich Nothdurft** is chief custodian of the Botanic Garden and lectures at the Institute of Botany in Hamburg. He is co-author of the handbook *Mitteleuropäische Pflanzenwelt* (Flora of Central Europe).

THE ILLUSTRATOR: Allianora Rosse, who provided 128 of the 154 delicate, precise watercolours of perennials beginning on page 90 is a specialist in flower painting. Miss Rosse was trained at the Art Academy of The Hague in The Netherlands, and her illustrations of shrubs, trees and flowers have appeared in many gardening books.

GENERAL CONSULTANTS: Dr. C. Gustav Hard, Professor, University of Minnesota, St. Paul, Minn. Louis B. Martin, President, Chicago Horticultural Society. Albert P. Nordheden, Morganville, New Jersey. Staff of the Brooklyn Botanic Garden: Robert S. Tomson, Assistant Director; George A. Kalmbacher, Plant Taxonomist; Edmund O. Moulin, Horticulturist.

THE COVER: The late-summer colours of a perennial border make a striking combination: red, pink and yellow day lilies, deep lavender balloon flowers and on the left, flat golden heads of *Achillea*, or fern-leaved yarrow.

Portions of this book were written by Henry Moscow. Instructional drawings are the work of Matt Greene. Valuable assistance was provided by the following departments and individuals of Time Inc.: Editorial production, Norman Airey; Library, Benjamin Lightman; Picture Collection, Doris O'Neil; Photographic Laboratory, George Karas; TIME-LIFE News Service, Murray J. Gart; Correspondents, Maria Vincenza Aloisi (Paris), Jane Estes (Seattle), Margot Hapgood (London), Ann Natanson (Rome).

CONTENTS

The flowers that bloom year after year

Among the most rewarding traits of perennials is the fact that they come up unprompted year after year to offer the garden masses of colour in uninterrupted but ever-changing patterns from March to November. Perennials flower abundantly and multiply without being coaxed. Most of them are easy to grow. Some require spadework occasionally, but many will tolerate considerable neglect. In fact, one can see long-neglected gardens in Britain and Europe where broken paving and tumbled walls are adorned with centranthus, peonies and acanthus, thriving and spreading.

The perennials are numerous and diverse; they include such garden mainstays as delphiniums, columbines and daisies, and such oddities as cimicifugas with their curious spikes of white flowers that resemble bottle brushes. Some of the best of them appear at the very time that the garden needs them most. When the tulips and daffodils have faded and summer annuals still are seedlings, the bushy peony, the stately iris and the alluring, hairy-leaved Oriental poppy rise to perform spectacularly. And when autumn frosts and gales have driven everything else off-stage, chrysanthemums and Michaelmas daisies remain to flaunt their colours in a grand finale of the gardening year.

A perennial, in the broadest horticultural definition, is any plant that lives for three or more years. The definition covers a lot of species, embracing both dandelions and giant redwoods and thousands of species in between. But when gardeners talk about perennials, they almost always mean—as does this book—flowering garden plants with stems that are herbaceous (fleshy rather than woody) and that usually die down to the soil's surface before winter, while the roots remain alive and ready to send up new growth the next season. (Technically, bulbous plants such as tulips and daffodils are perennials, but they are generally classified separately because of their method of storing food for next year's growth.)

The main characteristic of perennials that sets them apart from annuals and from biennials—which make good companions

With the aid of a lantern, Japanese ladies admire chrysanthemums at night in a garden pavilion. Chrysanthemums, among the earliest perennials cultivated, have been raised in the Orient for 2,000 years.

for perennials and which are also covered in this book—is the durability of their roots. Annuals sprout from seed, bloom, bear fresh seed with which to reproduce, and die—all in a single year. Biennials, which include sweet william, foxglove, Canterbury bell and wallflower, also sprout from seed, but spend their first year growing and their second year flowering and producing seed—and then die. Many herbaceous perennials do produce seeds annually, but others do so only sporadically; they concentrate their efforts towards survival in their roots, often spreading them through the soil to multiply the species.

A LONG-LIVED FAMILY   A typical example is the herbaceous peony (*Paeonia officinalis*). It is native to eastern Europe and was widespread along the Mediterranean coastline in pre-Christian times. Double forms were known early in history in colours of dark red, deep rose and white, and were described by Pliny as the "oldest of plants". When the double forms reached the West in the 16th Century they were warmly acclaimed by gardeners; by 1551 William Turner was saying that they were "common thorow out all England", and in 1597 John Gerard reported: "all the sorts of Peionies do grow in our London gardens, except the double Peiony with white flowres, which we do expect from the Low-countries or Flanders". These same garden forms are today some of Europe's most valuable garden perennials; easy to grow and reliable on almost any type of soil. Instances are known where peonies have remained in the same garden for over 50 years.

Acanthus, the plant which inspired the architectural design for the Greek Corinthian capital, is another long-lived perennial. It will resist competition from other plants, the occasional beheading with a hoe and even extreme neglect. There are, of course, many others, like day lilies (*Hemerocallis*), veratrums and helianthus, as well as the gas plant (*Dictamnus albus*). All of these bloom on and on.

Not all perennials, however, live as long as those mentioned above. Delphiniums, for example, may thrive for as long as eight years where both winters and summers are moderate, but survive only a year where the climate is hot. Still, most perennials grow well in most parts of Britain and continental Europe; in regions where the weather is too warm for some of them, others will flourish. On the warm Mediterranean coasts, for example, day lilies do beautifully and some other perennials thrive, including coreopsis, acanthus, cotton lavender (*Santolina*), mallows and pearl everlasting (*Anaphalis*). The cooler northern areas do not lack for perennials either. It is true that such delicate plants as gazanias will not grow there, but peonies flourish. So do Oriental poppies, garden phlox, bearded irises, asters, chrysanthemums and many others.

Some perennials change their life styles to adapt to their

surroundings. Petunias and snapdragons are perennials in mild climates, but in cold regions their roots perish. So they must be grown and treated as annuals, sowing fresh seed each year. Conversely, some annuals become biennials and some biennials become short-lived perennials in regions where winters are mild. In addition, different varieties of some species, such as hollyhocks and forget-me-nots, may be annuals, biennials or perennials. Anomalies such as these make gardening more challenging and, to the dedicated gardener, more fun.

A perennial garden is a long-term and never static project that, ideally, incorporates both permanence and constant change. Its objective is to present a pleasant and even exalting array of colour from early spring to late autumn. But it is a rare perennial that blooms throughout the growing season. That is the first challenge—to obtain continuity of colour by planting different varieties to bloom harmoniously at different times.

SOME BASIC GOALS

Another challenge is to keep different types of perennials from overcrowding one another in the same beds and creating a horticultural slum. Some highly desirable perennials notably Michaelmas daisies, spread so fast that their population explosion requires drastic control measures, including regular digging up and division of the roots. Other equally desirable perennials never outgrow their allotted space, provided that they are given enough of it when they are planted. One such is the peony. Another is dictamnus, the gas plant, which has confined itself for more than 50 years to the same flower bed in The Fellows Garden of St. John's College at Oxford University.

This plant, which has dark green leaves and 45 to 60 centimetre ($1\frac{1}{2}$ to 2 ft) spikes of white or rosy-purple flowers, also secretes a highly volatile lemon-scented oil. This becomes apparent directly the foliage, seed pods or stems are handled: if a lighted match is held near the plant on a still day, the oil can be ignited without injury to the plant.

Most gardeners can spare only a few hours a week for their plants—and therein lies a third challenge: to obtain maximum results with minimum work. Before you begin to think of specific plants, or even of the overall colour and form that the garden will take, consider its potential sites from a purely practical viewpoint. Good perennial gardens require free circulation of air; plant diseases thrive in stagnant air, particularly when the weather is humid. They require, for the most part, abundant sunshine; some perennials, such as day lilies, columbines and leopard's-bane, will tolerate shade and some, such as Japanese anemones, plantain lilies, yellow corydalis, dicentras and *Brunnera macrophylla*, will thrive in it. But the majority will grow spindly stems with few flowers and fall victim to infections without ample sun. Finally, good perennial gardens require properly prepared soil—soil that is both well-drained and sufficiently moisture-retentive so that it will not bake hard; soil that is rich enough to withstand years of demand on its nutritive content. Most important of all, perennials need soil that is open and loose enough in structure to permit air as well as moisture to reach the roots; useful soil bacteria that assist the nutritional processes of plants cannot live without air. Not all gardens offer such ideal conditions naturally, but given the air circulation and sunshine, you can create the other essentials. (The preparation and maintenance of soil suitable for perennials is discussed at length in Chapter 2.)

LOCATING YOUR BEDS

Once you know whether you can grow perennials in your garden, consider where you should grow them, that is, where they will look their best. They ought, if possible, to be visible from the house and perhaps from the terrace or porch to increase your enjoyment of them. Because perennials bloom profusely and colourfully, the majority are most effective in masses, but they also serve very well when planted in small clumps to accent the hues of other flowers. They surpass themselves when they have a dark background that draws attention to them rather than to a distant landscape or, more likely in these days of suburban living, the house next door. One of the finest plantings of Christmas roses that I have seen—a Christmas rose is a lovely little plant with evergreen leaves and 7.5 centimetre (3 in.) white blossoms that open in late winter or early spring—snuggles in a corner backed by the dark green of yews. Many other evergreens as well as deciduous hedges, vine-covered walls and fences make first-rate backgrounds for perennials.

In Victorian England it used to be considered akin to indecent exposure to plant perennials in anything but a long,

A penchant for Perennials

Perennials have long been a favourite subject of flower painters the world over. In England during the 19th Century, demand for information about how to cultivate and care for perennials sprang up as gardeners began to specialize in formal herbaceous borders. To help meet this demand two volumes of the six volume The Ladies' Flower Garden, *one of the most popular illustrated gardening series of the day, were devoted to perennials. It is from the original 1843 edition of 'Ornamental Perennials' that the hand coloured lithographs reproduced on the following pages have been taken. They are the work of Jane Loudon* (left), *wife of the eminent horticulturist John Claudius Loudon. She not only illustrated all the volumes, but wrote them as well.*

A cluster of perennials from The Ladies Flower Garden *includes the once popular* Sida malvaeflora *(number six), now known as* Sidalcea malvaeflora. *A native of California, it was grown in many 19th-Century conservatories.*

Jane Loudon (1807-1858)

Pl.29.

1. *Hibiscus Moscheutos* _2. *Lavatera triloba* _3. *Lavatera Thuringiaca* _4. *Nuttalia digitata*.
5. *Nuttalia Papaver* _6 *Sida Malvaflora* _7 *Crotarea coccinea*.

Day & Haghe Lith to the Queen.

MONKSHOODS

CRANE'S-BILLS

BELLFLOWERS

COLUMBINES

LUPINS

1 Dianthus arbuscula — 2 Dianthus Caucasicus — 3 Dianthus Virgineus — 4 Dianthus Alpinus
5 Dianthus Liburnicus — 6 Dianthus Arenarius — 7 Dianthus Saxicaris

PINKS

1 Convolvulus sepium Americanus — 2 Convolvulus reniformis — 3 Convolvulus Bryoniafolia
4 Ipomœa bilobata — 5 Ipomœa cuculelata

CONVOLVULUS

1 Antirrhinum majus, var. Quadricolor — 2 Antirrhinum majus, var. stipula albida
3 Antirrhinum Barrani

SNAPDRAGONS

straight border, 2.5 to 4 metres (8 to 12 ft) wide, or to mix perennials with other plants such as annuals and biennials. The idea of the herbaceous border—consisting of plants of like nature—caught on after 1890 when Phillip Nicholson, Curator of the Royal Botanic Gardens, Kew, advised in his *Illustrated Dictionary of Gardening* that "the best results are obtained when the border is made up of hardy herbaceous perennials". The British climate suits perennials and Nicholson's suggestion proved highly successful. It was fostered by two great gardeners and prolific writers, Gertrude Jekyll and William Robinson.

In the earliest borders it was fashionable to mix a variety of colours, on the principle of medieval stained glass windows or richly woven tapestries. As more and more borders were laid out, a greater variety of planting schemes evolved. Single colour borders became popular in which all the flowers had white blooms, for example, or shades of blue. Some of these single-colour borders can still be seen today, notably the white borders at Crathes Castle in Scotland and Sissinghurst in Kent, and the orange and red borders at Hidcote in Gloucestershire.

Among the other variations are seasonal borders designed for peak viewing at a particular time of year. They have become the favourites of gardeners with holiday homes. You can also choose perfumed borders, in which all the plants have fragrant flowers or leaves; green borders containing mainly foliage plants and grasses; and non-staking borders where all the plants are sturdy enough to stand on their own without ties or artificial support.

There have been many swings between order and informality in the history of gardening, and many people no longer think it necessary to restrict perennials to the herbaceous border. Just as Johanna Schopenhaven, writing in 1812 about the 18th-Century formality of so many continental gardens, affirmed that "you find everything there except Nature", so gardeners nowadays are tending towards the cottage garden tradition. In such gardens perennials were grouped informally—even haphazardly—among shrubs or annuals or else relegated to wild parts of the garden. You greatly increase your options if you plant perennials in various kinds of beds and if you mix them with other flowers, so I am for putting them wherever they will look good and grow well without getting in each other's way—beside the front door to add colour to an all-green permanent planting, in a strip beside the garage, mingled with flowering shrubs or wherever else the conditions of sun, air and soil permit.

Most perennials, like other garden flowers, can also be grown in portable tubs and other containers, or in beds raised above the ground level. One gardener I know apparently took to heart the words attributed to a monk who lived 1,200 years ago: "Stooping is the worst thing for the ageing gardener, and how can one escape the backache except by raising the beds?" My friend, who had retired, used railway sleepers to build a raised bed rising 1 metre (3 ft) above the level of his lawn, and he grows his perennials there.

Certain perennials are natural plants for rock gardens and walls. A cousin of mine, who had no railway sleepers, but did have a stone retaining wall which supported a bank of soil, made the wall and the space on top of it into a perennial garden. The wall is of stone blocks, laid without mortar, and she has set moss phlox (*Phlox subulata*) and rock cress (*Aubrieta*) to grow between the stones and flow down the wall's face.

A few of the larger perennials can be used in small groups or even standing alone, filling a spot that might otherwise be occupied by a flowering shrub or evergreen. I have seen a plume poppy (*Macleaya*)—a plant that may grow 3 metres (10 ft) tall and bears huge plumes of small, feathery, creamy-white blossoms— towering beside a wrought-iron gate. Its huge grey-green leaves and airy millinery made a striking complement to the tracery of the dark ironwork.

In planning any major planting of perennials, it is a good idea first to work out its location, size, shape and combination of plants with pencil and paper. Start conservatively. Grandiose dreams by a fireplace in midwinter may be shattered in spring, summer and autumn, for even undemanding gardens need some weeding, some fertilizing and some loosening of the soil.

If you are planning a perennial bed that backs on to a hedge, wall or fence, leave at least 60 centimetres (2 ft) of space between it and its back-drop, and make it from 2 to 2.5 metres (6 to 8 ft) wide. There are good reasons for both suggestions. Where the bed lies in front of a hedge, the space will prevent competition between the plants' roots and those of the shrubbery; it will also allow for circulation of air and will give you room to work at the bed's rear. In addition, it will help to preserve the hedge's looks, because if the hedge's lower branches are shaded all summer by tall perennials, they will eventually die, leaving ugly gaps that will prove all too noticeable in winter. This holds true for plants set in smaller clumps close to evergreens and shrubs; give them breathing space too. Walls and fences, of course do not compete for soil nutrients or suffer from shading, but the 60 centimetre (2 ft) leeway is still a good idea because the plants need circulating air and room for their roots, and you need room to work at the back of them. Remember too that brick, stone and concrete walls, particularly those facing south or west, will reflect or absorb and re-radiate the heat of the sun. This may make conditions too warm for some plants. For one thing, the warmth can induce plants to sprout prematurely in spring, only to be nipped or even killed by late frosts.

PLANNING ON PAPER

Primrose: gem of the rock garden

The tiny primrose requires little space: the 25 varieties pictured here could all be grown together in a modest rock garden wherever the climate is suitably cool and moist. There are approximately 500 species of primrose (*Primula*)—all related to the wild primroses that grow in mountains and meadows from the Alps to the Himalayas—and in the hands of growers these have given rise to countless cultivars and hybrids. The diversity of primroses can be judged from this sampling of categories. The numbered varieties include the eye-catching auriculas (1-7), first bred from alpine flowers more than 400 years ago, as well as species primroses (9-12), little changed from their wild flower ancestors. The polyanthus (13-19) has clusters of flowers on a long stem; the acaulis (23-25), or English primrose, bears a single flower on a short stem. The garryarde (8) is a short-stemmed polyanthus hybrid from Ireland with unusual dark foliage, while the juliana (20-22) is a creeper that thrives in rocky crevices.

The width of the bed from front to back is as important in your plan as the 60 centimetre (2 ft) space behind it, because the ease with which one can obtain continuous colour in a perennial bed increases in direct proportion to the width. Suppose you made the bed 1 metre (3 ft) wide. It could comfortably accommodate only two rows of plants, say low sweet williams in front and taller chrysanthemums at the back. The sweet williams would cease flowering in July and the chrysanthemums would show only green foliage until early autumn, leaving the bed colourless most of the summer. But a bed 2 to 2.5 metres (6 to 8 ft) wide will provide room for as many as six different kinds of plants from front to rear, and if you use early, mid-season and later flowering varieties, the bed can display colour continuously.

When you are planning the width of the bed and allowing for the needed open space at the rear, you should at the same time consider the area in front. Perennials have a way of growing exuberantly—that is one of their charms—and frequently plants in the foreground will billow over the edges of the bed. If the bed is fronted by a lawn, as is often the case, mowing close to the bed becomes difficult or impossible and the grass grows up messily through the plants. The best solution is a broad edging or separating strip, over which the plants can spill with abandon without creating maintenance problems. This edging can be a garden path, or a single or double row of bricks laid flat and perpendicular to the line of the bed, or a 30 to 45 centimetre (1 to 1½ ft) strip of flagstones, or a heavy decorative mulch such as gravel or granite chips. The irregular incursions of the plants on to this edging strip merely add to the natural informality of the garden; moreover, grass is easily mowed without hand trimming if one wheel of the lawn mower is run along the strip.

CHOOSING PLANTS

Once you have determined the location and shape of your beds, you can start considering specific flowers. The illustrations and notes in the encyclopaedia chapter (*pages 91-150*) show you what they look like and how and where they can be grown, and the chart on pages 151-154 provides a ready reference to height, colour, flowering season and preferences in light. Choose your plants sparingly. In large gardens there is room for a great variety of plants, even those that bloom briefly, because they can be surrounded by others that will take over later. But the small garden cannot afford such luxury; every plant must pay its way by flowering for a long time and by displaying ornamental foliage after the flowers fade.

The first step in laying out plants in a perennial bed is to try to think of them not as individual plants, but as masses of shapes and colours, both of flowers and foliage, which, appearing at various seasons, allow you to paint an ever-changing garden picture. Simplicity should be the keynote; intricate designs

PLANNING A PERENNIAL BORDER

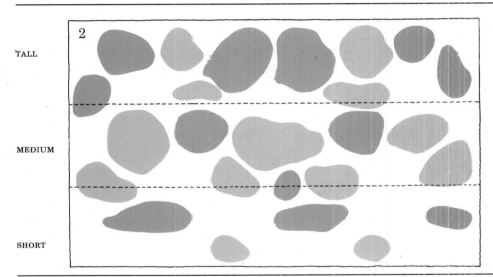

TALL

MEDIUM

SHORT

AUTUMN

To make sure of an attractive combination of flowers blooming in a perennial border through spring, summer and autumn, sketch the locations of plants on sheets of tracing paper laid over an outline of the bed. On the first sheet select tall late-flowering varieties (see the encyclopaedia, pages 91-150, and the chart on pages 151-154); draw these in as clumps (dark green) spaced along the back. Then add complementary autumn plants (also indicated in dark green), placing medium-sized ones in the centre and short ones at the front.

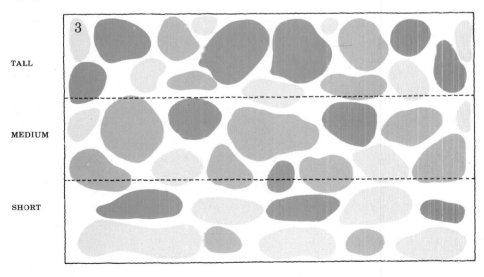

TALL

MEDIUM

SHORT

SUMMER

On a second sheet of tracing paper laid over the first, plan your mid-season blooms. Since most plants that flower in summer are medium-sized, select these first as your main display; draw them in as clumps, concentrating them in the centre of the bed and locating the plants (indicated in paler green) in some of the open areas not already occupied by the autumn flowers. Then place at the front and back a few short and tall summer-blooming perennials whose colours will complement the flowers you have chosen for the centre.

TALL

MEDIUM

SHORT

SPRING

On a third sheet of tracing paper laid over the other two, plan your spring-blooming plants (light green) in the remaining spaces. As most spring perennials are short, they naturally look best at the front of the bed. Some medium-sized and tall spring-flowering plants should be interspersed in the centre and back. Now you can trace the outlines of your autumn and summer displays through to the top sheet, or a fresh sheet, as a final buying and planting plan, filling in any remaining gaps with bulbs or annuals in desired quantities.

usually fail to come off as well in reality as they do on paper, and they add measurably to maintenance. Colour should be used in bold groups, not spotted here and there. Bright colours such as orange and red, however, have to be handled with some skill; most gardeners use them less lavishly than they do pastels, saving them as accent colours here and there to bring life to the more subtle shades.

DRAWING THE PLAN
In planning the garden's fine points, you must carry a number of different factors in your head simultaneously, so it is a good idea to use a sketch pad to keep them straight. I find it useful to make three copies of my plan, each depicting the garden at a different peak season, to permit me to envisage the changes that will take place as new flowers open and old ones fade (*drawings, page 19*). Some gardeners cut out pictures from garden catalogues or magazines and move them about on their plans to give them a rough idea of various effects. Others use bits of coloured paper, and some even fill in planting areas with coloured crayons.

Whether or not you use such aids, I suggest you work backwards. It might seem logical to plan flowers first for spring, then for summer and autumn, and to work from the front of the bed to the back. You can do this if you know your plants well, but I find it easier to work the other way round, going from October to May, and from the back of the bed to the front. The reason is fairly simple. In the most common kind of bed or border against the hedge or wall, the tallest plants, 1 metre (3 ft) or more high, naturally go at the back (with a few placed forward here and there to dramatize them as accents and to avoid monotony). Since the majority of tall plants flower in late summer or autumn, they are logically the backbone of the late-season garden. You will have a wide choice that includes Michaelmas daisies, tall chrysanthemums, sunflowers, Japanese anemones and boltonias. With the help of the encyclopaedia, decide on a tall autumn-flowering plant that particularly appeals to you; one that will grow well in your climate and the sun and soil conditions of your bed. Working from left to right (simply because that is the way you read and write and is easiest for most people), place one group of this type of plant at the rear left of the bed, then establish a pattern by placing a second group of the same plant in the rear centre and a third at the rear right. With autumn colour assured for the back of the bed, move to the centre and select one or two types of middle-sized autumn-flowering plants, in the 60 to 90 centimetre (2 to 3 ft) range, that will go well with those in the back row when both are in bloom; repeat these, too, at intervals. Two favourites here would be pompon chrysanthemums and late phlox. In the front of the border, select one or two smaller autumn-blooming plants such as *Sedum spectabile* or penstemon, which will complement those in the middle and back rows.

Now move to summer-flowering plants. The emphasis here will probably be on the middle of the border, because the majority of the most spectacular plants that bloom in summer are in the middle height range of 60 to 90 centimetres (2 to 3 ft): Shasta daisies, day lilies, foxgloves, salvias, heleniums and garden phlox. Choose among these or others mentioned in the encyclopaedia, setting groups of them to the left, centre and right of the middle row. Then fill in your summer garden picture with some taller back-row accents such as the globe thistle and heliopsis and a few spots of colour in the front row—lamb's tongue and catmint, for example.

Now move to spring-flowering plants. Here the emphasis will be on the front of the border, because the majority of plants that bloom at this season are low growing, under 60 centimetres (2 ft). Try to choose plants that not only bloom early, but that either bloom over a long period or retain attractive foliage after the flowers have faded so that they will continue to adorn the garden; the front of a bed or border, after all, is a highly conspicuous part of the overall design. Hybrid bleeding hearts, for example, are a good choice because they start blooming early and continue to bloom most of the summer; many pinks not only flower a long time but keep their handsome grey-green leaves through the growing season. Having established the main spring-blooming pattern at the front of the border, fill in the middle and back rows with other spring-flowering plants such as columbines and doronicums.

After a certain amount of experimenting on paper to arrive at the best combination, you can draw up a master planting plan, indicating the names, quantities and positioning of individual plants. From this you can make a shopping list of the plants you need to start your garden before turning to your local nursery, garden centre or your mail order catalogue. You may not want or be able to buy all of them at once, but with a plan as a guide you will at least be able to develop your plantings over a period of two or three years with some goal in mind, filling in bare spots with inexpensive annuals as the need arises, trying different combinations of colours and textures, making additions and corrections as you go. And that process of developing, experimenting and changing in perennial gardens can be half the fun.

WHERE TO SEE PERENNIALS
Gardeners can see outstanding collections of perennials—newly developed strains, uncommon kinds and established borders—at the major European flower shows, botanic gardens, National Trust properties and in many private gardens open to the public. Good collections are on view at various seasons at the following centres:

GREAT BRITAIN
Flower Shows:
Royal Horticultural Shows at Vincent Square, Westminster; Chelsea Flower Show; Shrewsbury Floral Fete; Southport Flower Show; Cardiff Horticultural Show
Botanic Gardens:
Kew; Edinburgh; Glasnevin (Dublin); Liverpool
Gardens:
Royal Horticultural Society Gardens, Wisley, Surrey; Harlow Car; National Trust gardens; private gardens
Nurseries:
Bressingham Gardens, Diss, Norfolk; Carliles. Twyford, Berks

FRANCE
Botanic Gardens:
Jardin des Plantes, Paris
Gardens:
Villa Roquebrunne, Cap Martin; Parc Floral, Orleans La Source

BELGIUM
Ghent Floralies; Salon du Jardin, Brussels

HOLLAND
Botanic Gardens:
Leiden; Wageningen; Amsterdam
Gardens:
Westbroekpark, The Hague
Nursery:
Ruys, Dedemsvaart

GERMANY
Botanic Gardens:
Bremen; Munich; Berlin—Dahlem Hamburg; Nordpark, Düsseldorf; Palmengarten, Frankfurt

The fine art of bordermaking

Among the most pleasant garden sights are beds of perennials lining the paths, lawns and terraces of thousands of homes, sending forth waves of colour from early spring until the frosts of autumn. Natural as they generally look in their surroundings, these planting schemes originated during the 19th-Century Victorian era in England. They were conceived by William Robinson, an influential gardening writer who felt that the ornate geometrical designs then in fashion, often filled with plants from distant lands, were unnatural and excessive. Instead, he championed the use of long straight-sided beds, which he called borders, planted with inexpensive and easy-to-grow perennials, many of them bred from native wild flowers like the common daisy and columbine. "There is no arrangement of flowers more graceful, varied, or capable of giving more delight, and none so easily adapted to almost every kind of garden," he wrote in 1883.

This free, informal credo was soon picked up by Gertrude Jekyll, a talented artist and gardener of the day who transformed border making from a concept into a practical horticultural art. In some 350 borders that she designed around the turn of the century, Miss Jekyll perfected the technique of blending and contrasting many different types of flowers as well as foliage. She also advocated the practice of mixing into perennial gardens other kinds of flowers—bulbs, annuals and biennials—that she felt were "right in colour and that make a brave show where a brave show is wanted". From the end of the 19th Century interest in the perennial borders quickened and nurseries specializing in hardy plants were established. One of the largest and most complete was Thomas Ware's establishment in Tottenham, North London, where many famous nurserymen received their early training.

Most gardeners today want not only a brave, but an extremely varied show. They generally follow Miss Jekyll's practices and aim to provide a succession of blooms from spring to autumn. But no two borders are quite alike; the enormous diversity of sizes, shapes, colours, foliage and blooming cycles among perennials gives each gardener almost unlimited material with which to suit his own taste. Whatever his choice, the flowers he selects will have one thing in common: they will repeat their performance faithfully the next year, and the next, and the next.

The perennial borders of a garden path, seen in late summer, are dominated by plantings of pale pink and mauve phlox.

Planning a succession of blooms

By choosing perennials with an eye to their flowering times, a gardener can plan his border to provide blooms whenever he wishes. He can, for example, plant a border that will bloom only in spring and autumn if he normally goes away during the summer—and at his holiday home he may enjoy another border planted only with summer-blooming perennials. Or if he is at home most of the summer he can plan a perennial border that will be filled with flowers from spring to autumn, simply by selecting and locating plants—including some bulbs and annuals—to bloom in the desired succession. Gardeners with only one border can nevertheless appreciate many different patterns as it matures and alters over time. The four pictures below, each showing the same border, indicate how such planning produces a garden that changes strikingly with the seasons.

SPRING

Early-blooming irises, in purple, white, yellow and lavender, dominate the border in front of the first red spikes of lupins. In the foreground are white petunias and marguerites (both grown as annuals in northern gardens).

EARLY SUMMER

The lupins and the blue spikes of delphiniums emerge from behind the foliage of the faded irises. In front of the border are white sweet williams (foreground), pink border carnations and contrasting maroon sweet williams.

MIDSUMMER

The rear of the border blooms with tall clumps of deep pink bergamots behind pink and white phlox. In the foreground are clumps of white feverfew. Bright colours are provided by such annuals as red snapdragons and orange-red salvias.

AUTUMN

Clusters of low-growing, late-blooming chrysanthemums at the front lead off the border's final show of the year. Behind them and in the foreground taller pink dahlias, growing from tubers, replace the summer annuals.

Choosing shapes and colours

The huge family of perennials includes virtually every flower shape and colour known; below are the delicate cup-like blossoms of pink Oriental poppies, on the page on the right are the bristly spheres of pale blue globe thistles, the daisy-like rays of yellow rudbeckia and the flowering spikes of pinkish-purple lythrum. But such a bonanza can also be a challenge for the gardener planning a perennial border. For while some shapes and colours go well together, others clash; some look best when massed, others when loosely grouped. In planning a border, many gardeners work much as a designer does, mixing and matching sizes, shapes and colours—and keeping in mind good combinations of flowers and foliage. Often the most effective combinations are the simplest, like the understated, but striking juxtaposition pictured on the following pages.

The spectacular but short-lived blooms of the Oriental poppy, seen here against a background of distinctively shaped irises, are often 20 cm (8 in.) or more in diameter; the plants should be widely spaced to provide the best effect.

The rudbeckia, or coneflower, with daisy-like blossoms 7.5 to 10 cm (3 to 4 in.) across, is a relative of the black-eyed Susan. Planted in a mass, as seen here, it provides a brilliant splash of colour.

The bright spikes of lythrums, which grow up to 1.2 metres (4 ft) tall, make a handsome display in small airy clusters. They look best when used as a background for short rounded plants.

The globe thistle—whose botanical name Echinops means "hedgehog-like"—is an unusual midsummer perennial that grows 1 to 1.5 metres (3 to 4 ft) tall. Planted in small groups, it provides a striking accent.

The tiny-flowered plumes of astilbe, or false spiraea, lend a pleasing contrast to the foliage of a perennial border in midsummer.

Astilbe, which comes in many colours, also provides a lacy screen to plants with larger individual blossoms such as Shasta daisies.

SPRING March and April	LATE SPRING April and May	EARLY SUMMER June
DOMINANT FLOWER LEOPARD'S BANE	ORIENTAL POPPY	CHINESE PEONY

TALL

		DELPHINIUM TALL BEARDED IRIS
CORSICAN HELLEBORE	FOXTAIL LILY LUPIN	FOXGLOVE GIANT SCABIOUS
		MULLEIN

MEDIUM

	SOLOMON'S SEAL	PYRETHRUM SWEET WILLIAM
LENTEN ROSE	COLUMBINE GEUM	BURNING BUSH CENTRANTHUS
	PYRETHRUM	BAPTISIA

SHORT

BERGENIA	BARRENWORT	GLOBE FLOWER
LUNGWORT ENGLISH DAISY	BLEEDING HEART SIBERIAN BUGLOSS	VIOLA PINKS
POLYANTHUS	VIOLA	CORAL BELLS

30

Probably the most popular way to plan a perennial border is to build the display for each season around a favourite flower. For early spring there are a few low-growing perennials such as polyanthus primroses and evergreen candytufts, but the great burst of colour comes later with plants such as those shown here. Listed beneath each picture are plants that bloom at about the same time as the illustrated flower. Many perennials start earlier or remain in flower longer than the periods in which they are listed and a few, like coral-bells (*Heuchera*) and pinks will bloom spasmodically all summer.

MIDSUMMER July and August	LATE SUMMER September	AUTUMN September and October
FERN-LEAVED YARROW	RED HOT POKER	MICHAELMAS DAISY

CLARY HOLLYHOCK PLUME POPPY MONKSHOOD MEADOW RUE	PERENNIAL SUNFLOWER MICHAELMAS DAISY GOLDEN ROD GOLDEN GROUNDSEL MIST FLOWER	JAPANESE ANEMONE GOLDEN ROD BUGBANE
JACOB'S LADDER GERANIUM BEE BALM ASTILBE SCABIOUS PHLOX	OX-EYE CHAMOMILE HELIOPSIS CONEFLOWER PURPLE LOOSESTRIFE SNEEZEWEED PINK TURTLE-HEAD	GEUM GAILLARDIA SNEEZEWEED CHRYSANTHEMUM
PINKS CAMPANULA TREASURE FLOWER CATMINT MASTERWORT STOKES' ASTER	DWARF MICHAELMAS DAISY TREASURE FLOWER BLAZING STAR	STONE CROP LILY-TURF

A plan comes to life

After selecting a succession of dominant and companion flowers, the gardener's next step in designing a perennial border is to draw up a plan like the one on the left of this picture, indicating where each group of perennials, as well as some annuals and bulbs, will be planted. The photograph, taken in late spring, shows a seasonal combination of blossoms —white peonies, on the left and right, with tall blue Italian buglosses (*Anchusa*) behind them on the right. They are accompanied by white and pink sweet williams, which continue to bloom along the front of both borders. Later the beds will be highlighted by phlox and globe thistles. Substitutes for the buglosses could be delphiniums, which do better in moist soil, with pinks or columbines taking the place of sweet williams for more permanent effects.

1 DAHLIA (tuber)
2 ITALIAN BUGLOSS
3 LANTANA (annual)
4 SWEET WILLIAM
5 GLOBE THISTLE
6 PEONY
7 PHLOX
8 IRIS
9 LEADWORT
10 HOLLYHOCK
11 BALLOON-FLOWER
12 SHASTA DAISY
13 COLUMBINE
14 FOXGLOVE
15 ASTILBE
16 ORIENTAL POPPY
17 JACOB'S-LADDER
18 ASTER
19 BELLFLOWER
20 PANSY
21 CHRYSANTHEMUM

A double border is dominated by tall blue Italian bugloss (Anchusa). Nearest the path are clusters of white and pink sweet williams. The tall creamy-white spikes of foxgloves have begun to bloom in both borders.

When the border is a border

"Herbaceous border" has come to mean any long and narrow bed of perennials, but perhaps its most appealing form is still the original one: a band of mixed flowers and foliage flanking a swath of lawn. Along the grassy path to an ivy-covered arcade of the garden (*below*), an imaginative choice of plants—selected as much for their distinctive leaves as their blossoms—has produced a pleasant effect in muted tones of green, silver, lavender and white. Such a border is easily adapted to a garden area in which curves are more natural than straight lines—the curving border on the right, which is set against a low wall to provide a flowery frame for the garden of another home. Its evergreen-punctuated symmetry forms a striking backdrop for green grass and silver birch trees.

1 ARTEMISIA
2 SEA LAVENDER
3 IRIS
4 BLEEDING HEART
5 SUNDROP
6 DAHLIA (tuber)
7 BUTTERFLY WEED
8 PHLOX
9 PLUME POPPY
10 LILY (bulb)
11 GLOBE THISTLE
12 PEONY
13 MONKSHOOD
14 BUGBANE
15 MEADOW RUE
16 BEDSTRAW
17 BABY'S-BREATH
18 CANDYTUFT
19 ASTILBE
20 BLUE FALSE INDIGO
21 ALLIUM (bulb)
22 LAMB'S TONGUE
23 PANSY
24 BROWALLIA (annual)
25 PENSTEMON

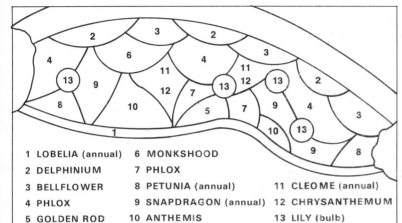

1 LOBELIA (annual) 6 MONKSHOOD
2 DELPHINIUM 7 PHLOX
3 BELLFLOWER 8 PETUNIA (annual) 11 CLEOME (annual)
4 PHLOX 9 SNAPDRAGON (annual) 12 CHRYSANTHEMUM
5 GOLDEN ROD 10 ANTHEMIS 13 LILY (bulb)

*A curving border, effectively
combining several perennials with
a variety of annuals and bulbs,
separates the small lawn from the
hidden wall of this garden. The
tall blue and purple spikes of
delphiniums and monkshoods
rise above white and red phlox in
the centre background. They will
be replaced later by autumn-
blooming chrysanthemums.*

*A muted blend of foliage and
flowers lends subtle beauty to
this double border. Contrasts of
colours are provided by plants
like the pale lavender-and-white
monkshood in the left foreground
and clumps of silvery artemisias
like the one in the right foreground. Adding bits of
brightness to the right-hand
border are the creamy plumes of
astilbes, clumps of orange-
flowered butterfly weeds and
white garden phlox. Seen in the
far left background are tall sprays
of lavender-pink meadow rues.*

Perennials in a formal garden

While perennials are not usually associated with formal garden designs, it is possible to incorporate them quite effectively in formal beds and borders like the ones shown here. These beds are made up of a relatively small number of varieties that blend well with annuals and produce compact masses of flowers of uniform size and colour. Notably absent are large and rampant types like hollyhocks and sunflowers. Yet, despite their tidiness, these beds require no more attention than the informal designs shown on the previous pages; the dominant pink phlox is one of the longest blooming and most trouble-free of the perennials. The accompanying plan for one of the beds (*right*) illustrates how a few well-chosen varieties of perennials and annuals can produce a rich blend of colours, shapes and textures in any garden.

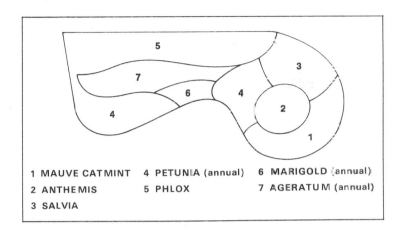

1 MAUVE CATMINT   4 PETUNIA (annual)   6 MARIGOLD (annual)
2 ANTHEMIS   5 PHLOX   7 AGERATUM (annual)
3 SALVIA

A series of asymmetrical beds makes up the borders of this lawn. The view, from behind one of the phlox-dominated beds, shows yellow anthemis on the right above mauve catmint in the opposite border.

Planting and caring for perennials

Because a perennial garden is a long-term project and because the soil for it must be prepared thoroughly enough to serve for a decade or more, I went to special pains a few years ago when my wife, Margaret, hinted that she wanted a small perennial garden of her own. I was determined to give her the best possible start; so when I had dug up the area, I spread 10 centimetres (4 in.) of a very rich compost on top of it, instead of the usual 5 centimetres (2 in.), and worked it in well. Then my wife planted, among other perennials, a cultivar of white Siberian iris that normally grows 60 centimetres (24 in.) tall and a few bulbs of the *Lilium auratum*, which in most gardens rises 120 to 150 centimetres (4 to 5 ft) and bears blossoms 15 centimetres (6 in.) across. Because of my generous use of compost, though, my wife's irises soared to nearly 120 centimetres (4 ft), and the gold-band lilies to 2.5 metres (8 ft) with blooms 30 centimetres (12 in.) across. They were spectacular, all right, but they were not quite what she expected.

I confess the incident only to emphasize how important soil preparation can be in starting a perennial garden—much more important than in preparing a bed for annuals, which blossom for a single season and die. Many perennials reach their peak only when they are three years old and may—as in the case of peonies and day lilies—flourish where you put them long beyond your own lifetime. All those years they use up nutrients from the soil. You can replenish the nutrients with fertilizers, of course, but once you have planted long-lived perennials you cannot change the structure of the soil—which is every bit as important to their well-being as fertility, for it controls both drainage and moisture retention. Soils that are heavy with clay tend to become compacted and this can mean death for perennials. Such soils must be opened and loosened so that air as well as moisture can reach the plants' roots. Light sandy soils, on the other hand, must be made spongy enough to trap and retain moisture and dissolved nutrients that otherwise would drain away.

Fortunately you can improve either type of soil by digging in a 5 to 10 centimetre (2 to 4 in.) layer of organic material such as

An array of vigorous perennials bears testimony to well-drained, well-prepared soil. Behind the mauve catmint in the foreground are yellow sundrops, purple salvias and creamy-yellow thermopsis.

moss peat, rotted compost, decayed farmyard manure, or leaf-mould, which consists of rotting leaves. Any of these will do, but moss peat is the most generally sold at nurseries and garden centres. Peat is naturally acidic and contains considerable quantities of nitrogen, although most of this is inaccessible to plants. It is weed-free, easily spread, clean to handle and breaks down slowly in the ground, thus improving aeration and drainage of heavy soils and retaining both food salts and moisture in light, quick draining soils.

Peat is commonly used in seed and potting composts and is also excellent for mulching borders. It often comes compressed in bales, which should be broken down and thoroughly moistened before use. Unlike some other organic materials, it does very well the job of moisture control for which it is intended.

So does compost—if you have space for a compost heap in your garden. Making one (*drawings, below*) is not nearly the job that people thought it had to be when I was a boy—in those days it involved digging a deep pit. Through the alchemy of a compost heap, you can convert your leaves and other organic debris into clean, odourless, rich fertilizer with less effort and cost than it takes to stuff them into plastic bags for refuse collection. Properly made compost is at least equivalent in plant food value to the best animal manure.

A COMPOST HEAP FOR PERENNIALS

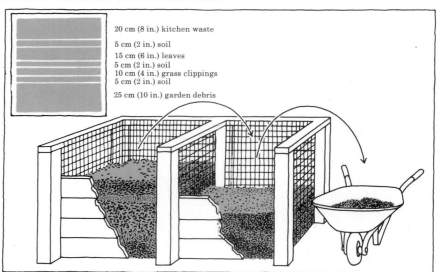

20 cm (8 in.) kitchen waste

5 cm (2 in.) soil

15 cm (6 in.) leaves

5 cm (2 in.) soil

10 cm (4 in.) grass clippings

5 cm (2 in.) soil

25 cm (10 in.) garden debris

An unending supply of compost is provided by twin bins, the backs and sides made of wire mesh to admit air, the fronts of removable boards to allow easy access. In one, the "brewing" bin, organic matter is alternated in layers (inset), dusted with fertilizer and an activator, wetted and sealed with soil. As the material decays, it is forked over; after three to six months it is transferred to the other bin, ready for use.

Compost-making speeds up the natural decay of organic materials by increasing the supply of nitrogen to the bacteria that attack and digest the materials. It has been found that the addition of an activator and lime also speeds up the process. (Lime, in the form of ground chalk or limestone, needs to be added to correct the natural acidity of most organic matter, but should not be used if the compost is to be used for acid-loving plants.) To get the needed chemicals, simply use a sprinkling of any ordinary lawn or garden fertilizer such as sulphate of ammonia, or a proprietary compost accelerator.

Compost heaps can be built in pits, on the open ground or within enclosures. I prefer enclosures because they hold the material in place and because they can be made attractive, or at least inoffensive—a consideration for both you and your neighbour if you live on a suburban estate. The material to be composted can consist of almost any non-woody organic matter, such as leaves, lawn clippings, old plant stems, egg-shells, weeds, corn stalks, beet or carrot tops, ruined fruit or vegetables, animal manure or even paper. All of these materials will decay much faster if they are cut up or shredded before being composted. Do not use toothed leaves, such as holly and rose clippings.

There are various methods of composting; one good way is to put the material down in layers, the thickness depending on the coarseness or fineness of the material. Leaves for example, should be put in layers about 15 centimetres (6 in.) deep, grass clippings 7.5 to 10 centimetres (3 to 4 in.) deep. Spread out each layer on the heap, making sure the centre is slightly concave to catch rainwater, and sprinkle an activator or fertilizer and limestone alternately between layers of refuse. To make sure there is enough moisture to aid decomposition, dampen the heap for a few minutes with a hose, then top it off with a 5 centimetre (2 in.) layer of soil from your garden. This soil layer will help to settle the heap, seal in the heat generated during decomposition and add bacteria to speed decay. Continue sandwiching alternate layers of soil and organic material sprinkled with fertilizer and limestone until the heap is 1 to 1.2 metres (3 to 4 ft) high. It will take anywhere from three to six months for the composting process to be completed.

If rainfall is light, hose down the heap from time to time to replace evaporated moisture. Turn the heap over with a garden fork after four to six weeks so that the outer material becomes incorporated into the centre and has a chance to decay. A second turning in another four to six weeks will help to speed the process, but it is not essential. The compost will be ready to use when it is dark in colour and the material from which it was made either loses its original form entirely or crumbles when touched. A 5 centimetre (2 in.) application of compost each year will make any soil enormously productive.

There is more to preparing the soil, of course, than the addition of organic material. But just what it will require in the way of extras can be determined only by a soil test. Your local agricultural office will give you an exact analysis for a nominal fee, or you can make one yourself, accurately enough for practical purposes, with an inexpensive soil-testing kit obtainable at chemists or garden centres. Such a kit will permit you to ascertain your soil's pH value—that is, whether its chemical balance is acid, alkaline or neutral—and the availability in the soil of the three essential plant nutrients: nitrogen, phosphorous and potassium.

The pH value of your soil can make the difference between success and failure with perennials. It is measured on a scale that runs from 0, for extremely acid, to 14, for extremely alkaline. A pH value of 7 is neutral. In those parts of Europe that have abundant rainfall—southern Ireland and the west coast of Scotland—soil is apt to be acid. In normally dry areas such as the South of France it is usually alkaline since the chemicals that make a soil alkaline are not leached away by rain. But you cannot rely on such generalizations. Areas that are broadly alkaline may have pockets of acidity, and vice versa.

Most perennials do best when the pH value is around 6.5 (slightly acid) to 7.0 (neutral), but soils in parts of Europe and North America, for example, range from 4.5 to 8.5; so some correction may be needed. A soil analysis will tell for certain.

The most effective and inexpensive material to raise the pH value of an acid soil is ground limestone. I prefer dolomite limestone to other ground limestone because it also contains magnesium, a trace element that many soils lack. If your soil is too acidic, and of medium consistency, you will need to raise the pH value by approximately $\frac{1}{2}$ to 1 unit. On the other hand, if your soil is heavy with clay, or if you plan to add large quantities of an organic material that is acid—as most moss peat is—you will require one-third more limestone.

To lower the pH value of excessively alkaline soil, two materials are available, and the special needs of the soil and the time you have before planting will help you determine which to choose. One material is finely ground sulphur. It is slow acting, but long lasting. The other is ferrous sulphate. It works quickly, but not over as long a period, for it washes out of the soil easily. Its merit is that it contains iron as well as sulphur. Iron, deficient in many soils, encourages the production of healthy, deep green foliage and richly coloured flowers. One hundred and fifteen grams (4 oz) sulphur, or 750 grams (1$\frac{1}{2}$ lb) ferrous sulphate, will lower the pH value of 5 square metres (about 50 sq. ft) of soil by $\frac{1}{2}$ to 1 unit. It is helpful to spray foliage with a weak solution of ferric chloride to bring back its green coloration, or to water roots with an iron chelate (sequestered iron) according to the maker's recommendations.

When you are considering the texture and acidity of your soil, you should consider its nutritive content. If you made a complete soil test, it probably showed your soil to be deficient in one or more of the three major fertilizer components: nitrogen, phosphate (the phosphoric acid in packaged fertilizers) or potassium (potash). Labels on fertilizers use a numerical rating to identify the amounts of nitrogen, phosphate and potash in the mixture and the sequence on the labels is always the same: 5:10:5 means the fertilizer contains 5 per cent nitrogen, 10 per cent phosphate, and 5 per cent potash. The balance, in inorganic fertilizers, consists of inert material to dilute the chemicals (which would be too strong in their pure form) and to make them easier to spread.

Nitrogen stimulates rapid, lush green growth and a lot of it is essential, for example, in a lawn fertilizer. But perennials, which take their time about growing, need very little nitrogen; in fact, if they get too much they will produce weak, succulent stems and big, floppy leaves rather than flowers. The most important fertilizer element for perennials is phosphate: it builds strong roots and stems, is important to the production of blossoms and provides both flowers and foliage with rich colour. Potassium helps plants to resist diseases and cold—an important factor to any vegetation that lives for years in one place.

A good general fertilizer for perennials should be dug into the soil when the bed is prepared at the rate of 0.75 to 1 kilo (1½ to 2 lb) per 5 square metres (about 50 sq. ft). If your soil requires only the addition of phosphate, bonemeal is an excellent source: fork in 0.75 to 1.5 kilos (1½ to 3 lb) per 5 square metres (about 50 sq. ft). Wood ash from the fireplace or charcoal ash from the barbecue are rich in potassium and provide a good free supply of that vital element. A thin, even scattering of weathered ashes, worked into the soil of the bed, will usually supply all the potassium your plants need.

A friend of mine who, like so many of us, is concerned about ecology asked me the other day why I didn't recommend such natural organic fertilizers as cow manure. Of course I do recommend them—well-rotted cow manure, at least one year old, is a splendid fertilizer; when I was a youngster living on a farm, I used nothing else on my plants. Such natural manures are not as concentrated as manufactured inorganic fertilizers—they often have only a tenth or a fifth of the strength—but they work wonders because they contain micro-organisms that release nutrients already in the soil and make them available to vegetation. But unless one lives near a dairy farm, natural stable manures are not easy to find. Dried cow manure, bonemeal, seaweed manures, dried blood, hoof and horn and powdered fish fertilizer are much more easily obtained in garden centres and they are all the next best thing. Best of all is the compost from your heap. I use a combination of natural and chemical fertilizers in my own garden. The natural ones are the basic fertilizers I use year after year for long-range plant feeding. When a plant needs a quick pick-me-up I scatter a bit of quick-acting, water-soluble chemical fertilizer around it.

PREPARING THE BED A good time to get the basic soil-conditioning aids into the ground is several months before you plan to plant: summer digging is fine for autumn planting, and autumn digging for spring planting, to give a chance for the soil to settle and the pH modifiers to become effective. If your soil is dry and heavy, as clay soils are, water it thoroughly with a hose two days before you start to dig. The soaking will make it easier for you to work. If the soil is light but dry, moisten it a day ahead of time, for the same reason.

Some gardeners insist that the only proper way to prepare a plant bed—for perennials, at least—is "double digging". This involves digging up the area to the full depth of a spade, removing and setting aside the soil clod as you go, and then digging deeper until the hole goes down 60 centimetres (2 ft). The soil clod is then tossed back into the bottom of the hole, too far down

EDGING A BED OR BORDER

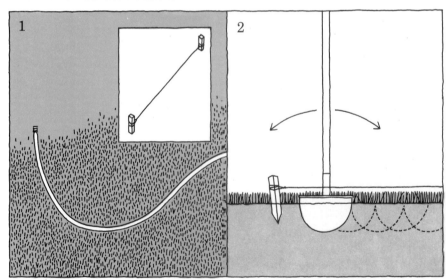

The easiest way to give a perennial bed a gracefully curved edge is to lay out the shape you want with a garden hose. To create a straight edge, simply stretch string between stakes (inset) and tie it tautly at both ends.

Before preparing the bed (page 46), cut around the edge with a half-moon edging tool thrust into the ground. Rock the edger from side to side (arrows) to drive it down all the way —10 cm (4 in.). Overlap the cuts.

for any weed roots to sprout again—decaying, they provide organic matter and nutrients for the deep-ranging roots of some perennials. This method certainly works. The finest large perennial borders I have ever seen are at the botanical gardens in Edinburgh, and some of the best small ones are in the Cotswolds, where hollyhocks often tower as high as the thatched roofs of the cottages. Presumably all of these beds in the park and around the cottages were dug extra deep.

I belong to the school of thought that believes digging 30 centimetres (1 ft) is enough. It is true that the roots of some perennials do reach down as far as 60 centimetres (2 ft), but most of the feeding roots are in the top of the soil, and if drainage is adequate the 30 centimetre (1 ft) depth suffices. In any case constant mulching increases the depth of the fertile top soil.

The easiest way to dig a large plot is with a rotary power cultivator (I prefer the self-propelled type with tines mounted in a housing behind the wheel because it leaves the surface of the soil smooth as it digs). These can be rented from many garden supply shops. Cultivators can bite through turf and tough-rooted weeds, chopping them to bits as they go. But you had better not take advantage of that capability. Every little hunk of root from a dandelion, a bell-tine and scores of other undesirables can reproduce another full-sized nuisance. So before you put the rotary cultivator to use, strip the turf off your projected bed with a sharp spade, chip it up and put it on your compost heap. If you do not have a compost heap and do not want to start one, use the turf to fill in any bare patches in your lawn. If you are lucky enough not to need such patching, shake the soil loose from the turf to fall back on the bed, then discard the grass. Dig out every vestige of weed root with a fork. Whatever time you spend on the task will be short compared to the time it would take to uproot weeds once they and the perennials are fully grown.

When you are satisfied that the site is weed-free, make an initial run over the bed with the cultivator; this will break up the soil to a depth of 10 to 15 centimetres (4 to 6 in.). Rake it over and pick out any weed roots you may have missed. Then spread your soil additives—fertilizer, moss peat. lime or sulphur—over the surface, and till again, mixing them all into the standard 30 centimetre (1 ft) depth.

Some spots in the garden—where, for example, you may plan to set a single clump of perennials in front of an evergreen—will prove too small to accommodate a cultivator. There you will have to dig by hand. If the area has been covered by grass, remove this with a square-nosed spade, which will slice cleanly through the roots. Eliminate weed roots as you did in the large bed, then dig (*drawings, page 46*). If the area has been cultivated before, use a spade or fork to turn the soil over to a depth of 30 centimetres (1 ft), then dig in the 5 to 10 centimetres (2 to 4 in.) of moss

PREPARING THE SOIL FOR PLANTING

1. *To prepare a bed in a grassy area, strip off the turf with a sharp flat spade (either discard the turf, or add it to your compost heap). Because the richest soil lies close to the surface, try to take only 2.5 cm (1 in.) of it with the turf.*

2. *With a fork, dig up and remove grass and weed roots so they will not sprout again. The likelihood of uncovering any large roots near the surface is slim if the bed is located properly—a minimum of 1 metre (3 ft) away from neighbouring trees or shrubs.*

3. *Use the spade to work the soil in small beds, but a rotary cultivator is advisable for large beds. Turn over the soil to a depth of 20 to 30 cm (8 to 12 in.), taking a slice no more than 10 cm (4 in.) thick with each spadeful. Toss each slice beyond the hole and break it up with the spade.*

4. *When the entire bed has been dug, work it again with a metal-pronged rake to level the top and pulverize the clods of soil on the surface. At the same time remove any remaining roots as well as any stones, sticks or other rubble.*

5. *With the fork, work into the soil a layer of moss peat 5 to 10 cm (2 to 4 in.) thick, a good general fertilizer, as well as any limestone or sulphur required to change the soil's pH factor (pages 41-42). Mix all these with the soil down to a depth of 20 to 30 cm (8 to 12 in.).*

6. *If the border is to be planted immediately, tread the soil firm with your feet and smooth the surface with the back of the rake. If planting is to be delayed for several weeks, the soil will settle naturally without treading.*

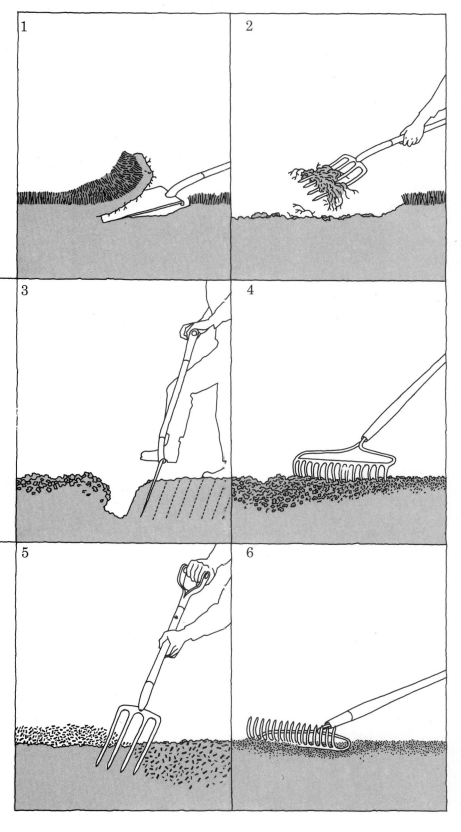

peat or whatever other organic material you have chosen and any other soil additives needed.

All the digging and the incorporation of organic matter will leave the soil too soft and loose for immediate planting. If you have prepared the bed well in advance, as you should, you do not have to do anything more about it for a while. The soil will settle by itself with the help of rain and frosts, and, in the interim before planting, you will need only to pluck out an occasional weed. But if you are going to do any planting right away, you will have to firm the soil to eliminate air pockets in which roots would dry out. One way is to tread back and forth on it, using a rake afterwards to smooth the surface. (Do not do this if the soil is wet or sticky, for it will become excessively compacted and negate the benefits of the organic matter; wait until it dries out.) A second way, which works well with light soils but not with heavy ones, consists of hosing the soil thoroughly to settle it and eliminate air pockets.

Regardless of when you prepare the bed—in summer for autumn planting or in autumn for spring planting—two factors determine the best planting time for perennials—the growth habits of each species and the region in which you live. The timing also depends on how you acquire your plants. Many garden centres stock perennials already growing in containers. These can be set out at any time they are available. But the same plants can often be bought as dormant bare roots. Nearly all perennials grow from crowns, which consist of a number of stems joined together at the base, sometimes in firm clumps, as in the case of garden phlox, and sometimes loosely, as in the case of chrysanthemums. The feeding roots extend below the stems. In autumn when the plants approach dormancy, the stems die, but the crowns from which they rise begin to form small buds. During dormancy the buds remain inactive, becoming new stems in the next growing season. When you buy a dormant perennial from a nursery, it may still have the stubs of the previous season's stems attached and the buds may or may not be discernible; in most cases they are less easy to see in autumn than in the spring. Many gardeners prefer to buy their perennials like this—they are less expensive than container plants, and dormant roots can be moved with virtually no risk of loss.

But dormant perennials must be set out at the times the plants' growing habits and the climate dictate. In general autumn is the best planting time in areas where winter temperatures do not fall appreciably below freezing, and spring in areas that habitually experience severe frosts. But there are exceptions: bearded iris is best planted as soon as possible after flowering because that is the time when the old feeding roots die; about a month after flowering, new roots begin to grow, pro-

PLANTING TIMES

47

DIVIDING AND PLANTING BEARDED IRIS

1. *Bearded irises need to be divided as shown here every three years to keep their vigour. Soon after the flowers have faded, pry the entire clump gently out of the ground with a fork.*

2. *After washing the soil from the rhizomes, trim the leaves to a length of 10 to 15 cm (4 to 6 in.); remove any shrivelled leaves and dead stalks. If plants show any signs of pests or disease (pages 56-59), discard or burn the stalks and leaves; do not put them on a compost heap.*

3. *With a knife, cut off the fleshy outer roots as shown by the dotted line, so that you get V-shaped pieces, each with two fans of leaves. Discard the old centre rhizome. If pieces contain pests, cut these out; dust the cuts with an all-purpose fungicide.*

4. *Plant each root division in a hole made by plunging a trowel to its hilt into the soil, then pulling it up and towards you. Hold the division against the straight side of the hole, with the top of the rhizome just above the surface. Fill in and firm the soil.*

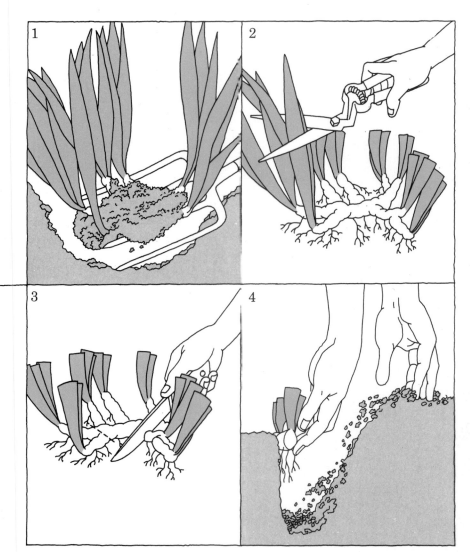

vided the plants are in moist earth. During that interval there is practically no risk involved in transplanting. Oriental poppies constitute another exception; they are unique in being extremely difficult to move when they are in active growth and nearly impossible to kill when they are dormant; dormancy comes in early summer when the tops die to the ground, and poppies can be moved at that time without loss. Peonies also have a special planting season; the best time to move peony roots is in early autumn. By then the leaves will have nearly finished replenishing the strength in their roots for another year. Peony roots are long, slender and somewhat brittle; be especially careful not to break off the bright pink buds on the crown. Plant the roots so that the tips of these buds are no more than 5 centimetres (2 in.) below the surface of the soil. No part of peony culture is more important than the depth of planting. Whenever anyone tells me his peonies fail to bloom, I immediately suspect that they were planted too deeply, and this generally proves to be the case. There are some other exceptions to the general rule on planting times, and these exceptions can be found in the encyclopaedia section (*pages 91-150*).

How you plant is as important as when you plant. Three factors are critical to good planting. One of them is space for the roots. Do not dig tiny holes and try to cram the roots into them. If you have prepared the bed properly, the soil will be soft and it will be easy to scoop holes big enough to accommodate the roots without crowding. Spread the roots outwards as well as downwards, so that they can begin to establish themselves and take up nourishment immediately. If a crown is large, build a little mound of firm soil in the centre of the hole, set the crown on it, and drape the roots over the edges; this prevents the possibility of having an air pocket underneath the crown.

A second and equally critical factor is depth of planting. If you buy perennials growing in containers, you have no problem; simply set them at the same depth at which they were growing. If you buy them as dormant plants, place them at the depth at which the plant grew the previous season. You can determine this easily on crowns that still have old stems, because the soil will have left its mark on them; on crowns that have started new growth, the new shoots will be lighter in colour below the old soil level than above it. But some dormant plants, such as those of Oriental poppies, have no such guiding marks because they have neither old nor new stems at planting time. Consult the encyclopaedia for their proper planting depths. (Proper depth of planting is so important for two perennials that are basic to perennial borders—bearded irises and peonies—that drawings are devoted to them on pages 48 and 50.) A third critical factor in planting is the firmness of the soil. There must be no pockets of air in which roots can dry out, for dried roots die. After you have set the crowns in the ground with the roots spread and the tops at the proper depth, firm the soil by treading it. Pressing it with your hands is not enough: you cannot apply enough pressure to eliminate air pockets.

Precautions against drying out are particularly necessary when you are transplanting. Mark the new site for each plant in advance with a stake and dig your new holes before you dig up your old plants. If you have to keep the plants out of the ground for any length of time, moisten the roots and keep them covered with damp hessian until you can plant them again.

Whether you plant your perennials in autumn or spring, mark every site where you have set a plant. If you trust your memory, you may find yourself digging into and ruining some slow starters when you are hoeing weeds or starting other plants. For plant markers, I generally use 20 centimetre (8 in.) wooden labels, stuck 7.5 or 10 centimetres (3 to 4 in.) deep in the soil beside each plant. In addition, I identify each group of plants with a stake bearing an indelible label.

CARING FOR PERENNIALS   Perennials, whether they are old plants or young, respond well to shallow cultivation in early spring: cultivated plants grow faster than uncultivated ones. Use a Dutch hoe and lightly move the top 2.5 centimetres (1 in.) or so of soil, working backwards so as to obliterate footmarks. Be careful not to damage surface roots of perennials; it is better to pull out weeds by hand rather than hoe too close to emerging plants. Other cultivating tools preferred by some gardeners include the swoe, which has a swan-neck attachment to one side of the handle that makes it easier to get around plants; and small hand cultivators with two, three or four prongs set at right angles to the handle. All of these uproot weeds and allow air to get into the soil for healthy growth. Unless the bed is a new one and already fertilized, work in fertilizer containing nitrogen, phosphate and potassium around each plant (from year to year the soil's natural nitrogen content is depleted so some should be added). If you are using a general fertilizer, a level tablespoonful suffices for an initial spring feeding of a small clump. Older and larger plants may need more

DIVIDING AND PLANTING PEONIES

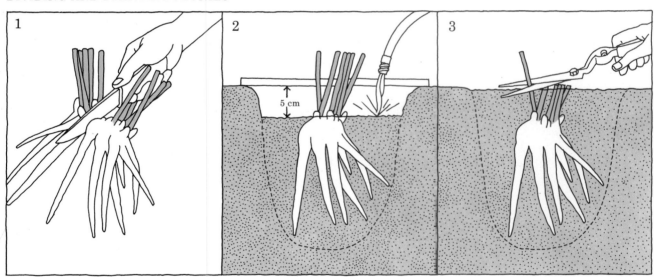

To propagate a peony, dig up and cut apart the clump in early autumn, taking care not to break its roots. After washing, the roots should be divided so that three to five prominent buds remain on each new division.

Using a board as a guide to get the buds about 5 cm (2 in.) below ground level, set each division into a hole containing prepared soil (page 46). Then fill the hole to the level of the buds and water thoroughly.

When the water has drained away, firm the soil with your hands to press out any air pockets that may remain under the plant, then fill the hole to ground level. Cut off the peony stems close to the surface of the soil.

fertilizer—the amount depends on the size of the plant and the strength of the fertilizer, but it is better to err on the side of caution. Scatter the fertilizer on the soil's surface, keeping it off the leaves and crowns so it cannot burn them, and work it into the soil with the cultivator.

Foliar feeding, which consists of spraying the leaves with nutrients, can be used to correct deficiencies of iron or magnesium, and to supply a balanced nitrogen, phosphate and potash feed. There are various proprietary makes available for the purpose; they are used with a spreader or wetting agent to give even coverage.

Two other jobs remain to be done immediately after spring fertilizing and cultivating. One is mulching to conserve moisture and keep down weeds. The other is staking to support those plants that might be blown over or snapped off by the wind or splattered with mud when they bend too low. I detest the appearance of stakes, and I cherish the grace of a hollyhock stalk that grows in a natural curve. But I fear the havoc that a summer thunderstorm can wreak, and I recognize that staking is unavoidable. So I keep it to a minimum and do it as inconspicuously as possible. I delay any staking until the plants have filled out sufficiently to conceal the stakes, at least in part (*drawings, page 52*).

A clump of hybrid delphiniums may be as much as 1.5 metres (5 ft) high when its blossoms open, but I wait to stake it until the mass of foliage at the base has grown nearly to its full height and the flower spikes have begun to stretch upwards. Then I choose slender green stakes of bamboo or reed that are long enough to reach about three-quarters of the way up the ultimate height of the plant, and about halfway up the expected height of the flower spikes. I insert three or four stakes in the ground, concealing them among the plant's leaves as best I can. I weave soft green twine into a sort of cat's cradle from stake to stake about 30 centimetres (1 ft) above the soil and repeat the weaving 30 centimetres (1 ft) higher; individual stems are not tied, but are allowed to grow up between the strands of twine. This kind of staking suits any tall plants. Different staking works better for lilies, young delphiniums and young monkshoods that send up only one or a few stalks. Each of these stalks needs its own bamboo stake, about three-quarters as long as the plant is tall and set at an angle to follow the natural bend of the stem. For tying the stem to the stake, I use green or tan twine or raffia fibre. Be careful not to constrict the stems in tying them to the stakes, or to force them into unnatural positions. Tie the twine or raffia securely to the stake, but loosely around the stems.

The best staking for peonies is a ring of heavy wire on legs that rise 38 to 45 centimetres (15 to 18 in.) above ground. Such

STAKING FOR SUPPORT

supports can be purchased at garden centres as well as from garden sundriesmen. The elevated ring holds the centre stems of the peony upright and allows the outer stems to bend naturally and gracefully, but keeps the heavy blossoms from touching the ground and becoming splattered with mud.

For weak-stemmed plants such as gaillardia, coreopsis, sneezeweed, lupin and Michaelmas daisy, all of which tend to flop over in the wind and rain, the best support consists of, twiggy branches. They should be set around the plants when the stems are still quite low, so that the foliage can grow around and conceal them before the flowers open.

MULCHING AND WATERING

Whether or not your plants need staking, they will benefit from a mulch, applied immediately after the spring fertilizer application, to conserve moisture and discourage weeds. There are many

FOUR WAYS TO STAKE PERENNIALS

1. *Tall floppy perennials such as lupins and coreopsis can be held upright by pushing twiggy branches into the ground around them. Foliage will hide the branches before the flowers open.*

2. *Clumps of spiky perennials such as delphiniums are best supported by garden twine wound around stakes three-quarters as tall as the plants' expected height; set four stakes around each clump. When the blossoms begin to appear, weave the twine between the stems at 30 cm (1 ft) intervals.*

3. *If a perennial has only a few slim stalks, as does this young monkshood, tie each of them to a reed or bamboo stake three-quarters the height of a fully grown plant. Loop soft twine or raffia loosely around the stalk, but tie it tightly to the stake (inset).*

4. *To restrain thick bushy clumps of perennials such as peonies, use a three-legged circular wire stand, available at many garden shops. Place the stand around the plants when they are about 30 cm (1 ft) tall and push the legs firmly into the ground.*

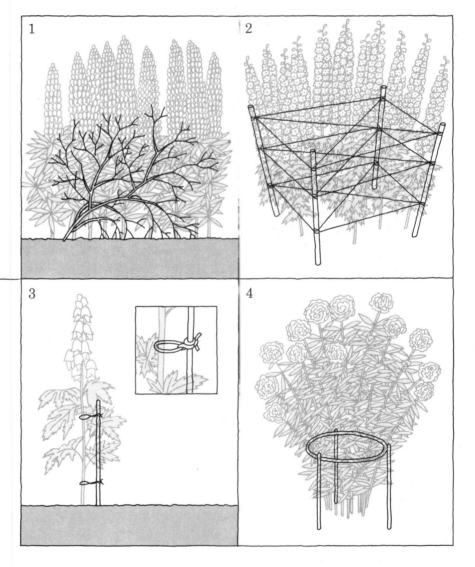

mulching materials that will do this job satisfactorily, but I prefer those that gradually disintegrate during a season and by the following spring can be easily worked into the soil during cultivation and the application of fertilizer. Suitable materials include ripe compost, well-rotted farmyard manure, moist moss peat, leaf-mould and rotted grass clippings; but layers of newspaper—well-watered and hidden from sight with a thin layer of peat or soil—also conserve moisture. Spread these materials about 2.5 centimetres (1 in.) thick between the plants, tapering this off close to the stems of the plants so that the crowns do not rot after rain. Use most of the mulch on the ground between the plants—this is where the weeds are most likely to appear (*drawing, on the right*).

Mulch will help keep your perennial border moist in mid-summer, but it cannot do the job alone. So many plants growing in such close proximity use enormous quantities of water, and if nature does not supply it, you must. Without an adequate supply of water, perennials cannot mature and flower properly because their stems become woody and stunted.

Watering should be done so that it goes to the roots rather than on to the foliage. Regular wetting of the foliage makes the plants vulnerable to fungus diseases such as mildew that mar their appearance and sap their strength. If you spray your garden with a hose, give it a thorough soaking and do it early enough in the day so the water dries off the foliage before nightfall. I water my perennial garden with a porous canvas hose that soaks the soil slowly, or with a sprinkler hose with pin-point holes; I keep the holes aimed down at the ground and the pressure low so that the water just seeps into the earth. Your plants will indicate when they need water by wilting—be sure to water them immediately when this happens. Garden phlox is so sensitive to drought that you can use it the way coal miners used canaries to indicate the presence of gas in a mine. If the lower leaves of your garden phlox wilt, water the whole garden right away—even if all the other plants look fine.

With such basic care, your perennials should flower bountifully. But you can control the size and production of blooms by several methods illustrated on page 55. First of all, you can double or even triple the number of flowers that appear by pinching out the growing stems of certain plants, forcing them to send out three or four stems where there was only one before. The stems will be shorter and the flowers will be smaller, but both will be far more numerous than without a pinching out. This procedure is especially advantageous with autumn bloomers such as chrysanthemums, sneezeweed, Michaelmas daisies and boltonias that have a long growing season to develop many stems and buds. In reducing the height of plants, pinching out makes them less

MULCHING FOR SUMMER

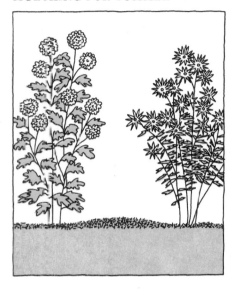

To hold the moisture that plants need, to protect shallow roots from sun and to keep down weeds that compete for nourishment, mulch the perennial bed in late spring, following the application of fertilizer. Lightweight organic materials work best: chunky moss peat, leaf-mould, compost or grass clippings. Spread the mulch about 1 cm ($\frac{1}{2}$ in.) deep directly beneath the plants, and cover the spaces between them—where the sun hits the ground—with a layer 2.5 to 5 cm (1 to 2 in.) thick. The mulch will gradually disintegrate during the winter; in spring work it into the soil around the plants with the application of fertilizer—replace the mulch later in the season with a fresh layer.

PINCHING OUT AND THINNING

vulnerable to wind, so they may not have to be staked for support.

To obtain large flowers rather than many smaller ones, thin out the stems rather than pinching them out; by restricting each plant to only a few stems, you force it to produce fewer but bigger blossoms. The common garden phlox, which blooms in midsummer, is often treated this way. Ordinarily, a clump two years old or older sends up at least a dozen stems, each bearing a 7.5 to 10 centimetres (3 to 4 in.) flower cluster. But gardeners who want to make their phlox resemble the magnificent specimens pictured in garden catalogues remove all but four or five stems per clump early in spring. The results are large individual blossoms growing in impressive clusters, which may develop a span as great as 25 centimetres (10 in.).

DISBUDDING FOR BIG BLOOMS

There is a special kind of thinning that is called disbudding: instead of eliminating entire stalks, you remove only the side buds in order to concentrate all of the strength of each stem into producing a single magnificent flower. Disbudding is often practised with peonies, and the solitary blossom that develops could win a first prize at a show. But for each splendid bloom, two potential flowers—at least—have been sacrificed. Each plant produces only a few flowers, and most of them open and fade about the same time. In the interest of continuing colour in the garden, I prefer not to disbud, but to snip out the central flower as soon as it fades and to let the side buds develop into smaller— but no less lovely—blooms that will greatly prolong the plant's flowering season.

PROLONGING FLOWERING

The obvious reason for removing faded flowers is that it improves the appearance of the garden. But there are other less obvious and equally important reasons. One of them is that by removing the waning blooms before seed is produced, you can almost always obtain a second crop of flowers from such perennials as delphiniums, lupins and garden phlox, all of which would otherwise have only one flowering period in a season.

It works this way: when these flowers fade, they go to seed, and with the production of seed, the plant completes its life cycle for the season. If you remove the flowers before the seeds form, the plant tries again, bearing new flowers to make seed. But the timing of the flower removal must be precise—after the flowers have faded and before they have produced any seed. The method must also be precise, and it varies for different plants. With phlox, coreopsis and anthemis, snip off only the top one-third of the stalk from which the flowers grew. Side branches will develop below the cut and will form new flowers. With delphiniums and lupins, first cut off the stalks just below the faded flowers, leaving as much of their foliage as possible. In a few weeks, new stalks will rise from the soil. Then you can cut off the old stalks at

(continued on page 60)

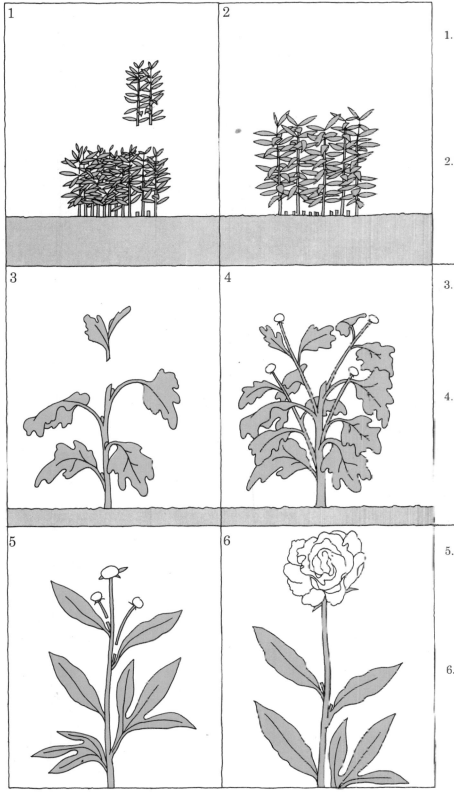

HOW TO GET MORE OR LARGER BLOSSOMS

1. *To increase the size of flowers on garden phlox and on other perennials that produce a dense thicket of stems, remove young shoots in spring when they are 10 to 15 cm (4 to 6 in.) tall. Snip the stems near ground level, leaving four or five shoots.*

2. *With fewer stalks to feed, the plants will grow vigorously and foliage will quickly spread to fill the gaps left by thinning. The flower clusters on the remaining stalks may become two or three times their normal size.*

3. *To double the crop of flowers from autumn-blooming perennials such as chrysanthemums, pinch out the tip of each stem, including the main one, when the plants are approximately 15 cm (6 in.) tall.*

4. *Within a week new shoots will appear at the leaf joints. Pinch out these shoots each time they grow about 15 cm (6 in.). Stop pinching out in midsummer to allow flower buds to develop. Pinching out produces more flowers and bushier plants that may not need staking.*

5. *To produce a show-sized peony or chrysanthemum, pinch off the side buds close to the stem as they appear, leaving only the large top bud. This process forces the plant to put all of its energy into nourishing and developing the remaining flower.*

6. *The single blossom that results from disbudding may be a giant —20 cm (8 in.) across instead of the normal 12.5 cm (5 in.) in some peonies. For display, cut the blossom as soon as the petals begin to open, leaving several lower leaves on the stem.*

Controlling pests and diseases

Although perennials are among the healthiest of garden plants, some types are susceptible to disease and to damage by various pests. In combating such threats, a little prevention is worth more than masses of chemicals. Regular clearing of accumulated weeds and dead stalks robs pests of their favourite breeding places, and well-drained plant beds eliminate the moist conditions favoured by fungi. When plants first show signs of damage, simple measures are often effective: knocking

PEST	DESCRIPTION	METHODS OF CONTROL
	APHIDS Among the most familiar of garden pests, aphids are tiny plant lice, ½ to 1 mm (1/16 to 1/18 in.) long, yellowish green to black in colour, which are found clustered on new shoots. They suck a plant's juices, stunt its growth and cause deformities like curling leaves, and they also secrete a sticky fluid called honeydew. If no measures are taken, aphids may produce many generations in one growing season. SUSCEPTIBLE PLANTS: CHRYSANTHEMUM, COLUMBINE, POLYANTHUS, VIOLET	Spray with dimethoate, malathion, BHC or pirimicarb as soon as aphids are noticed. Pirimicarb does not harm beneficial insects such as ladybirds.
	CAPSID BUGS These small, bright green bugs suck sap from leaves, young stems, fruit and flowers. Attacked plants fail to grow properly and the leaves become tattered and distorted. Eggs are laid on woody plants, and the nymphs feed on these in spring. When adult they fly to herbaceous plants or weeds. A second generation appears in summer, and the adults return to the woody plants and lay eggs. SUSCEPTIBLE PLANTS: CHRYSANTHEMUM AND RELATED PLANTS, PHLOX, PRIMROSE	Spray plants that show signs of leaf damage (small brown spots or holes) in spring with dimethoate or formothion. Capsid bugs on herbaceous plants can be controlled with dimethoate, BHC or carbaryl sprays. Keep down weeds in July to prevent them from becoming hosts.
	LEAF HOPPERS Wedge-shaped insects 1 to 4 mm (1/16 to ¼ in.) long, leaf hoppers damage foliage by sucking sap from the leaves. Their presence is signalled by a white stippled effect on the leaf surface. Some leaf hoppers transmit virus diseases. The insects get their name from their habit of jumping away quickly when disturbed. SUSCEPTIBLE PLANTS: CATMINT, PRIMULA, SALVIA, FOXGLOVE, POLYANTHUS	If infestation is severe, spray with nicotine, derris, pyrethrum, malathion or carbaryl, particularly the undersides of leaves.
	EELWORMS These are microscopic, worm-like animals that can be seen only under a microscope. They live and feed inside the stems and leaves, causing distortion and death of the tissues. In phlox, their presence is revealed by split stems and leaves that are reduced to thin strips. Chrysanthemums develop brown, wedge-shaped markings on their leaves. SUSCEPTIBLE PLANTS: CHRYSANTHEMUM, DAHLIA, PHLOX, SALVIA	Burn infected plants and change the site for replacement stock. Eradicate weeds. Propagate phlox from root cuttings. Chrysanthemums for propagation should be heat-treated when dormant. Stand the stools in hot water for 5 minutes then immerse them in cold water.

insects off plants with water from a garden hose or snipping off diseased leaves. The wise gardener avoids powerful non-specific insecticides that can eliminate both beneficial and harmful insects and leave residues that may eventually affect animals and even humans. Formulas compounded to control specific pests and diseases, available under various brand names, are preferable. In many cases it is possible to control pests by introducing into your garden their natural enemies (*page 59*).

PEST	DESCRIPTION	METHODS OF CONTROL
	SNAILS AND SLUGS The chief differences between these two members of the mollusc family are size and shell—snails are usually 15 to 40 mm ($\frac{1}{2}$ to $1\frac{1}{2}$ in.) long and have complete shells, while slugs can be up to twice as large and have only slight humps. Both emerge at night to feed on low-hanging leaves. Leaving a tell-tale slimy trail behind them, they chew large holes and may completely devour young shoots. SUSCEPTIBLE PLANTS: BELLFLOWER DELPHINIUM, PANSY, POLYANTHUS, HOSTA, IRIS	Because slugs and snails find it difficult to crawl over rough surfaces, lay protective strips of coarse sand or cinders around plant beds. The pests can be lured to a drowning death by placing shallow bowls of beer or grape juice near plants. Use metaldehyde or methiocarb if damage is heavy.
	SPIDER MITES Tiny members of the spider family, barely visible to the naked eye, spider mites are ubiquitous, hot-weather pests that build small webs on the undersides of leaves. By sucking sap from the leaves, they stunt growth and cause yellow, grey or brown discolorations. A smaller family member, the cyclamen mite, attacks Michaelmas daisies. SUSCEPTIBLE PLANTS: CLEMATIS, HOLLYHOCK, PRIMROSE, VIOLET	Destroy spider mite webs with strong jets of water from a garden hose. If this treatment proves ineffective, spray weekly for several weeks with dicofol, malathion or derris.
	LEAF MINERS These tiny larvae of certain flies hatch from eggs laid on the undersides of leaves. The young larvae then tunnel between the tissues and consume the leaves' tender interior, leaving prominent, serpentine trails called mines. When fully fed they pupate at the end of a larval mine or in the soil. Meanwhile the leaves shrivel and fall. If badly infected, the plant may die. SUSCEPTIBLE PLANTS: CHRYSANTHEMUM, COLUMBINE, DELPHINIUM, SHASTA DAISY	Remove badly affected leaves and burn them before a new generation of flies can emerge. Sow-thistle is host to chrysanthemum leaf-miners so destroy these weeds also. Control as soon as mines appear by spraying the undersides of the leaves with diazinon or BHC.
	THRIPS These barely visible winged insects, about 1 mm (1/18 in.) long, scrape open the tissue of leaves, petals and buds and drink the sap, causing discoloration and deformities and leaving behind distinctive brown or silvery streaks on the outside of leaves. They breed continuously under favourable conditions, especially in hot, dry weather. SUSCEPTIBLE PLANTS: CARNATION, CHRYSANTHEMUM, GLADIOLUS	Unlike many pests, thrips infest gardens unpredictably, sometimes appearing one year and not the next. Infestations can be readily controlled by spraying with malathion or dimethoate; the latter is a systemic insecticide which should not be used on chrysanthemums.

DISEASE	DESCRIPTION	METHODS OF CONTROL
LEAF SPOT	Various fungi and bacteria cause spotting of leaves on weak plants, especially when humidity is high; the resultant disease is known as leaf spot or blotch. The dark brown or black spots may join to produce large irregular blotches before the leaves wither and die or fall prematurely. Affected plants may be weakened severely or killed. SUSCEPTIBLE PLANTS: CHRYSANTHEMUM, DELPHINIUM, HELLEBORE, LUPIN, PHLOX	Remove old leaves, stems and other plant debris. Cut off infected leaves or rake up those which have fallen, and burn them. Spray with benomyl, Bordeaux mixture, captan, dichlorofluanid, maneb, thiophanate-methyl or zineb as first leaves unfold or when disease is first seen.
GREY MOULD	Also called botrytis, this disease can be troublesome during long periods of humid, sunless weather, causing the death of stems, leaves, flowers and bulbs. Affected tissues are soft and discoloured and soon become covered with a greyish, velvety mould, consisting of masses of microscopic spores. The fungus overwinters in the form of small, round or elongated, hard, black resting bodies (*inset*). SUSCEPTIBLE PLANTS: EUPHORBIA, PEONY, PYRETHRUM AND MOST BULBOUS PLANTS	Remove and burn diseased portions. Avoid over-watering. Thin out plants so they get more light and air or move them to a dry, sunny position. Dust with dry Bordeaux powder, or spray with benomyl, captan, dichlorofluanid, maneb, thiophanate-methyl, thiram or zineb.
POWDERY MILDEW	This type of fungus, usually more unsightly than harmful, shows as a white powdery coating on leaves, stems and flowers. Affected leaves wither and may fall, thus causing loss of vigour, but the disease does not kill plants. The fungus is encouraged by a humid atmosphere, but plants are susceptible to infection when the soil is dry. SUSCEPTIBLE PLANTS: DELPHINIUM, GOLDEN ROD, LUPIN, MEADOW SWEET, MICHAELMAS DAISY, PHLOX, VERBASCUM	Cut out diseased shoots at the end of the season and burn them. Avoid dense growth by thinning if necessary. Mulch and water before the soil dries out completely; avoid late afternoon sprinkling. Spray with benomyl, copper, dinocap, thiophanate-methyl or triforine.
SOIL-BORNE DISEASE	Various fungi and bacteria in the soil can attack many kinds of plants either below or just above ground level, causing them to wilt or topple over. The disease of seedlings known as damping off occurs in unsterilized compost or where contaminated water from a butt is used. In older plants shoot and root rot—or wilt—occurs if the soil has become infected. SUSCEPTIBLE PLANTS: SEEDLINGS OF MOST PERENNIALS, OLDER PLANTS OF DELPHINIUM, LUPIN, MICHAELMAS DAISY, PHLOX	Use sterilized or new soil for seed sowing under glass, and keep water butts clean. Sow seeds thinly and ensure that they have good ventilation. Water soil in boxes or pots with captan, Cheshunt compound or zineb. Dig up and burn affected plants together with the soil attached to the roots.
RUST	The appearance of raised spots called pustules marks the onset of the fungus disease known as rust. The pustules are usually found on the undersides of leaves and on stems; they produce masses of powdery spores, often orange in colour, but sometimes yellow, pale or dark brown and occasionally black. In severe cases shrivelling of the leaves or even of the whole plant may occur. SUSCEPTIBLE PLANTS: AQUILEGIA, ARTEMISIA, CAMPANULA, HOLLYHOCK, HYPERICUM, SIDALCEA, THRIFT	Remove and burn rust-infected leaves. Spray every two weeks throughout the growing season with maneb, thiram or zineb. When the flowering season is over, cut infected plants to the ground and burn the stalks at once. Do not use them for compost.

Using nature's pest killers

An increasingly attractive alternative to chemical spraying and dusting—and one that avoids their possibly harmful side effects—is the introduction into the garden of certain insects and disease-carrying bacteria that prey almost exclusively on pests. Some of the natural controls listed below provide broad protection—ladybirds devour any number of different plant-eating pests—while others are more specific. The larvae of chalcid wasps attack the scale stage of white fly.

NATURAL CONTROL	DESCRIPTION	GARDEN TREATMENT
LADYBIRD	There are about fifty species of ladybirds, chiefly red with black spots, but sometimes yellow. Their presence on plants usually indicates an infestation of aphids. Both the adult beetles and their black or grey, alligator-like larvae feed voraciously on aphids and also attack scale and related insects. There is usually one brood a year, but occasionally a second small brood in June. INSECT VICTIMS: APHIDS, LEAF WORMS, MEALY BUGS, MITES, SCALE INSECTS	Protect ladybirds whenever possible; many are destroyed by contact sprays such as nicotine and derris. In some countries, ladybirds are bred and sold in packages of 10,000 or so—enough for a small garden. These can be stored in a refrigerator and released in batches as required.
LACEWING LARVAE	The adult lacewing is rather handsome, about 1 to 2 cm ($\frac{1}{2}$ to $\frac{3}{4}$ in.) long with gauze-like wings and large glittering eyes. But it is the ugly little larvae, called aphid lions, that are most useful as pest killers. In their two-week larval period they feed almost constantly on aphids and other insects. As adults, only a few species continue to eat insects. The rest live on aphid honeydew and flower nectar. INSECT VICTIMS: APHIDS, LEAF HOPPERS, MITES, THRIPS, WHITE FLIES	The eggs are laid on slender stalks near aphid colonies. In the United States lacewing eggs are sold in vials by insect farms for scattering on infested plants.
LARGER CREATURES	Among the larger beneficial creatures frequently found in European gardens are hedgehogs, nocturnal in habit and voracious feeders on snails, slugs and insects. The sow produces one litter (sometimes two) a year with four to seven young and hibernates under leaves, moss or beneath a shed or similar refuge. Other insect eaters are shrews, toads and frogs, whilst many birds help the gardener by preying upon caterpillars and insects. INSECT VICTIMS: APHIDS, BEETLES, CATERPILLARS	Frogs and toads breed in water and they appreciate a pool or long grass as a refuge against hot sun. Hedgehogs can be enticed and tamed by putting out a saucer of bread and milk each evening; birds can be encouraged by the provision of water in summer and food in winter.
GARDEN FRIENDS	The gardener has many friends that are often overlooked, for example the numerous small predators that prey on harmful pests. These include the well-known centipede which is carnivorous and feeds on many soil pests, and the larvae of chalcid flies which attack the scale stage of white fly. The grubs of ichneumon flies are parasitic on leaf-eating caterpillars, and the larvae of hover flies attack aphids. INSECT VICTIMS: SOIL PESTS, APHIDS, WHITE FLIES	It is important to recognize and respect these friends. The quick-moving centipede —unlike the harmful millipede which curls up like a watch spring—should always be spared. Plants should not be sprayed when in flower for fear of injuring the friendly grubs.

ground level as shown in the drawings below. (If you cut the old stalks to the ground before the new ones have appeared, the plant will probably die.) The new stalks will produce a new crop of flowers.

Even if a plant will not flower a second time, faded blooms should be removed. Producing seeds taxes the strength of a plant and unless seeds are needed, it is better to channel the plant's energy into building a stronger root system for the following year. Unwanted seeds that are allowed to ripen fall to the ground, where they may sprout like weeds and eventually compete with the parent plant for food and moisture. Worse, many such seedlings—particularly those of the brilliantly coloured garden phlox—bear little resemblance to the lovely flowers whence they came, reverting instead to the duller colours of their ancestors.

PERENNIALS AS CUT FLOWERS

One way you can multiply the pleasure of perennials is to harvest some of them for use indoors, both as freshly cut flowers and for dried arrangements. Many gardeners raise peonies, delphiniums, chrysanthemums and pyrethrums in special beds just for cutting, but the list of perennials that will survive well in vases indoors is a gratifyingly long one. It includes, to name only a few, lupins, Oriental poppies, salvias, scabious, artemisias, yarrows, monkshoods, centaureas, globe thistles and coreopsis.

MAKING DELPHINIUMS AND LUPINS BLOOM IN LATE SUMMER

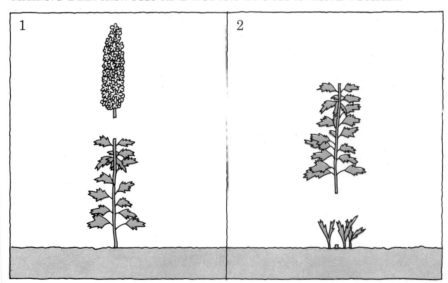

For a late crop of delphiniums and lupins, remove spring flower spikes as soon as they fade. Cut just below the spike base. Hoe in fertilizer around the roots to encourage new stalks, but leave old foliage intact.

When the new growth has reached a height of about 15 cm (6 in.), cut the old foliage stalks to the ground. The new stalks will produce flowers—smaller than previously —within about two months.

Cut flowers are not dead flowers—they continue to live and grow for a while; how long depends in part on the treatment they get. Their chief requirement is water, which not only carries food to their cells, but also fills the cells, keeping the stems sturdy and the blossoms upright. The best time of the day for cutting flowers is in the early morning or late afternoon. Use a sharp knife or secateurs and choose stems with buds that are half or three-quarters open; full-blown blossoms will not last long. Strip off the stems' lower leaves. The reason for this is that plants give off moisture through their leaves and removal of some of the leaves will help to conserve it.

When I step into the garden to cut flowers, I carry a wide-necked vase three-quarters full of warm water, and plunge each stem into it immediately after I have severed it. When the vase is full, but not to the point of crowding, I take it indoors and put it in the coolest place in the house for a couple of hours. Only after that do I begin to arrange the flowers. At this point, I remove any remaining leaves that would be below the water level in the vase, because they would decay and foul the water with bacteria. Then I trim the stems to the desired length, and it does not matter a bit whether the cut is straight across or slanting. What does matter is that the cut should be a clean one, made with extra-sharp scissors and without squeezing the stems—that could impede the intake of moisture. Some plants, such as poppies, ooze a substance that tends to clog the stems; in such cases, the stems should be seared for an instant over a lighted match, a candle or a gasflame; this searing will prevent clogging, thus enabling the cut flower to absorb water.

Many gardeners believe that the lives of cut flowers can be lengthened by the addition of aspirin or sugar or even copper coins to the water. Aspirin and coins do neither good nor harm, but sugar used alone actually is harmful: it stimulates the growth of bacteria, which clog the open cells at the ends of the cut stems. Most of the commercial cut-flower foods, however, do work. They contain sugar to provide quick energy, but they also contain substances that inhibit the growth of bacteria, maintain colour in the petals and slow the flowers' metabolism so that they will survive longer. If you use a material of this kind, put it in the vase before you go out into the garden, so that the flowers can start benefiting from it immediately. With a cut-flower food it is necessary every day to add water containing the same solution in order to replace what the flowers have consumed. When it is not used, you should remove the flowers from the vase every day, rinse the vase clean and then refill it with warm water.

For centuries, gardeners have been extending their enjoyment of certain perennials—baby's-breath, sea lavender and cupid's-dart, to name a few—by turning them into permanent dried

HOW TO DRY FLOWERS

arrangements. Methods used include hanging the cut flowers in a dry place until the stalks are quite dry, or burying them in sand or borax to absorb their moisture. A faster and more reliable method has now been developed, one that also preserves the true colour of flowers that cannot be dried successfully by the old methods. It involves the use of silica gel, a substance widely employed in industry to protect dehydrated foods and sensitive instruments from dampness. Silica gel looks like sugar and can absorb water equivalent to 40 per cent of its own weight. Ordinarily blue, it turns pink when saturated, but dries out again and reverts to blue after half an hour's warming in a 130°C (250°F) oven. When the silica gel is not in use, it must be stored in an airtight container to keep it dry. You will find that large biscuit tins are ideal for this purpose, for they do double duty: they serve both as storage units and again during the flower-drying process itself.

Flowers that are to be dried should first be stripped of foliage and fragile stems. The heads of the flowers are then placed, facing up, on a layer of silica gel about 4 centimetres (1½ in.) deep on the bottom of the tin, and more silica gel is sprinkled over them until they are covered. The lid is put on and sealed with masking tape. Within four to seven days the flowers will have dried and can be gently removed from the gel. (If you lose a petal, stick it back on, using a toothpick to apply transparent glue.) Blossoms that are not going to be used in arrangements can be stored immediately in a tightly covered glass jar with a teaspoon or two of silica gel to keep them dry. When you are ready to do your dried flower arranging you can mount the flower heads on stems made of florists' green wire. First run a length of wire up through the head of each flower, then bend the top of the wire to make a small hook and, finally, pull the bent wire down into the flower head so that the hook is concealed. You can then bend and twist the stems which will enable you to make a variety of different arrangements, with dried grasses for a foliage effect.

WINTER PROTECTION Perennials have little trouble surviving winter where snows start early and stay late, or where the climate is mild all year. But they need some special care in areas where wind and cold arrive when the ground is still bare and where winter thaws may be followed by sudden freezes that can push the roots out of the ground and damage them. In exposed areas, leave the old stems on the plants (to protect them) until spring; also cover the crowns with fine branches, bracken or dry leaves. In more favourable climates, cut all the old stalks right to the ground after the leaves have withered in autumn, chop them up and put them on the compost heap. At this time it is easy to discern which plants are encroaching on their neighbours and should therefore be divided.

A few that are cold resistant can be divided then and there (*Chapter 3*); the others should wait until spring.

Next, replace missing stakes and labels to avoid mistakes and lapses of memory next season. Then scatter a handful of bonemeal around the patriarchs such as peonies and gas plants that are not scheduled to be dug up, divided and replanted in newly fertilized soil. The phosphoric acid it contains will strengthen their roots. Now wait for the ground to freeze.

In cold weather areas, perennials do best when they are frozen solid and remain completely dormant all winter. So where there is danger of alternate freezing and thawing, they should be covered, not to keep them warm, but to keep them cold; for this reason the perennial bed should be mulched after the ground has frozen—never before it has frozen. By then any mice that might have been tempted to nest in the mulch will have found homes elsewhere and will be less likely to gnaw the roots. The ideal mulch is light enough to permit air to penetrate, but substantial enough to shade the soil and keep it from thawing every time the sun shines. A good mulch consists of evergreen boughs. Some gardeners buy up left-over Christmas trees, cut off their springy branches and lay them over the perennial bed. Two layers of boughs, criss-crossed, should suffice. They admit air to the ground, but keep out the sun. If no such mulching material is available, you can use a 20 centimetre (3 in.) blanket of straw or bracken to cover the dormant plants.

In the spring, I remove the winter mulch in two stages, three or four days apart, just as the first new shoots appear; this permits the tender new growth to become gradually acclimatized to the chill spring air. I use a long-handled fork to lift the straw or the boughs rather than pulling them off with a rake, whose tines might damage the tender growth that has already started to push up through the surface of the ground. Then my perennials are almost ready to reward me with lovely blossoms. And, with only a little more effort on my part, these plants will multiply and fill not only my garden—but, they will enhance and fill the gardens of my friends as well.

THE PEONY'S MAGICAL PAST

The offhand way modern gardeners cut peonies for indoor bouquets would have shocked the ancients, who endowed the plant with magical powers. To the Greeks, the flower was a charm against evil spirits and had to be plucked with care: it was thought to be watched over by a woodpecker; if it was taken in daylight, the woodpecker would peck out the eyes of the gardener. The Greeks, consequently, picked peonies in the middle of the night, when any sensible woodpecker is sound asleep. The Romans were even more cautious in handling peonies. They thought that the plant emitted a soft groan as it emerged from the earth, and that anyone close enough to hear the groan would die. To pull up a peony, a dog was tied to the plant. Enticed with meat, the animal pulled up the plant as humans stayed out of earshot.

Prestige Showcase where the grower's art is in full bloom

To knowledgeable gardeners everywhere, "Chelsea" is not just a place but an event: the Chelsea Flower Show, the biggest and best-known show of its kind in Europe. For four days every May thousands of visitors from all over the world flock to the grounds of the Royal Hospital overlooking the Thames in London's Chelsea district, crowding into a vast marquee that encloses one and a half hectares (3½ acres) of dazzling displays.

The show's appeal transcends horticulture; it is invariably attended by members of the British royal family and marks the opening of the London social season. But for all its fashionableness, flowers remain the primary attraction, among them the finest and most colourful perennials that breeders can produce: delphiniums in every tone of blue, irises of deepest purple and pure white, peonies in a profusion of tints, Oriental poppies bobbing their heads of blazing colours over carnations, pinks, chrysanthemums, each bloom nurtured for this moment of glory.

International competition for the top awards has grown tougher year by year since the first Chelsea Flower Show in 1913. Amateurs with single, treasured blooms vie with commercial nurseries and professional gardeners from many different countries. The flowers are judged the day before the show opens to the public. New varieties are considered separately—and cautiously. As many as 20,000 individual plants may have to be grown to produce a new variety and even then the breed may finally prove to be unstable. Thus it is rare for a new perennial to receive any award grander than a Certificate of Commendation on its first appearance before the judges. And years may pass before it wins one of the 30-odd medals.

Exhibitors spend months preparing their displays. Autumn-flowering plants are forced forward with heat and artificial light while spring flowers are held back by refrigeration to ensure that each bloom is at its peak of perfection when it arrives at Chelsea. Some plants travel halfway around the world. Transporting orchids from Barbados or bonsai trees from Japan takes careful planning. Even local growers have to stake and wrap individual blossoms to protect them on their trips to the show. No effort is too great when the prize might be a gold medal from the Royal Horticultural Society—the supreme accolade for any plant.

On the Chelsea show's first day, viewers discuss the merits of feathery astilbes, stately foxgloves and golden verbascums.

Ranks of regal delphiniums

Among the most popular perennials at Chelsea are delphiniums, which have been cultivated since the days of the pharaohs. Then they were valued for their seeds, thought to destroy body lice, but nowadays their appeal is in the arresting beauty of their towering columns of blossoms. The stately Elatum hybrids (*on this page and opposite*) are particular favourites, their spikes of semi-double flowers—ranging from white through mauve to royal blue—often standing more than 1 metre (3 ft) high. Delphiniums may bloom for as little as a week, so timing is critical. Exhibitors grow many more plants than they plan to show to make sure enough will be at their prime on judging day.

An exhibitor attaches a name card to a 'Molly Buchanan', a delphinium that has been popular since it was first displayed at Chelsea in the mid-1960s.

'WHITE KNIGHT'

'BLUE NILE'

Delphiniums like these blossom in shades of blue, purple, pink and white, all with prominent contrasting eyes. Experimental breeding work in the mid-1970s promised to produce cultivars in red and yellow as well.

With the aid of his assistant, an iris breeder (right) prepares his exhibits at Chelsea for judging. Great care must be taken as the twine is cut away and the cotton wool removed (above), to ensure the flower opens out to a perfect shape.

For iris growers Chelsea presents special problems. The flowers are so delicate and easily bruised that each bloom has to be individually protected for shipment. The petals are carefully gathered up, swathed in cotton wool, and then tied with special Chinese twine. The job requires great skill and patience and can take as much as three days for a single exhibit. But the results are well worth the effort. The *Iris* genus, named after the Greek goddess of the rainbow, displays myriad colours. The classic bearded irises, often known as flags (*here and overleaf*), are probably the most widely grown and exhibited. Their brilliantly coloured blooms are often deliciously scented.

The great variety of colour and size displayed by irises like these results from cross-fertilization experiments by growers.

'WABASH'

'RED BOURNE'

'JANE PHILLIPS'

'MAGIC HILLS'

'LADY MOHR'

'HENNA STITCHES'

Exultant crowds of foxgloves

Wild foxgloves, common in Europe, bear only faint resemblance to the sophisticated varieties seen at Chelsea. In the wild, the bell-shaped blossoms grow only on one side of the stem and hang downward. Popular hybrids have flowers all around the stem, lifting their heads to reveal striking interior markings. Foxgloves must be half-open before arrival, as the diffuse light inside the marquee is too weak to bring buds to bloom.

The visual exuberance of the foxglove hybrids (left and below) is reflected in their name: Excelsior. Introduced in the early 1960s, they are now prized throughout the world and are regularly exhibited at Chelsea.

Glamorous peonies

Peonies appear at Chelsea in such wide and exotic variety that the blossoms seem sometimes not to represent the same genus. Some plants bear rose-like clumps of soft pink petals while others sport brilliant scarlet cups tufted with golden stamens. Peonies normally are at their best during the week of the show, and do not need to be forced or held back. But their heavy blooms on long stems are accident-prone and must be individually supported by "travelling canes" for the trip to Chelsea. They are just beginning to open when they arrive. Were they already in full bloom, they would not survive five days of display in the heat inside the marquee.

'MADAME CALOT'

'INSPECTOR LAVERGNE'

'KELWAYS BRILLIANT'

'BALLERINA'

'GLOBE OF LIGHT'

A nurseryman carefully cuts the tops
from canes tied to the stems of these
fully double, delightfully scented peonies
so that the blossoms can be viewed in
unobstructed glory while still being
supported for the duration of the show.

A Chelsea gathering of peonies (clockwise from left) include the ruffly 'Madame Calot'; the shallow-cupped 'Pink Delight'; the

large pink 'Bowl of Beauty'; the red, glossy 'Silver Flare'; the tasselled 'Globe of Light'; and in the centre foreground, 'Strephon'.

Propagating new plants for your garden

Perennials proliferate like kittens and, as with kittens, some people always have too many and are eager to find good homes for them. Producing new plants is perhaps the most exciting aspect of gardening. Admittedly one does sometimes get carried away with enthusiasm, but the surplus can often be used for the benefit of others—those with less knowledge of propagating plants, or less time or space in which to raise them. Young plants will always find a saleable market at local horticultural societies or garden clubs; flower arrangers are always on the lookout for new sorts of material. Many friends of mine, and I myself, find such local garden sales a great help in keeping gardens young. And many a beginning gardener, once he realizes that most of the plants that he has purchased or has seen on sale were produced from someone's existing garden plants, decides to try propagating his own. In this way he can not only enlarge his garden, but also replace old overgrown specimens with vigorous free-flowering ones at little or no expense.

Once you decide to try your hand at propagation, you have a choice of several different methods. In the case of some plants, such as delphiniums and lupins (*encyclopaedia*), you can get excellent results if you propagate biologically, that is, by means of seed from one plant that has been fertilized by pollen from another. However, except in the case of species, that is naturally occurring forms, you must buy seed properly produced by seedsmen to breed true; there is no predictability in propagation by seed taken from flowers in your garden. The offspring may display undesirable characteristics of one or more forebears. More reliable results, however, can be depended upon if plants are propagated vegetatively, that is produced from pieces taken from a single parent plant. Vegetative propagation ensures that the offspring will inherit all of the traits of its single parent plant. This is particularly helpful in expanding or rejuvenating a perennial border, for example, since the gardener can be certain that his new plants will duplicate precisely the colour patterns, sizes and heights of the old plants from which they come.

This long, stately border of hostas, prized as much for their foliage as for their lily-like flowers, grew in eight years from just four plants. Divided and replanted, they spread to form an impressive display.

The most common method of vegetative propagation, and the one with which most amateurs begin, is division, which is simply breaking up a large plant into several smaller ones. This operation does not harm the plants; in fact, most perennials will stay healthier if they are dug up, divided and replanted periodically. An old, and still good, rule of thumb is to divide plants every third flowering season. There are exceptions: peonies and gas plants, for example, which are slow-spreading and slow to re-establish themselves after division, should remain undisturbed as long as they thrive; Korean and Rubellum chrysanthemums, on the other hand, spread so fast that they should be divided every year (how often to divide each type of plant is noted in the encyclopaedia section). It may take a good deal of will-power, I know, to dig up a clump of flowers that looks in its prime, but that is the way to keep your garden young over a period of years.

The reasons for digging and dividing are twofold. First, fast-growing perennials overrun and crowd out their neighbours, so they must be kept under control for the sake of the garden as a whole. Equally important is the need for growing space for all parts of each plant. As a plant spreads, the new roots and stems on the clump's periphery thrive in the fresh soil and ample breathing space, but in the centre, competition for nutrients, water, light and circulating air becomes increasingly intense and roots and stems weaken. The result is a ring of healthy flowers around a dying heart. Wise gardeners avoid this unsightly result by dividing the old clump and leaving in its place only as many vigorous roots and stems as the available space can support in good health. The remaining healthy parts of the clump can be immediately replanted; the dying centre should be discarded.

The best time to divide depends on the kind of plant and where you live. Generally, spring-blooming plants such as primroses and moss phlox should be divided in early summer after they have flowered. Summer-blooming plants such as sea-pinks and garden phlox do well when they are divided in late summer or early autumn. Autumn-blooming plants such as chrysanthemums, mist-flowers and sneezeweed should be divided in spring when they will have a whole growing season ahead of them.

However, this rule has its exceptions. Where winters are severe, it is advisable to divide most plants in very early spring before they begin to produce new growth. They are then sure to have enough time to develop a strong root system and anchor themselves firmly in the earth before cold weather arrives again. If they are divided and replanted later in the year, they may be forced out of the ground to die in the alternate freezing and thawing of the soil in late winter and early spring.

HOW TO DIVIDE PLANTS   With plants such as bergamot, sneezeweed or Michaelmas daisy, which have relatively shallow roots that may be reached and

80

lifted with little difficulty, the easiest way to divide a clump is to dig with a sharp spade at the clump's periphery, using the spade to cut away outer sections of the plant and as much soil as will adhere to them (*drawings, below*). Many perennials have eyes, or buds, in their upper roots that are easily visible in spring and often visible in autumn. With such plants, cut each section, called a division, to include two to four eyes; from them stems will grow eventually. The rest of the clump should then be dug up and the old centre discarded.

To replant a division where the old plant was growing, do not simply stick it back in the hole. Turn the soil thoroughly to a depth of at least 30 centimetres (1 ft) and work into the soil a 5 to 10 centimetre (2 to 4 in.) layer of moss peat and a dusting of fertilizer. Then set the division in the hole at the same depth that its parent was, spreading the roots loosely; cover them with soil, firm with your feet and water thoroughly. If you are doing the job in late summer or early autumn, the plant being divided will have live stems and leaves. Cut the stems back by half before you plant; the new roots could not support full-sized stems. Plants that are divided in early spring, when their top growth is still only a few centimetres in height, do not require any cutting back.

The method of division that you use will be dictated in part by the plants. The roots of day lilies, for example, are so inter-

DIVIDING SHALLOW-ROOTING CLUMPS OF PERENNIALS

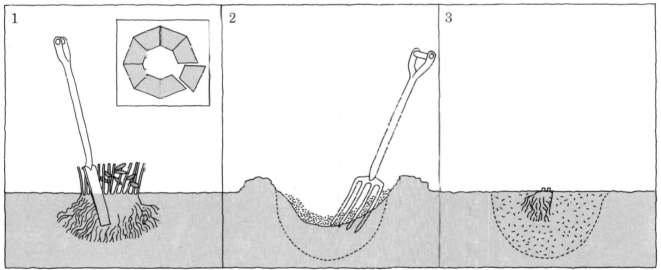

To revitalize a sneezeweed or any perennial that spreads to form a large clump surrounding a dying centre, cut the clump into segments (inset) with a sharp spade. Discard the old centre.

With a fork, loosen the soil in the bottom of the original hole and drop in a little moss peat and a light dusting of fertilizer. Then mix the fertilizer and the moss peat thoroughly with loose soil.

Replant one segment, or division, in the old hole, other divisions elsewhere in the garden. Cut off the old stems close to ground level and water well. Each division will eventually fill the allotted space.

twined that it requires two forks back to back (*drawings, below*) to pry them into segments after they are out of the ground. But primroses come apart easily and their roots can be separated gently with the fingers. In every case, though, prepare the soil properly and water the plants thoroughly after planting.

TAKING STEM CUTTINGS Propagation by division serves the garden well when a clump has outlived, or is about to outlive, its usefulness. But occasionally you will want to multiply an attractive still-young clump that is doing so well where it is that you hesitate to dig it up and divide it, or one that should be left alone and never divided. In either case you can create new plants by cutting segments of stems from the plant and inducing them to produce roots of their own (*drawings, page 84*). Stem cuttings, like plant divisions, produce young perennials that duplicate their parents precisely in both the colour and shape of their blossoms. This is an important consideration in modern cultivated perennials, which are often erratic in producing seed—and the seeds, when they do appear, produce plants that may revert to the less desirable shape and colour of an ancestor. Unlike plant divisions, stem cuttings allow you to have your clump of prized flowers and multiply it too, with only temporary damage to the parent. This method works well with Michaelmas daisies, anthemis, pinks and solidasters.

THREE WAYS TO DIVIDE PERENNIAL CLUMPS

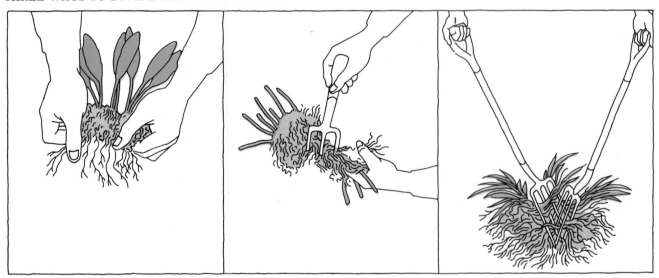

Shallow-rooted plants such as primroses are easy to pull apart by hand. After digging them up, shake off the soil and gently separate the clump into small plant segments, each with a few leaves intact.

Long whiskery roots like those of phlox may be prised apart with a hand fork. Replant only those segments with strong roots; shrivelled pieces from the centre of the clump must be thrown away.

Thickly intertwined roots such as those of day lilies must be forcibly separated. Thrust two forks, back to back, into the clump and, using the handles of the forks as levers, pry the roots apart.

The best season to take stem cuttings, sometimes referred to as soft cuttings, or "pips" in the case of border pinks, is in spring or early summer. To make a cutting, choose a stem that is straight and firm, but not yet hardened and woody. Use a sharp knife or razor blade to slice off a 5 to 15 centimetre (2 to 6 in.) shoot immediately below a joint, called a node, where a leaf sprouts from the stem. If the tip of the cutting has buds or flowers, pinch the tip off; this operation forces the cutting to concentrate on root production rather than on top growth. Carefully remove the lower leaves of the cutting so that about 2.5 centimetres (1 in.) of bare stem will go below the surface of the ground when you plant, but do not remove the upper leaves— the cutting will need them as a source of energy while it continues its growth processes. Fresh cuttings tend to wilt quickly when the weather is warm and they should be planted immediately. If you cannot do so speedily, moisten them slightly and keep them in a plastic bag in a cool place.

Do not attempt to plant a stem cutting in the garden; it must be started in a container where you can provide conditions conducive to rooting. For a few cuttings, a 10 centimetre (4 in.) flowerpot will serve. For a large number, you can use a bigger pot or any container—such as a shallow box or an alpine pan— that is at least 10 centimetres (4 in.) deep, and has provision for drainage. Fill the pot or pan to within 12 millimetres ($\frac{1}{2}$ in.) of its top with a porous rooting medium such as coarse builders' sand, vermiculite, equal parts of moist peat and coarse sand, or shredded sphagnum moss that will admit plenty of moisture and air. Moisten the rooting medium thoroughly. Sand should be wetted, tamped, and wetted again before the cuttings are set; the alternative materials should be wetted but not firmed before the cuttings are inserted.

When you have the rooting medium and the container ready, prepare the cuttings for insertion. A few, delphiniums and phlox for example, may not take root easily, but you can help the process by dipping their ends first in water and then in a hormone rooting powder (a root stimulating chemical obtainable from chemists and garden centres). Most herbaceous perennials should not need such aid. Use a dibber or blunt stick about the size of a pencil to make holes in the compost and insert the cuttings, firming gently around them so that they are not sitting in an air pocket. Label the container and water well.

Ideally the container should now go into a propagating case that provides bottom heat to stimulate rooting. The case should have a glass or plastic cover to maintain humidity. Small electric models can be bought from garden centres, but bottom heat can also be contrived by putting the container in a box which has 5 to 7.5 centimetres (2 to 3 in.) of moist peat at the bottom. If this is stood over a warm radiator and covered with a polythene sheet,

THE MEASURE OF LOVE

An old name for Bellis perennis, *the familiar English daisy, is "measure of love", a tribute to generations of lovelorn maidens who plucked the petals of the daisy one by one to the rhythmic chant of "he loves me, he loves me not". To make it come out right, the trick is to begin with "he loves me" on the first petal—for reasons botanical and mathematical. Since virtually all daisies have an odd number of petals, the words "he loves me" will almost invariably coincide with the tearing-off of the last petal if they are also used for the first.*

humidity will be maintained and the cuttings will soon root. If neither of these aids are available, rooting will take longer and some cuttings may rot if the weather turns cold. Keep the cuttings in a light place, but protect them from direct sunlight. If glass is used as a covering it should be removed daily and wiped, the cuttings should be lightly sprinkled with water and the glass returned after an hour.

When the cuttings show small new leaves, an indication that roots have developed, open the glass or plastic cover a little to let in fresh air; the new plants will then become acclimatized before the cover is removed. Gently pry loose one or two cuttings from the rooting medium; if new roots are 12 to 25 millimetres ($\frac{1}{2}$ to 1 in.) long, the cuttings are ready to move to the garden. I put mine first in a reserve garden, a small home nursery that I keep beside my vegetable garden. There the young plants can

STARTING NEW PLANTS FROM STEM CUTTINGS

1. *To propagate perennials from stem cuttings, take 5 to 15 cm (2 to 6 in.) segments from the tips of stems, cutting immediately below a leaf joint. Remove the lower leaves. To prevent wilting, sprinkle the cuttings with water, place them in a plastic bag and set them in a cool place.*

2. *Stimulate root growth by dipping the bottom 12 mm ($\frac{1}{2}$ in.) of each stem in rooting powder; tap off the excess. Do not dip the stem in the container; if diseased it can contaminate the remaining powder.*

3. *Using a dibber, make holes 2.5 cm (1 in.) deep and 2.5 to 5 cm (1 to 2 in.) apart in a tray or pot with a 10 cm (4 in.) bed of moist vermiculite, sand and peat or sphagnum moss. Insert cuttings, firm rooting medium and water.*

4. *Cover the seed tray with glass or, as here, with clear plastic tucked under the tray. Fit a plastic bag over pots. Set the cuttings in a bright place. When the new growth appears, open the plastic to admit air. Transplant when the roots are 12 to 25 mm ($\frac{1}{2}$ to 1 in.) long.*

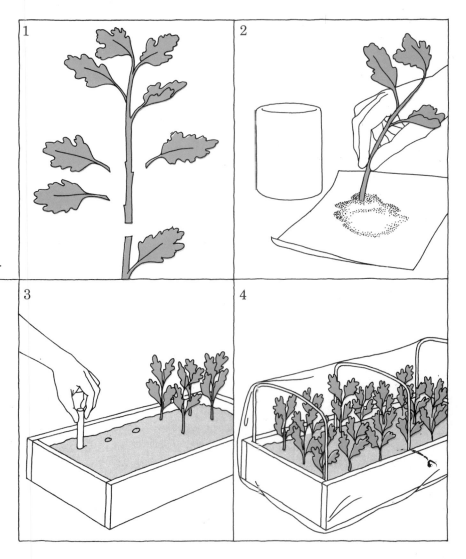

be spaced out in easy-to-tend rows to continue their growth without being overwhelmed by larger, older plants. When they have become big enough to hold their own in the main garden, they are transplanted to go on display there.

Another way to increase some of your cherished plants is to take cuttings from roots rather than stems. Nature uses this technique on occasion, as I learned back in 1934 when I was working for a nurseryman who specialized in perennials. It was an exceptionally cold winter and there was no snow on the ground to act as insulation for the nursery plants; many hardy species were killed outright. Even the garden phlox, normally extremely tough, suffered disaster—all the buds (the points at which stem and root merge) and central crowns perished, and the nurseryman wrote them off as a total loss. But late in spring, a circle of tiny new plants appeared around each dead crown. The tiny roots farthest from the crowns, although cut off by the cold, had survived on their own, and where each large plant had stood there were now dozens of small ones.

Horticulturists employ this regenerating characteristic of tiny roots to reproduce such plants as Japanese anemone, butterfly weed, *Primula denticulata* and blanket flower. They snap off bits of roots, in autumn or winter, either when they have lifted plants for division or by digging into the ground around them. If you try this method (*drawings, page 86*), use a sharp knife or scissors to cut off tips of the roots. The size of the root pieces and the manner of replanting them differ with various plants. For most species, pieces of root 2.5 to 5 centimetres (1 to 2 in.) long will be large enough; such pieces should be laid on their sides in light soil or coarse sand in a wooden seed tray or other shallow box with drainage holes. Cover them with a little sand; firm the sand thoroughly over the root cuttings and moisten it. Finally, put the box in a cold frame for the winter. A cold frame is nothing more than an outdoor box that is heated by the sun and protects young plants from extreme cold and wind. It can be made out of bricks or boards of decay-resistant wood such as hardwood or cypress to enclose an area about 1 by 2 metres (3 by 6 ft). The back of the box, facing north, should be 45 to 75 centimetres (18 to 30 in.) high; the front, facing south, should be 30 to 60 centimetres (12 to 24 in.) high. The sides should slope slightly, and the entire frame should be topped with glass or heavy-gauge clear plastic. The sloped cover allows the rain to run off. Root cuttings, protected in such a structure, will send up shoots in spring. When they do, move them to a nursery bed; they will eventually grow large enough for the flower garden.

Some plants—Oriental poppy, bleeding heart and a few others specified in the encyclopaedia—require special treatment when roots are cut (*drawings, page 87*). Their root pieces should

TAKING ROOT CUTTINGS

be longer—7.5 to 10 centimetres (3 to 4 in.) and each segment should be potted separately and upright, in potting soil or in a mixture composed of $\frac{1}{3}$ sand, $\frac{1}{3}$ garden soil and $\frac{1}{3}$ moss peat or compost. Put the mixture into 15 cm (6 in.) pots and bury each root so the tip is nearly 2.5 centimetres (1 in.) below the surface. Be sure that the root is the right side up; the part of the root that was closest to the crown of the parent plant must be at the top. Moisten the soil thoroughly and then put the pots in a cold frame for the winter. The roots will develop growth buds at their tops and in the spring the new plants will begin to grow. But in most cases they will not flower until their second season, so they too should go into a nursery bed until they are ready.

Seeds, of course, are less expensive than nursery-grown plants but they can tax the gardener's patience—it takes from two to three years, for example, to bring a balloon flower into

TAKING CUTTINGS FROM SLENDER ROOTS

1. *To propagate phlox, Japanese anemones and other perennials that have roots no thicker than 6 mm ($\frac{1}{4}$ in.), first slice off the outer ends of the roots in autumn with a sharp spade, starting about 15 cm (6 in.) from the clumps. Root pieces can also be taken while the plants are lifted for division (drawings, page 82).*

2. *After hosing down the roots, cut off and discard the thin end and cut the healthy middle sections into pieces about 2.5 to 5 cm (1 to 2 in.) long.*

3. *Lay the root cuttings horizontally 2.5 cm (1 in.) or so apart in a seed tray filled with light soil or sand and cover them with 12 mm ($\frac{1}{2}$ in.) of sand. Firm the sand well and water thoroughly until the water seeps through the bottom of the tray. Set the tray in a cold frame (opposite) for the winter.*

4. *Remove the tray from the cold frame the following spring. When the new plants are about 7.5 cm (3 in.) tall, transplant them to a nursery bed, then in autumn transplant them again to selected positions in your bed or border.*

bloom from seed. Even peonies, normally grown from divisions of named cultivars, can be raised to maturity from seed, but it takes five to seven years for a peony seedling to blossom. Nevertheless, there is an immense satisfaction in seeing plants that you yourself have raised from seed come into blossom for the first time, and I am sure you will find it worthwhile to try this method of propagation with at least some of your perennials.

Neither divisions nor stem or root cuttings will work for multiplying biennials such as Canterbury bells, foxgloves and wallflowers, which so often supplement perennials in the garden. You have to start them from seed. Many perennials may also be grown from seed, among them gas plants, columbines, lupins and delphiniums. There are, however, many pitfalls in such an endeavour. Home-gathered seeds can reflect selective breeding only rarely—the bees in your garden are not choosy and pollinate

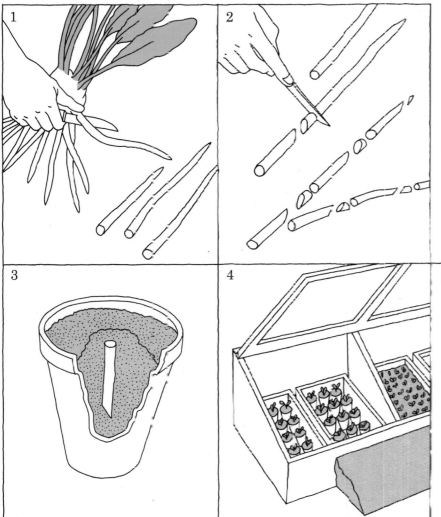

TAKING CUTTINGS FROM THICK ROOTS

1. *To propagate plants with roots 12 mm (½ in.) or so in diameter— Oriental poppy and bleeding heart, for example—dig them up in the autumn and slice off a few of the healthy outer roots with a sharp knife.*

2. *Cut the roots into 7.5 to 10 cm (3 to 4 in.) pieces in such a way that you can identify the top and bottom of each cutting. An easy way is to make a straight cut at the top end and a slanting cut towards the tapered bottom end from which new roots will grow.*

3. *Plant each cutting with its top, straight end up in a pot or box 12 to 15 cm (5 to 6 in.) deep filled with potting soil. Cover with 2.5 cm (1 in.) of soil and water thoroughly.*

4. *Stored over winter in a cold frame, the cuttings will start sending up shoots and leaves when spring arrives. Leave them in the frame until they are about 7.5 cm (3 in.) high. Then transfer them to a nursery bed to go on growing until their next dormant season, when they will be ready for permanent planting.*

both good and poor plants. Few home gardeners can ever hope to produce seeds with the noble pedigrees achieved by professional seedsmen. Also, many perennials are hybrids that are either sterile or whose seeds cannot be relied upon to breed true.

As I suggested at the beginning of this chapter, there is a way around the problem. The answer lies in buying seeds of named cultivars or strains that have been scientifically developed over a period of years. By using these you can be sure that the flowers you choose will perform in the way you wish. They offer far more than exciting colours; different ones often have different times of bloom and are available in varying heights. Delphiniums are a good example: rather than having only the familiar blue ones, the gardener can select strains that produce purple, lavender, pink or white flowers as well as specific shades of blue. By choosing a number of strains he can have delphiniums that bloom from spring to autumn and that grow from about 75 centimetres ($2\frac{1}{2}$ ft) to 1.5 metres (6 ft) tall.

For both biennials and perennials the techniques of reproducing plants from seed are the same, but the time for sowing them varies with the species. The seeds of biennials generally should be sown in midsummer so that the seedlings will have time to make strong growth before winter. (A few species such as pansies and English daisies as well as so-called annual strains of foxgloves, Canterbury bells and sweet williams will bloom in their first year if the seeds are sown early indoors but plants grown in this way do not usually produce as large or as many flowers as do those grown from seed sown the previous summer.)

Some perennials, such as pinks and hollyhocks, germinate quickly and are up and growing in a matter of days. Others, such as gas plants and primroses, may lie dormant for six months or more before sprouting. The seeds of some plants, such as delphiniums, should be sown immediately after their seed pods ripen, for their fresh seeds germinate more dependably than do old ones. The normal germination period for perennials is from 10 days to a month.

Unlike annuals, many of which can be permanently damaged by frost, perennials often grow better in very early spring than at any other time of the year. Since they do not need frost protection, there is no advantage in growing them indoors; in fact, indoor temperatures are usually too warm for them. Therefore the best way to start perennials, and biennials, from seed is outdoors. Preferably, the seeds should be sown within the protected area of a cold frame, not to protect the seedlings from cold as much as from too-strong summer sun and drying winds. For this purpose all you need is a simple temporary structure of boards with a piece of muslin tacked across the top. An alternative is an open seed bed about 1 metre (3 ft) wide (which is a convenient width to work) with the soil raised about 5 centimetres (2 in.)

above the surrounding ground to provide good drainage. Seeds sown in such a bed will do well, but will need more attention to watering whilst they are germinating and when the plants are small and young. Small quantities can be grown in pots, plunged up to their rims in sand or ashes in a cold frame.

Whether you use a cold frame or an open bed, prepare the soil carefully. Dig it about 15 to 20 centimetres (6 to 8 in.) deep, rid it of weeds and stones and break up lumps with a garden rake until the soil looks as though it has been pulverized. Add about 1 part moss peat to each 2 parts of soil, then dig the bed over again and rake it smooth. Do not add fertilizer; it would stimulate the seedlings to send up fast, very tender growth.

Sow your seeds in separate rows spaced about 15 to 20 centimetres (6 to 8 in.) apart; to make rows, use the edge of a draw hoe or a thin board to press shallow furrows into the ground to make a drill. This will make each row about 1 metre (3 ft) long and should give you space for as many seedlings of a particular cultivar as you could possibly want. For fine seeds, first fill the furrows with vermiculite and then sow the seeds sparingly on top; they will sift down slightly into the vermiculite. Sow larger seeds very thinly and cover them with about 6 millimetres ($\frac{1}{4}$ in.) of fine soil or vermiculite. Moisten the seed bed with a fine mist, then cover it with a piece of damp hessian to keep the soil moist. After four or five days lift a corner of the covering daily and peep under it for signs of green; some seeds germinate faster than the average. On the day the seedlings first appear, remove the hessian; uncover the seedlings late in the afternoon so that they will have the night to adjust to their new conditions and to the gradual appearance of light the next morning. The seedlings will need protection from strong sun until they have developed two or three true leaves (which, unlike the initial seedling leaves, are recognizably like those of the mature species). To provide temporary shade, fix a frame light or a section of slatted fencing a few centimetres above the seedlings on stakes set into the corners of the bed. During the seedlings' early growth the seed bed should be kept lightly moistened by sprinkling, but should never be allowed to become soggy, for fungus diseases fatal to seedlings thrive in excessive dampness. When the seedlings have three to four true leaves, they can be dug up gently with a little stick such as a plant label and reset in a nursery bed; space them 15 to 25 centimetres (6 to 10 in.) apart, depending on the size of the species you are growing.

When the young plants have become large enough to begin flowering, you can move them to the display bed that will become their permanent home. Like any plants you have propagated yourself—whether by seed, cuttings or divisions—they will give you a special thrill as you watch them grow up and add beauty to your garden year after year.

An encyclopedia of perennials and biennials

Perennials and their frequent companions, the biennials, are available in such a wealth of colours, sizes and flowering seasons that choosing the best ones for your garden might appear overwhelmingly difficult. The following encyclopaedia of 142 genera of plants, which include the outstanding perennials and biennials, should help to narrow the field. In addition to providing information about the plants—the areas in which they grow and the soil, light and moisture conditions they require—the entries indicate any unusual characteristics. There are, for example, several colourful varieties that can be planted in wooded, even swampy, areas and left untended to bloom indefinitely. There are perennials whose foliage is so distinctive that they are grown more for this reason than for their flowers. Many perennials can be enjoyed indoors as cut flowers.

Once you have made your selections, how do you begin in your garden? Most perennials are sold by nurserymen as container-grown or bare-rooted plants. Container-grown plants, which are sold actively growing in their own soil, can be planted at any time; bare-rooted plants, which are sold while dormant, are generally set out either in autumn or spring depending on the prevailing climates. For those gardeners who want to propagate their own plants from existing ones in their garden, the encyclopaedia entries note which of the methods described in Chapter 3 are best for each plant. The most common method is the division of mature clumps; this is generally done after the plants flower: in summer for spring-flowering plants, autumn for summer-flowering plants, and spring for autumn-flowering plants. In cold areas, plants that flower from midsummer on should be divided in early spring.

Plants are listed by their scientific names. In the case of white perennial flax (*Linum perenne* 'Album'), the genus name, *Linum*, is followed by the epithet, *perenne*; the third name, 'Album', indicates a white-flowered cultivar. A chart on pages 152-154 gives flowering characteristics, height, light and soil requirements of species in which each illustrated plant belongs.

The bounty of the garden, drawn by Allianora Rosse, includes the large, daisy-like flowers of a lavender aster and a yellow leopard's bane (centre), coral-bells (right) and bergamot (top left).

A

ACANTHUS

A. mollis; *A. mollis* var. *latifolius*; *A. spinosus* (spiny acanthus). (All also called bear's-breeches)

Although the flowers of acanthus are attractive, some gardeners remove the flower stalks as soon as they appear and grow the plants solely for their distinctive foliage, which was immortalized in the fifth century B.C. in the design for the capital of the classic Greek Corinthian column. The shiny dark green, deeply-lobed leaves rise directly from the ground and may be 60 cm (2 ft) long and 30 cm (1 ft) wide; those of the spiny acanthus are tipped with stout thorns and must be handled with gloves. In early summer, flower stalks 30 to 120 cm (2 to 4 ft) tall bear 2.5 cm (1 in.) spikes of tubular white, rose or lavender flowers with broadly flaring lips. Small leaves along the spikes and leaf-like bracts just under the flowers are often tinged with purple. The flowering season lasts about two months; spikes may be cut for indoor arrangements or dried for winter bouquets, although the original colours tend to fade within a short time.

HOW TO GROW. Acanthus grows well in all but the coldest areas and does best in very well-drained positions (too much moisture in winter can be fatal). In hot areas, it needs light shade but elsewhere it flourishes in full sun. Set plants about 1 metre (3 ft) apart. The stout, drought-resistant roots range far in good soil, so it is advisable to plant acanthus where the roots will be confined, as between a path, and a wall. New plants may be grown from seeds sown in spring but usually take three years to blossom; they may also be propagated from root cuttings.

ACHILLEA

A. filipendulina, also called *A. eupatorium* (fern-leaved yarrow); *A. millefolium* (common yarrow); *A. ptarmica* (sneezewort); *A. taygetea*; *A. tomentosa* (woolly yarrow)

Yarrows are easy-to-grow perennials that vary in size from creeping kinds suitable for rock gardens to 1 to 1.3 metres (3 to 4½ ft) tall types for the back of a border. Most bear fern-like foliage that has a pungent fragrance. Recommended cultivars of the showy fern-leaved yarrow, which blossoms from early summer to early autumn, are 'Coronation Gold', 1 metre (3 ft) tall, with flat-topped 7.5 cm (3 in.) clusters of mustard-yellow flowers; 'Gold Plate', 1.2 to 1.3 metres (4 to 4½ ft) tall with 15 cm (6 in.) clusters of deep yellow flowers; and 'Parker's Variety', 1 to 1.2 metres (3½ to 4 ft) tall with 7.5 to 10 cm (3 to 4 in.) clusters of deep yellow flowers. The blossoms are excellent for cutting and may be dried for winter decoration. The common yarrow, a European wild flower, has muddy-white flowers, but the cultivars 'Fire King' and 'Cerise Queen' bear clusters of bright red blossoms on 45 cm (18 in.) stems from midsummer onwards. Sneezewort, so named because its dried roots were once ground and used as snuff, is a white-flowered perennial that bears 7.5 to 15 cm (3 to 6 in.) clusters of small, fluffy, ball-shaped flowers in summer. The flowers, held high above shiny dark green, willow-like leaves, are dramatic in a border and excellent for cutting. Notable cultivars are 'Perry's White', and 'The Pearl', both of which grow about 60 cm (2 ft) tall, and 'Snowball', which grows about 38 cm (15 in.) tall. The woolly yarrow has fern-like, grey-green leaves and creeping stems, from which 15 to 30 cm (6 to 12 in.) flower stalks rise, bearing 4 to 5 cm (1½ to 2 in.) flat-topped clusters of bright yellow flowers from early summer to early autumn. *A. taygetea* 'Moonlight' has pale yellow blossoms.

HOW TO GROW. Yarrows thrive in full sun and well-drained soil and will tolerate drought; in windy places tall

BEAR'S-BREECHES
Acanthus mollis

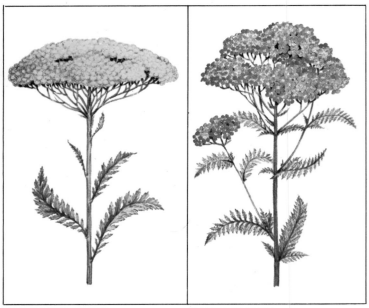

FERN-LEAVED YARROW
Achillea filipendulina
'Coronation Gold'

COMMON YARROW
Achillea millefolium 'Fire King'

cultivars may need staking. Set plants 30 to 60 cm (1 to 2 ft) apart. Cut to ground level in late autumn. Propagate by dividing clumps; this should be done every two to four years to prevent overcrowding.

ACONITUM

A. napellus (monkshood); *A. henryi* 'Spark's Variety'; *A.x cammarum*, also called *A.x stoerkianum* and *A.x bicolor*; *A. vulparia*, also called *A. fischeri* and *A. carmichaelii*; *A. volubile* (climbing monkshood)

A confused genus of herbaceous perennials with deeply cut, shiny palmate leaves and tall spikes of hooded flowers in midsummer. These are usually blue or purple, but white, yellow and bi-coloured forms exist. Monkshoods are valuable in perennial gardens, generally as tall accent plants; they make ideal informal plantings in moist, lightly shaded woodlands. The flowers are excellent for cutting. The roots, leaves and seeds are poisonous and very dangerous if eaten or if their juices get into scratches.

Among the most garden worthy are *A. napellus*, which today is largely superseded by its cultivars, particularly 'Bicolor', 1 metre (3 ft) tall, with blue and white flowers; 'Bressingham Spire', 1 metre (3 ft) tall and violet-blue; and 'Ivorine', 1 metre (3 ft) tall and ivory-white. These cultivars are often listed as *A.x cammarum* or *A.x stoerkianum*. The handsome, dark violet-blue 'Spark's Variety' is also referred to as *A.x cammarum* by some authorities, but it is more probably a form of *A. henryi*. *A. vulparia* is a handsome 1 metre (3 ft) tall Chinese species with spikes of yellow flowers in mid to late summer, and the climbing monkshood will grow to 3.5 to 5 metres (12 to 16 ft) if provided with twiggy pea sticks up which it may climb. The flowers are pale violet.

HOW TO GROW. Monkshoods do well in areas subjected to neither excessive cold in winter nor excessive heat in summer, in partial shade and a cool, moist soil enriched with compost or leaf-mould; they will thrive in full sun if the soil is moist enough. Space plants 30 to 45 cm (12 to 18 in.) apart with the crowns, or tops of the root structure, just beneath the surface. New plants can be started from seeds sown as soon as possible after they ripen; germination periods vary and seedlings take two or three years to produce their first flowers. The roots can also be divided and replanted during the dormant season.

ACTAEA

A. alba (white baneberry); *A. rubra* (red baneberry); *A. spicata*, also called *A. nigra* (cohosh)

Actaeas are members of the buttercup family with two outstanding features: spikes of small white flowers in spring and clusters of colourful poisonous berries in autumn. All have deeply cut leaves and grow 30 to 60 cm (1 to 2 ft) tall. *A. alba* has white berries, *A. rubra*, scarlet berries, and *A. spicata*, black berries.

HOW TO GROW. Actaeas grow in any but the coldest areas, in dappled shade and moist woodland soil. A mulch of peat or leaf-mould in summer is beneficial. Propagate by division of the roots in spring or sow fresh seed.

ADONIS

A. amurensis (Amur adonis); *A. vernalis* (spring adonis)

Rising from the soil as soon as the frost leaves the ground, these slow-growing, dwarf plants are useful for early blossoms at the front of the border. *A. amurensis* is mostly available in Europe in its double form 'Flore-Pleno', the round, golden blooms about 5 cm (2 in.) across on 20 to

Aconitum henryi 'Spark's Variety'

LEFT: RED BANEBERRY
Actaea rubra

RIGHT: WHITE BANEBERRY
Actaea alba

Illustration by Dorothy Bovey

93

SPRING ADONIS
Adonis vernalis

LADY'S MANTLE
Alchemilla mollis

LIGTU HYBRID
Alstroemeria ligtu

38 cm (8 to 15 in.) stems. Pink, white, orange and copper-coloured forms have been developed in its native Japan. They appear in late winter or early spring. The rather uncommon *A. vernalis* bears 5 cm (2 in.), single buttercup-yellow flowers on 22 to 30 cm (9 to 12 in.) stems which fade to green with age. Both types have feathery foliage.

After the seeds ripen in late spring, the leaves shrivel and disappear, and the plants rest beneath the soil until the following spring. Adonis is best grown in large clumps near the front of a border or in a rock garden.

HOW TO GROW. Adonis thrives in cool temperate areas; in any well-drained, but moist, garden soil in full sun or light shade. Set plants 15 to 25 cm (6 to 10 in.) apart. New plants can be started from seeds sown in summer; if homegrown seeds are to be used, sow them as soon as possible after they ripen. Seedlings usually require two years to reach flowering size. Clumps may be divided for propagation in early autumn. Otherwise, allow them to remain undisturbed for at least three to five years.

AGATHAEA See *Felicia*
AGROSTEMMA See *Lychnis*
ALCEA ROSEA See *Althaea*

ALCHEMILLA
A. mollis (lady's mantle)

This is a charming little plant for edging borders, or for growing in rock garden pockets or along a stream or pool so that its flowers are reflected in the water. Its blooms and foliage are also useful for flower decoration. The softly hairy, heart-shaped leaves resemble the capes worn by elderly ladies at the beginning of this century and have similar scalloped margins. The greenish-yellow star-like flowers are small but very prolific in 30 to 38 cm (12 to 15 in.) sprays in summer.

HOW TO GROW. Lady's mantles will grow in all but the very cold regions; they need moist but well-drained soil in full sun or light shade. Set the plants 38 cm (15 in.) apart. The seeds germinate readily around the parent plants. Transplant these or the divided roots in early autumn or spring after the frosts are over.

ALSTROEMERIA
A. aurantiaca (Peruvian lily); *A. ligtu*

For gracing summer borders Peruvian lilies have few equals, particularly when they are associated with lilies, campanulas, delphiniums and even floribunda roses. These South American perennials have brilliant, funnel-shaped flowers massed in terminal heads, smooth, rather twisted, narrow leaves and fleshy, tuberous roots. They are, however, notoriously difficult to establish and, once settled, difficult to eradicate. The secret lies in planting the finger-like roots fairly deep—15 to 20 cm (6 to 8 in.)—and being patient, for little growth is made the first season. The flowers of the Peruvian lily are rich orange, but cultivars of *A. ligtu*, commonly known as Ligtu Hybrids, vary from apricot, lilac, pink and flame to pale purple. The overall height is around 60 cm (2 ft).

HOW TO GROW. Peruvian lilies are hardy, but the Ligtu Hybrids may need winter protection with straw or a raised frame light supported on bricks. They do best in deep, well-drained, sandy soil in full sun. Staking is sometimes necessary. Plants should be set out in spring, 45 to 60 cm (1½ to 2 ft) apart, preferably using young seedlings. To propagate stock, seeds should be sown after ripening in boxes of peat, leaf-mould, soil and sand in equal parts, and kept in a frame until ready for planting out.

ALTHAEA

A. rosea, now more correctly called *Alcea rosea* (hollyhock)

Hollyhocks, with a history of cultivation going back more than 500 years, are thought to have originated somewhere in the eastern Mediterranean region, not in China as is frequently stated. They are commonly associated with English cottage gardens and certainly look most striking when grown against white walls or soft brick buildings, where they remain in character from midsummer until early autumn. The flowers are borne on long spikes; blossoming begins at the bottom of the stems and moves progressively upwards so that 45 to 60 cm (1½ to 2 ft) of each stem is covered with flowers throughout the season. Plants usually grow 1.5 to 2.7 metres (5 to 9 ft) tall from low clumps of hairy leaves 15 to 20 cm (6 to 8 in.) across and range in colour from white through every shade of yellow, pink, lavender and red to nearly black. In addition to the old-fashioned cup-shaped single flowers, there are spectacular new cultivars whose petals are fringed, ruffled or doubled. There is also a dwarf cultivar called 'Silver Puffs', which flowers from seed sown the same year and is a perfect 60 cm (2 ft) replica of its giant relatives.

HOW TO GROW. Perennial hollyhocks are best treated as biennials because of the widespread occurrence of hollyhock rust, a disfiguring disease which attacks the leaves, checking growth and sometimes defoliating plants. Spraying the seedlings with Bordeaux mixture helps to prevent this disease. They will grow in all but very cold areas and need full sun, moist, but well-drained soil and staking to support the fragile stems in windy situations. New plants are best started from seeds sown in summer for flowering the following year.

ANAPHALIS

A. margaritacea (pearl everlasting); *A. yedoënsis* (Japanese pearl everlasting)

The name pearl everlasting is appropriate for these species of *Anaphalis*: the button-like flowers, which grow in clusters 5 cm (2 in.) or more wide, are composed of tiny silvery white petals that retain their colour and texture when dried. Clumps of pearl everlastings grow 30 to 60 cm (1 to 2 ft) tall and blossom from midsummer to autumn. Because their slender 5 to 10 cm (2 to 4 in.) leaves are heavily coated with white hairs, the plants look silvery grey, a useful colour to contrast with other plants having darker foliage and flowers of brighter hues. Pearl everlastings are wild flowers in North America and Asia.

HOW TO GROW. Pearl everlastings grow in cool regions in full sun or light shade. They do well in almost any well-drained soil and will tolerate poor, dry soil. Set plants 30 to 38 cm (12 to 15 in.) apart. All can be divided for propagation purposes in autumn or spring.

ANCHUSA

A. azurea, also called *A. italica* (Italian bugloss, alkanet)

The bright blue blossoms of Italian bugloss are about 2.5 cm (1 in.) across and from early summer to midsummer are borne in clusters on stems that reach a height of 1 to 1.8 metres (3 to 6 ft). The leaves are large—the lower ones may be 30 cm (12 in.) or more in length—rough and tongue-shaped (the name bugloss is Greek for "oxtongue"). Cultivars such as 'Dropmore', 'Morning Glory' and 'Opal' grow 1.5 to 1.8 metres (5 to 6 ft) tall and are well suited to the back of a border. The gentian-blue 'Loddon Royalist' and 'Royal Blue' cultivars rarely exceed 1 metre (3 ft).

HOW TO GROW. Italian bugloss thrives when given deep, fertile but well-drained soil. Sand or weathered ashes

HOLLYHOCK
Althaea rosea

JAPANESE PEARL EVERLASTING
Anaphalis yedoënsis

ITALIAN BUGLOSS
Anchusa azurea 'Loddon Royalist'

JAPANESE ANEMONE
Anemone x *hybrida*

OX-EYE CHAMOMILE
Anthemis tinctoria 'Moonlight'

can be added to stiff clay soils to improve drainage and deter slugs. It grows in full sun or light shade. Set plants 45 to 60 cm (1½ to 2 ft) apart. Late in the autumn mound 5 to 7.5 cm (2 to 3 in.) of soil directly over newly set plants to divert moisture from them during the winter. If planted in soil that drains poorly—such as moist clay—plants may die in winter because their fleshy roots have a tendency to rot. The foliage of Italian bugloss becomes floppy and unattractive after the flowers fade. If leaves and stalks are cut to the ground at that time the plants will shoot up and blossom again, but less generously, in early autumn. In windy locations the stalks may need staking. New plants can be grown from seeds sown in spring or early summer, but will not be of the same quality as named cultivars grown from root cuttings taken in winter or early spring.

ANCHUSA MYOSOTIDIFLORA See *Brunnera*

ANEMONE
A.x hybrida (*A. hupehensis* var. *japonica* x *A. vitifolia*) (Japanese anemone)

In 1844 a British plant collector, Robert Fortune, introduced from Japan a semi-double, autumn-blooming anemone. Because Japan's ports had been closed to Europeans for some 200 years, Fortune had to accept hearsay evidence that the plant grew plentifully on the hillsides around the ports. On the strength of this it was named *A. japonica* and thought to be a true species. However, when at the beginning of the 20th Century a five-petalled plant called *A. hupehensis* was brought in from China, botanists realized that this was the type species of Fortune's plant. The latter then had its name changed to *A. hupehensis* var. *japonica*. Most Japanese garden anemones are hybrids derived from these plants and *A. vitifolia*. They include 'Honorine Jobert', a white single of 1.2 metres (4 ft); 'Queen Charlotte', a pink semi-double of 1 metre (3 ft); 'White Queen', which is 1 metre (3 ft); and 'Lady Gilmour', a 60 cm (2 ft) pink double. The 5 to 7.5 cm (2 to 3 in.) wide flowers are borne on branching stems between late summer and late autumn, and the leaves are cut into three or five lobes.

HOW TO GROW. Japanese anemones grow well in all parts of Europe. They do best in light shade and a well-drained soil that has been liberally supplemented with moss peat; they will tolerate sun if there is ample moisture during the growing season. Set plants about 45 cm (18 in.) apart. Do not disturb the roots except for purposes of propagation. New plants are started from root cuttings taken in winter and planted out in autumn of the same year.

ANTHEMIS
A. tinctoria (ox-eye chamomile)

Hybrid cultivars of anthemis are prolific and easy to grow, bearing yellow, daisy-like blossoms about 5 cm (2 in.) across in summer and early autumn. Most cultivars grow 60 to 75 cm (2 to 2½ ft) tall and have dense, fern-like foliage, pungent when crushed. They provide good cut flowers, and pests seldom bother them. Some recommended cultivars are 'Beauty of Grallagh', deep yellow flowers; 'Grallagh Gold', orange-tinged yellow flowers; and 'Moonlight', a soft primrose-yellow variety.

HOW TO GROW. Anthemis grows in all but the very coldest areas, in full sun and almost any well-drained soil. Set plants about 30 cm (12 in.) apart. Plants can be started from clump divisions or from stem cuttings taken in spring; they should flower the same year. Divide clumps in spring after two years of flowering.

AQUILEGIA

A. vulgaris (columbine), *A.x hybrida*; *A. caerulea*

Columbines have been cultivated in Britain for centuries and are mentioned by both Shakespeare and Chaucer. The flowers were at one time used medicinally and as a food flavouring until, according to Linnaeus, people died as a result. *A. vulgaris* is the true columbine, still to be found wild in Britain and characterized by 2.5 cm (1 in.) wide, distinctive short-spurred flowers of blue, white or purple, and deeply lobed, dark green leaves. Double forms, known as 'Granny's Bonnets', are common. In the late 19th Century, long-spurred forms were bred by a florist called Douglas, and today these and selected forms of the short-spurred types are grouped collectively under the name *A.x hybrida*. Various strains and races have been raised by seedsmen, of which Mrs. Scott-Elliot's long-spurred hybrids and McKana hybrids are deservedly popular. Both grow about 1 metre (3 ft) tall and have cream, pink, yellow, blue, red and crimson flowers in various combinations in midsummer. *A. caerulea* is the state flower of Colorado and grows 45 to 60 cm (1½ to 2 ft) tall with 5 to 7.5 cm (2 to 3 in.) blue and white flowers. Because the flowering season ends early, columbines should be planted where their fading leaves will be camouflaged by the developing foliage of other plants. The flowers are excellent for cutting.

HOW TO GROW. Columbines do well throughout Europe. They grow best in moist but well-drained soil in very light shade, but will tolerate full sun except in hot dry areas. Set plants 25 to 35 cm (10 to 14 in.) apart. Plants are best started from seeds purchased from a commercial grower—garden seeds may revert to a less desirable cultivar. They may also be divided in late autumn.

ARMERIA

A. maritima; *A. arenaria*, also called *A. plantaginea* and *A. alliacea*; *A. pseudoarmeria*, also called *A. cephalotes*. All called sea pink, thrift and armeria)

From late spring to midsummer, and occasionally until the end of summer, sea pinks, send up 15 to 45 cm (6 to 18 in.) stems topped with 2.5 cm (1 in.) globe-like clusters of pink, lilac, white or red flowers that are excellent for cutting. In temperate coastal climates, plants may bloom all year. Wherever they grow, their 15 to 25 cm (6 to 10 in.) tufts of grass-like, bluish foliage stay green the year round and always look neat. The size of sea pinks makes them suitable for planting in a rock garden, along a path or at the front of a border. *A. maritima* is the most common; its cultivar 'Vindictive' is an especially fine deep pink, and 'Düsseldorf Pride' is deep red. A cherry-pink cultivar of *A. arenaria* called 'Bees' Ruby' is also widely grown.

HOW TO GROW. Sea pinks can be grown in all temperate regions. They require full sun and excellent drainage, and do best in rather poor, dry soil; too much moisture and fertilizer diminish flower production. Set plants 22.5 to 30 cm (9 to 12 in.) apart. Common types are often grown from seeds sown in spring to blossom the same year, but seeds of named cultivars may not produce plants resembling their parents. These cultivars are best propagated by clump division in early spring or early autumn. Because old clumps tend to die out in the middle, all sea pinks should be divided after three years of flowering.

ARTEMISIA

A. ludoviciana ssp. *albula* 'Silver Queen' (wormwood, white sage); *A. lactiflora* (white mugwort) *A. schmidtiana*

Artemisias are valued more for their feathery aromatic leaves than for their flowers. 'Silver Queen', which grows

COLUMBINE
Aquilegia x *hybrida*

SEA PINK
Armeria arenaria 'Bees' Ruby'

97

WORMWOOD
Artemisia ludoviciana ssp. *albula* 'Silver Queen'

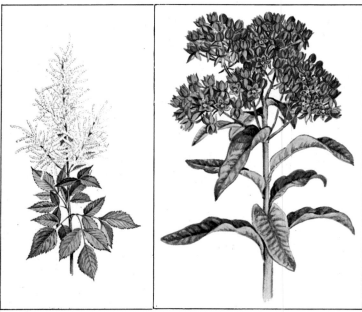

GOAT'S BEARD
Aruncus dioicus

BUTTERFLY WEED
Asclepias tuberosa

about 1 metre (3 ft) tall and produces insignificant white flowers in late summer, has silvery-white foliage excellent for softening the bright colours of other flowers. *A. lacti-flora* grows 1.2 to 1.5 metres (4 to 5 ft) tall and has dark green leaves, silvery underneath; from mid to late summer it bears plumes of tiny fragrant, creamy flowers along its upper branches. *A. schmidtiana* makes a cushion of silver 22 cm (9 in.) high with lacy, thread-like leaves and dull yellow balls of flowers enclosed with silvery bracts.

HOW TO GROW. Most artemisias grow well in all parts of Europe, in light, well-drained soil and full sun, but the white mugwort needs moist soil and will tolerate part shade. Plant artemisias 30 to 45 cm (12 to 18 in.) apart. Propagate 'Silver Queen' and white mugwort from clump divisions in autumn or spring.

ARUNCUS
A. dioicus, also called *A. sylvester*; *Spiraea aruncus* (goat's beard)

For two weeks in early summer, each 1.2 to 1.8 metre (4 to 6 ft) stalk of goat's beard is crowned with a 15 to 25 cm (6 to 10 in.) plume of tiny blossoms. Because the flowering season is relatively short and the foliage is tall, goat's beard is generally placed at the back of a border; but it is also dramatic when massed alone as a separate planting. Its tolerance to part shade and wet soil makes it popular in woodland gardens.

HOW TO GROW. Goat's beard does well in cool areas, in almost any soil, in sun or light shade. Set plants 45 to 60 cm (1½ to 2 ft) apart. To get new plants, divide clumps in spring or autumn.

ASCLEPIAS
A. tuberosa (butterfly weed, pleurisy root)

Too beautiful to be called a weed, butterfly weed probably achieved its name because it is a common wild flower in most parts of the United States and southern Canada; its second name, pleurisy root, recalls its use as a medicine by the American Indians. A single plant may send up 5 to 10 flower stalks, 30 to 60 cm (12 to 24 in.) tall, lined with slender 5 to 10 cm (2 to 4 in.) hairy leaves and topped by several 5 cm (2 in.) clusters of small, fragrant, vivid orange blossoms, which bloom from midsummer to early autumn. In autumn 5 to 7.5 cm (2 to 3 in.) canoe-shaped seed pods open to disperse clouds of silky seeds. The flowers are good for cutting and the pods are attractive when dried.

HOW TO GROW. Butterfly weed grows anywhere except in very cold areas, in full sun and well-drained sandy soil. Because its tap-root reaches deep into the ground, it can withstand drought. Set butterfly weeds 20 to 30 cm (8 to 12 in.) apart. New plants can be grown from seeds sown in spring or summer to blossom in two years. The long tap-roots make these plants difficult to divide, and clumps should remain undisturbed indefinitely.

ASPERULA See *Galium*

ASTER
A. amellus; *A.x frikartii* 'Wunder von Stäfa'; *A. novae-angliae* (New England aster); *A. novi-belgii* (New York aster), both also called Michaelmas daisy; *A. tongolensis*, also called *A. yunnanensis* 'Napsbury'

Perennial asters range in height from 30 to 180 cm (1 to 6 ft). The predominant colours are blue, lavender and purple; but among the hybrids are white cultivars and every shade of red from pink to crimson. *A. amellus* grows 45 to 60 cm (18 to 24 in.) tall and produces numerous 5 cm (2 in.) blossoms from mid- to late summer. In addition to the basic species which has purple flowers, there are such fine cultivars as 'Moerheim Gem' and 'King George', both bright blue, and 'Sonia', clear pink; all have bright yellow centres and are fragrant. *A.x frikartii* is a name coined for a race of blue-flowered hybrids between *A. amellus* and *A. thomsonii* raised by the Swiss Monsieur Frikart; 'Wunder von Stäfa' is one of these, 75 cm (2½ ft) tall with lavender-blue, gold-centred flowers. In cool areas *A. amellus* blossoms from spring to autumn, but in frost-free climates bears occasional flowers throughout the year.

The most important selections of the New England aster, which produces masses of 4 to 5 cm (1½ to 2 in.) flowers from late summer to early autumn, are 'Harrington's Pink', clear pink; and 'September Ruby', ruby red; both become 1.2 to 1.5 metres (4 to 5 ft) tall. The flowers of all New England asters close at night. New York asters, which produce flowers of similar size from late summer to early autumn, include 'Autumn Glory', 1 to 1.2 metres (3 to 4 ft) tall, claret red; 'Crimson Brocade', 1 metre (3 ft) tall, bright red; 'Eventide', 1 to 1.2 metres (3 to 4 ft) tall, purple; 'Marie Ballard', 1 to 1.2 metres (3 to 4 ft) tall, pale blue; 'Patricia Ballard', 1 metre (3 ft) tall, pink; and 'White Lady', 1.5 to 1.8 metres (5 to 6 ft) tall, white. Aster 'Napsbury', a cultivar of a Chinese species, grows about 45 cm (18 in.) tall, from a 20 to 30 cm (8 to 12 in.) mound of dark green leaves and produces 7.5 cm (3 in.) orange-centred, bright blue flowers, one to a stem, from mid-spring to summer.

HOW TO GROW. Michaelmas daisies are hardy in most cool areas, but need a well-drained and fertile soil which will not dry out in summer. They appreciate full sun and should be planted between October and March, as the weather permits, the *A. amellus* types preferably in spring. Taller cultivars of *A. novi-belgii*, in particular, may need staking. Propagate Michaelmas daisies by clump division in spring or early autumn, or from soft cuttings rooted from forced plants stimulated under glass in early spring. Many of them will flower the following autumn. Set tall growing asters about 60 to 75 cm (2 to 2½ ft) apart, low growing ones 30 to 45 cm (12 to 18 in.) apart.

ASTILBE
A.x arendsii (astilbe, false spiraea)

For two months in midsummer, astilbes bear on their 60 to 90 cm (2 to 3 ft) stems, spectacular spire-like plumes 20 to 30 cm (8 to 12 in.) tall. These are composed of myriads of tiny flowers. The flowers are good for cutting if they are allowed to open fully before being picked. The deeply divided leaves are dark green, with coppery tints when young. Outstanding hybrid cultivars include 'Bridal Veil' and 'Deutschland', white flowers; 'Fanal' and 'Red Sentinel', deep red blossoms and bronzy foliage; 'Rosy Veil' and 'Peach Blossom', pink flowers; and 'Serenade', rosy-lilac flowers.

HOW TO GROW. Astilbes can be grown in areas that are not exceedingly hot in summer, in moist soil supplemented with moss peat or leaf-mould. Although they will get along in full sun, it is easier to grow them in light shade so that they do not dry out rapidly in summer. They require well-drained soil, particularly during the winter months, when the plants are resting. Plant astilbes 38 to 45 cm (15 to 18 in.) apart. Astilbes are what are called "gross feeders". They multiply rapidly and exhaust the soil around them, then become straggly and produce few flowers. For this reason, the clumps should be dug up and divided in spring every two or three years. Before re-setting the plants,

ASTER
Aster x frikartii

MICHAELMAS DAISY
Aster novi-belgii

ASTILBE
Astilbe x arendsii 'Rosy Veil'

MASTERWORT
Astrantia carniolica

FALSE INDIGO
Baptisia australis

ENGLISH DAISY
Bellis perennis

replenish the soil with moss peat or leaf-mould, and a dusting of general fertilizer. Many florists force astilbes into flower in the spring; after such plants have finished blooming, they can be set outdoors and will flower the following year.

ASTRANTIA
A. carniolica; *A. major* (both called masterwort)

Although not very showy these are interesting plants with 2.5 cm (1 in.) wide, round flowers in compact heads, set off by a ruff of white bracts. They look like miniature Victorian posies. In *A. carniolica*, the flowers are white streaked with green on branching 45 to 60 cm (1½ to 2 ft) stems and greenish-pink in *A. major*. Both plants bloom in midsummer and have much-divided, slender, pointed, mid-green leaves.

HOW TO GROW. Masterworts grow best in a shaded position, but will grow also in a sunny spot, provided it does not dry out in summer. Plant them about 60 cm (2 ft) apart. Divide in late spring or late summer.

B

BAPTISIA
B. australis (false indigo)

False indigo grows 1 to 1.5 metres (3 to 5 ft) tall and from mid-spring to early summer sends out 22.5 to 30 cm (9 to 12 in.) spikes of purplish blue 2.5 cm (1 in.) flowers, followed by fat 5 to 7.5 cm (2 to 3 in.) seed pods; it has blue-green, clover-like leaves composed of three segments, each 5 to 7.5 cm (2 to 3 in.) long.

HOW TO GROW. False indigos grow in any but the very coldest areas, in almost any soil in full sun or very light shade. They grow best if started from seeds sown in autumn or spring; the plants begin to blossom when they are two or three years old. Space flowering-sized plants 45 to 75 cm (1½ to 2½ ft) apart. To encourage false indigos to produce more blooms, pinch off faded flowers before they form new seeds. False indigos almost never need dividing, for although the clumps increase in size, the long tap-roots reach deep and do not spread.

BELLIS
B. perennis (English daisy)

The English daisy, immortalized by poets, is a delightful 15 cm (6 in.) tall plant with pink or white flowers 2.5 cm (1 in.) across. The species, however—a scourge of English lawns—is never deliberately grown, except in its cultivated forms. These are treated as biennials (occasionally annuals) and used for edging borders, under-carpeting bulbs and other spring flowers, and in rock garden pockets. They may also be grown as pot plants for winter flowers. The blooms are larger than the species, up to 5 cm (2 in.) across, and the stems 12 to 15 cm (4 to 6 in.) tall. There are single forms with rich yellow centres, semi-doubles and doubles with white, pink or deep red flowers. Others have quilled petals and there are small double daisies, such as the elfin 'Dresden China'. None of these should be allowed to set seed except for reproduction purposes, as they can invade lawns in the same way as the species. They flower with great freedom from May to July.

HOW TO GROW. English daisies grow in full sun or light shade in moist soil that has been well supplemented with moss peat. Set plants 20 cm (8 in.) apart. Seeds should be sown outside in early summer, in a small bed and covered with 6 mm (¼ in.) of soil. After germination, prick out the plantlets 7.5 cm (3 in.) apart and plant out in their flowering positions in September. Alternatively, sow the seeds in late summer where they are to flower, and thin to the required distances. They may also be grown as annuals by sowing the seeds under glass in early spring, hardening off the seedlings in a cold frame and planting them out 10 cm (4 in.) apart in early summer for flowering the same season. New plants can also be obtained by dividing the clumps in spring.

BERGENIA
B. cordifolia; *B. stracheyi*; *B. crassifolia*. (All formerly classified in the genera *Megasea* and *Saxifraga*)

Bergenias appeal to gardeners because of their large, handsome leaves and their 7.5 to 15 cm (3 to 6 in.) clusters of robust flowers, which appear in spring. Colours range from deep red-purple to pale pink and white. The leaves of *B. cordifolia* are 20 to 25 cm (8 to 10 in.) across, with toothed edges; flowers are borne on nodding stems that barely extend above the foliage. *B. crassifolia* has oval leaves of similar size; its flowers bloom on stout stems 30 cm (12 in.) or more above the foliage. *B. stracheyi* has rounded leaves and branched heads heavy with pink flowers on 22.5 to 30 cm (9 to 12 in.) stems; there is also a white form.

The following cultivars are freer flowering than the species and have a wider colour range, 'Abendglut' syn. 'Evening Glow', rich crimson, almost double flowers on 22.5 cm (9 in.) stems; 'Silberlicht' syn. 'Silver Light', white flowers with bronze-red foliage 30 to 38 cm (12 to 15 in.) tall; and 'Ballawley', bright crimson, the leaves turning purple in winter, 45 cm (18 in.) tall. Because the leaves are attractive even after the flowers fade—they remain green throughout the year in warm climates and turn a handsome bronze in winter in cold areas—the plants are often planted near the front of a border or along a path and are also much used by flower arrangers.

HOW TO GROW. Bergenias thrive in almost any soil in full sun or light shade, although they prefer light shade in hot areas. They tolerate a wide range of moisture conditions, growing slowly in dry areas and rapidly in constantly wet spots, such as beside a stream or pool. Set plants 30 to 38 cm (12 to 15 in.) apart. New plants can be started by dividing and replanting mature clumps when they become overcrowded, usually after about three or four seasons of flowering.

BOCCONIA See *Macleaya*

BOLTONIA
B. asteroides (white boltonia)

Plants of similar habit and closely related to Michaelmas daisies; *B. asteroides* produces 1.5 metre (5 ft) stems which branch at the top into small star-like daisies of white to lilac or violet-purple in the more showy variety *latisquama* Flowering is from midsummer until early autumn.

HOW TO GROW. Boltonias grow in almost any soil in full sun or light shade. Plants should be 45 to 60 cm (1½ to 2 ft) apart. New plants can be started from division of clumps in spring. Boltonia clumps increase rapidly; in order to prevent overcrowding, clumps should be divided every other year.

BRUNNERA
B. macrophylla, also called *Anchusa myosotidiflora*, *Myosotis macrophylla* (Siberian bugloss)

BERGENIA
Bergenia cordifolia

PINK BOLTONIA
Boltonia asteroides var *latisquama*

SIBERIAN BUGLOSS
Brunnera macrophylla

Siberian bugloss is a relative of the forget-me-not, as is apparent from its tiny, yellow-centred, blue flowers, which bloom on 30 to 45 cm (12 to 18 in.) stems from early spring to early summer. The long-stalked leaves are 10 to 12.5 cm (4 to 5 in.) across in spring, increasing to about 20 cm (8 in.) by midsummer. There is also a form with cream variegated foliage. Siberian bugloss is a good choice for the middle of a shaded border, and it is also often planted to grow untended, as if wild, in wooded areas.

HOW TO GROW. Siberian bugloss does best in light shade in soil that has been well supplemented with moss peat or leaf-mould and is kept constantly moist. Set new plants 30 to 38 cm (12 to 15 in.) apart. Siberian bugloss is best propagated from self-sown seedlings which may be lifted when small and separated; it can also be divided in autumn or spring.

C

CALLIRHOË
C. digitata (poppy mallow); *C. involucrata.* (Both also called wine-cup)

Poppy mallows bear 5 cm (2 in.) blossoms from early to late summer and occasionally even until frost; the slender flower stalks, about 30 cm (12 in.) tall, rise from sprawling stems that become as long as 60 cm (24 in.). The blossoms of the two species are almost identical, but their foliage differs: *C. digitata* has smooth, deeply cleft leaves while the leaves of *C. involucrata* are hairy and less deeply notched. As both species have heavy, carrot-like roots that tend to rot if planted in poorly drained situations, they are best suited to the crevices of a rock wall or for carpeting a dry bank.

HOW TO GROW. These plants grow in full sun and almost any well-drained soil; because they have deep roots, they can tolerate dry locations. Set plants about 45 cm (18 in.) apart. New plants may be grown from seeds sown in early spring; flowers will bloom late the same year. Leave established plants undisturbed indefinitely.

CAMPANULA
C. carpatica (Carpathian bellflower, tussock bluebell); *C. glomerata* (clustered bellflower); *C. medium* (Canterbury bell); *C. persicifolia* (peach-leaved bellflower). (All also called bellflower)

Bellflowers of both the perennial and biennial species are among the mainstays of a flower garden. All are undemanding in their care and reliable and prodigious in their blossoming.

The Carpathian bellflower is one of the most dependable and delightful species of bellflowers. It forms neat clumps of foliage 10 to 15 cm (4 to 6 in.) tall. Wiry 15 to 20 cm (6 to 8 in.) stems rise from the clumps and are topped by 5 cm (2 in.) flat-cupped blue or white flowers from early summer until late autumn. Among the better cultivars are 'Blue Moonlight', clear medium blue; 'Cobalt', deep blue; 'Chewton Joy', pale blue; and 'White Star', white.

The clustered bellflower grows 30 to 60 cm (12 to 24 in.) tall and bears dense clusters of 2.5 cm (1 in.) upward-facing white, blue or purple bell-shaped flowers from late spring to early summer. 'Joan Elliott' is a handsome cultivar with deep violet flowers; 'Alba' is a cultivar with white blossoms.

Canterbury bell is a biennial species of bellflower. During the second year of its life cycle, it sends up flowering stalks 45 to 90 cm (1½ to 3 ft) tall, each bearing many bell-shaped flowers about 5 cm (2 in.) long. The flowers come in white or shades of pink, mauve or blue, and bloom from late

POPPY MALLOW
Callirhoë digitata

PEACH-LEAVED BELLFLOWER
Campanula persicifolia

spring to midsummer. Some strains of Canterbury bells have one bell set within another; this type of flower is called hose-in-hose. Still another blossom type, often listed as *C. medium calycanthema*, is called cup-and-saucer, an apt description of the shape of its blossoms. All are splendid for cutting.

The peach-leaved bellflower is a particularly durable species. The cultivar 'Telham Beauty' has 5 to 7.5 cm (2 to 3 in.) porcelain-blue bells that bloom along the top half of the 1.2 metre (4 ft) flower stalks in early to mid-summer; 'Pleniflora Alba' is an excellent similar cultivar that bears white flowers.

HOW TO GROW. Bellflowers grow in full sun or light shade in almost any well-drained garden soil. Set bell-flowers 30 to 45 cm (12 to 18 in.) apart. New plants of the perennial types may be started from clump divisions in early spring. The biennial Canterbury bells should be started from seeds sown in early summer to bloom the following year; some perennial cultivars will blossom the first year from seeds sown indoors about six months before the flowering season, but they do not approach the magnificence of the biennial strains.

Carpathian bellflowers and peach-leaved bellflowers are slow to spread and should generally be divided after three to five years of flowering. The clustered bellflower spreads more rapidly, however, and may need to be divided every two or three years.

CASSIA
C. marilandica (wild senna)

Wild senna is a striking 60 to 120 cm (2 to 4 ft) shrubby plant that blooms in late summer and dies down in winter. The 2.5 to 7.5 cm (1 to 3 in.) clusters of tiny bright yellow blossoms have conspicuous, chocolate-coloured, pollen-bearing anthers. The fern-like, light green leaves are 15 to 25 cm (6 to 10 in.) long, and the foliage is so attractive that the species would be worth growing even if it had no flowers. The height of wild senna makes it especially suitable for the backs of borders.

HOW TO GROW. Wild senna grows in all areas in full sun or light shade in any well-drained soil. Set plants about 60 cm (2 ft) apart. New plants are easy to grow from imported seeds; they rarely ripen in Europe.

CATANANCHE
C. caerulea (Cupid's-dart)

The 5 cm (2 in.) flowers of cupid's-dart are highly unusual; they look as if the ends of the petals have been clipped with pinking shears. The flowers bloom at the top of 60 cm (2 ft) wiry stems in mid to late summer and occasionally later, and are excellent for cutting and in dried winter bouquets. The low, attractive clumps of grey foliage, with leaves 20 to 30 cm (8 to 12 in.) long, make the plants particularly suitable for use at the front of a border. Some of the recommended cultivars of cupid's-dart are 'Major', blue; 'Alba' and 'Perry's White', white; and *C. caerulea* 'Bicolor', whose blue-centred petals are tipped with white.

HOW TO GROW. Cupid's-dart does well in almost any soil, but requires full sun and excellent drainage—especially in winter. Space plants 20 to 25 cm (8 to 10 in.) apart. Start new plants of named varieties from root cuttings taken in the autumn to blossom the following year. Cupid's-darts may also be grown from seeds sown in early spring to produce flowers in summer, but seed-grown flowers vary greatly in colour and many turn out to be unattractively pale.

WILD SENNA
Cassia marilandica

CUPID'S-DART
Catananche caerulea

CENTAUREA

C. dealbata (Persian centaurea); *C. gymnocarpa* (dusty miller, velvet centaurea); *C. macrocephala* (yellow hardhead); *C. montana* (mountain knapweed); *C. rutifolia*, also called *C. cineraria* and *C. candidissima* (dusty miller)

The several species of centaureas include widely different plants whose foliage colours, flowers and hardiness have little in common.

The Persian centaurea grows 45 to 90 cm (1½ to 3 ft) tall and bears 5 cm (2 in.) feathery-petalled flowers from midsummer to early autumn or even later into the autumn. The flowers are lilac to purple in colour and are excellent for cutting. The fern-like foliage is smooth on top and covered with silvery hairs underneath.

The dusty millers, both *C. gymnocarpa* and *C. rutifolia*, grow 30 to 60 cm (12 to 24 in.) tall and are so outstanding with their spectacular silvery-white foliage, which is also fern-like and covered with soft velvety hairs, that many gardeners cut off the small yellow or purple flowers even before they open in summer to focus attention on the dramatic leaves.

The yellow hardhead sends out 7.5 cm (3 in.) bright yellow flowers above sparse foliage on stiff, leafy 90 to 120 cm (3 to 4 ft) stems in early summer to midsummer. The mountain knapweed looks like an annual cornflower except that its flowers are twice as large, about 7.5 cm (3 in.) across. The plants grow about 60 cm (2 ft) tall on weak stems that need staking. They blossom from early summer to early autumn and are excellent for cutting.

HOW TO GROW. Persian centaureas, yellow hardheads and mountain knapweed thrive in cool and temperate areas; dusty millers, although useful as annuals anywhere, can be grown as perennials only in some warm regions. All need sun and well-drained soil. Set 30 to 45 cm (12 to 18 in.) apart. New plants can be started from clump divisions or from seeds sown in spring or summer to bloom the second summer. To prevent overcrowding, most centaureas should be dug up and divided every two to four years; the mountain knapweed, a particularly rapid grower in good soil, may have to be divided and replanted every other year.

CENTRANTHUS

C. ruber (red valerian)

Red valerian, a dependable plant even for gardeners who claim to have no green fingers, almost never fails to put forth great clusters of tiny red, pink or white flowers high on its 60 to 90 cm (2 to 3 ft) stems from early summer to midautumn. The oval, glaucous leaves have an unpleasant cat-like smell when bruised.

HOW TO GROW. Red valerian grows well in full sun or light shade in almost any well-drained soil. Space plants 30 to 38 cm (12 to 15 in.) apart. New plants can be started from seeds sown in spring to flower the following year, or from clump divisions in spring.

CEPHALARIA

C. gigantea, also called *C. tatarica* (giant yellow scabious)

The giant yellow scabious grows 1.5 to 1.8 metres (5 to 6 ft) tall, with branching stems carrying deeply-toothed leaves and many large, yellow, scabious-like flowers. These are good for cutting. The plant's height makes it useful at the back of a border.

HOW TO GROW. The giant scabious is hardy in mild, temperate areas; it prefers well-drained but fertile soil and full sun or light shade. Plant in spring, setting the plants 1 metre (3 ft) apart. Propagate by division in spring or sow seeds outside in April.

MOUNTAIN KNAPWEED
Centaurea montana

RED VALERIAN
Centranthus ruber

Illustration by Dorothy Bovey

GIANT YELLOW SCABIOUS
Cephalaria gigantea

104

CERATOSTIGMA

C. plumbaginoides, also called *Plumbago larpentae* (leadwort)

Leadwort grows 22.5 to 30 cm (9 to 12 in.) tall; its clusters of small blue flowers, almost 2 cm (¾ in.) across, bloom from late summer until the frosts. At the end of the blooming season, the upper leaves turn reddish bronze. Leadwort makes a fine, carefree ground cover.

HOW TO GROW. Leadwort grows in all but the very coldest areas, in full sun or light shade. It needs well-drained soil supplemented with moss peat or leaf-mould; good drainage is essential during the winter months because the dormant plants cannot tolerate soggy soil. Set plants 45 to 60 cm (18 to 24 in.) apart and shorten the old stems to ground level in early spring. For winter protection in areas prone to frost, apply a light mulch of straw or bracken. Propagate by dividing the clumps in early spring just as new growth becomes evident.

CHEIRANTHUS

C.x allionii, also called *Erysimum* x *marshallii* (Siberian wallflower); *C. cheiri* (English wallflower)

A few true perennial wallflowers are useful in borders because of their extended period of flowering during spring and early summer. They include several *Erysimum* cultivars—commonly, but erroneously, referred to as *Cheiranthus*—such as 'Harpur Crewe' with massed spikes of small, double, fragrant, golden flowers on dumpy 45 cm (18 in.) stems; 'Moonlight', a single yellow; and 'Bowles Mauve', a rich purple on 60 cm (2 ft) stems. All of these are propagated from cuttings. The Siberian wallflower, now more correctly *Erysimum* x *marshallii*, grows 38 cm (15 in.) tall and has bright golden flowers; it comes true from seed. True wallflowers, *C. cheiri*, are much valued for their fragrance, early blooms and wide colour range from white, cream, yellow, orange, pink, bronze, purple to carmine. All make good cut flowers.

HOW TO GROW. Wallflowers do well in European countries except in very hot regions in full sun. They grow best in well-drained soil with a pH of 6.0 to 8.0. As biennials, wallflowers are generally started each year from seeds sown in a nursery bed in early summer. When they are 2.5 to 5 cm (1 to 2 in.) tall, dig them up, pinch off the tip of the tap-root of each plant to encourage a fibrous root system and replant 15 cm (6 in.) apart. When the plants are 7.5 to 10 cm (3 to 4 in.) tall, pinch out the stem tips to encourage multiple branching. In mild areas transplant to the garden in late summer. For winter protection in cold parts, dig up the plants with as much soil as possible clinging to the roots and set them closely together in a cold frame; transplant to the garden in early spring, setting them 15 to 30 cm (6 to 12 in.) apart.

CHELONE

C. lyonii (pink turtle-head)

Pink turtle-head grows 60 to 90 cm (2 to 3 ft) tall and in late summer and early autumn bears short spikes of rose-purple 2.5 cm (1 in.) flowers and dark green leaves. Turtle-heads are easy to grow, pest resistant and especially suitable for planting in areas that get little sun.

HOW TO GROW. Turtle-heads grow well in a sunny or partly shaded area, but must have moist or wet soil. Mulch the plants with 5 to 7.5 cm (2 to 3 in.) of compost or moss peat in summer to help moisture in the soil during the blooming season. Set new plants about 45 cm (18 in.) apart. The most practical method of propagation is to divide the clumps in early spring every two or three years.

LEADWORT
Ceratostigma plumbaginoides

ENGLISH WALLFLOWER
Cheiranthus cheiri

PINK TURTLE-HEAD
Chelone lyonii

PYRETHRUM
Chrysanthemum coccineum

CHRYSANTHEMUM

C. coccineum, also called *Pyrethrum coccineum*; *C. roseum*, also called *Pyrethrum roseum* (pyrethrum); *C. frutescens* (marguerite); *C. maximum* (Shasta daisy); *C.x hortorum* (hardy chrysanthemum, florists' chrysanthemum); *C. parthenium*, also called *Matricaria eximia*; and *Pyrethrum parthenium* (feverfew)

The wide variety of plants in the *Chrysanthemum* genus share one quality: all are long lasting when cut. In addition, most have a pleasing fragrance. But from there on, dissimilarities abound.

Cultivars of pyrethrum range from 20 cm to 1 metre (8 in. to 3 ft) in height and bear red, pink or white flowers on slender stems. The flowers appear from early summer to midsummer, although a few scattered blossoms open now and then until frost; they may be single with one ring of petals, or double with overlapping rings of petals, or they may have raised pincushion-like centres similar to those of anemones. The dark green, fern-like foliage forms a soft mound a few centimetres high.

The marguerite is a perennial in southern parts of Europe, where it flowers throughout the year; elsewhere it is popular as a house plant or as a white or yellow summer-flowering annual. The foliage forms a mound 60 to 90 cm (2 to 3 ft) tall with an equal spread.

The Shasta daisy has become a mainstay of perennial gardens. Cultivars range from 30 cm (1 ft) to more than 1 metre (3 ft) tall; some begin to bloom in early summer and others continue until frost. The flowers, as large as 15 cm (6 in.) across, come in single, double and anemone forms, and are nearly always snow white with occasional tinges of yellow. Superior cultivars include 'Esther Read' and 'Cobham Gold', both 7.5 cm (3 in.) double types; 'Snow Cloud', a 10 cm (4 in.) anemone-centred double; and the spectacular 'Thomas Killin', a 15 cm (6 in.) anemone-centred semi-double.

Most garden chrysanthemums originated from two Chinese species—*C. vestitum* syn. *C. morifolium* and *C. indicum*. For many centuries these have been used in the Orient to produce cultivars, the Chinese having bred chrysanthemums since 500 B.C. The first of such plants reached Europe in the 18th Century, but the hardier types, like the Koreans and Rubellums, did not arrive until the 20th Century. Forms from the latter races carry masses of single or double flowers 5 to 8 cm (2 to 3 in.) across on branching 60 to 90 cm (2 to 3 ft) stems and exhibit a wide colour range from white and yellow to pink, red, bronze and crimson. There are also low growing 'cushion types'. All make good cut flowers, are hardy in Britain and many parts of Europe, and associate pleasantly in the garden with Michaelmas daisies, coreopsis and other late-blooming perennials.

The late-blooming hardy or florists' chrysanthemums are among the most varied, dependable and useful of all perennials. Older types bloomed so late that frost often came before some of the buds opened; today this defect has been eliminated. New attractive cultivars come into flower as early as August. Colours include white and many shades of yellow, pink, lavender, red and bronze; many blossoms combine more than one colour, and on some the second colour appears on the backs of the petals. These cultivars offer a number of different flower types and shapes.

Among the florists' chrysanthemums are hardy and half-hardy kinds for the border as well as the greenhouse types. As the latter bloom late in the year under glass, they are not within the range of this book. Florists' chrysanthemums are further sub-divided into seven main groups, according to the type of bloom and the way the petals are arranged: 1). Incurved: all the petals curve inwards to make a globe-shaped flower. 2). Reflexed: the petals fall outwards and downwards, the outer florets often drooping. 3). Intermediate: similar to incurved, but with irregular incurving and looser packing of the petals. 4). Single: daisy-petalled single flowers with flat or slightly rounded central discs. 5). Anemone-centred: single or double blooms with raised pin-cushion-like centres. 6). Pompon: round button flowers, singles and doubles, 2.5 to 5 cm (1 to 2 in.) across on 60 cm (2 ft) stems. Other types include thread-flowered blooms which have long tubular, spoon-shaped petals, often lighter in colour at the flared ends; quill-flowered are similar but the ends of the tubular petals are closed. Spray, cascade, and spider chrysanthemums are also included in this sub-division.

Unlike these challenging hardy chrysanthemums, fever-fews are easy to grow. Cultivars rise 30 to 90 cm (1 to 3 ft) tall from clumps of pungent foliage and bear 2.5 cm (1 in.) yellow or white flowers in mid to late summer. Some of the flowers are doubles; others have no petals at all, only a central disc.

Pot-grown chrysanthemums obtained from florists can be planted in the garden and are most likely to grow successfully if they are small-flowered types; most large-flowered cultivars bloom late and their buds may be killed by frost. These florists' plants, which have been induced to blossom out of their normal season, will revert to their natural flowering season if later planted in the garden. Potted chrysanthemums are often treated by florists with a chemical that shortens their height without reducing their blossom size, but the dwarfing lasts only one season and the plants then revert to their normal size.

HOW TO GROW. Pyrethrums, Shasta daisies and the hardy chrysanthemums recommended for gardens do well in most areas, but marguerites thrive as perennials only in warm regions; elsewhere they are treated as annuals. Feverfews are generally hardy, except in cool areas where they may be grown as annuals. All chrysanthemums need soil that has been thoroughly cultivated and enriched with organic material such as compost, leaf-mould or rotted manure. The plants require ample watering during the growing season and good drainage while they are dormant in winter. Space plants 30 to 60 cm (1 to 2 ft) apart, depending on the size of the cultivar.

To multiply named cultivars of pyrethrum and Shasta daisies, divide and replant clumps in spring. Marguerites may be propagated from stem cuttings at any time; they will usually blossom within a few weeks. To prolong the bloom of Shasta daisies, pick off flowers as soon as they fade. To prevent overcrowding, divide pyrethrums and Shasta daisies after three or four years of flowering, fever-fews after one or two years.

Hardy chrysanthemums require more care than most perennials because best results are obtained when plants are raised new each year. Start by buying growing plants for your garden. When they become 15 to 20 cm (6 to 8 in.) tall, feed them with a proprietary fertilizer at the recommended rate; repeat the feeding every week to 10 days until the buds show colour, then discontinue. To make hardy chrysanthemums bushier and sturdy enough to eliminate the need for staking, pinch out the tops of the stems; cushion chrysanthemums, which form many stems by themselves, do not need to be pinched out, nor do plants that are to be disbudded. Start pinching out when the plants are about 15 cm (6 in.) tall (page 55) and repeat the process until early summer every time the stems make 15 to 20 cm (6 to 8 in.) of growth. Dig up one or more plants of each cultivar of hardy chrysanthemum in autumn, each with its own clump of soil and set them in a cold frame;

SHASTA DAISY
Chrysanthemum maximum 'Snow Cloud'

HARDY CHRYSANTHEMUM
Chrysanthemum x hortorum

BUGBANE
Cimicifuga simplex 'White Pearl'

HERBACEOUS CLEMATIS
Clematis heracleifolia var. *davidiana*

place each cultivar in a separate shallow box and label it. Put a light mulch of straw over the plants after the soil freezes. To propagate new plants from those saved in the cold frame, cut off as many stolons, or underground stems, as you desire. The stolons, lighter in colour than the rest of the roots, spread out at the base of the plants and are tipped with small, new leaves. Only one stolon is needed to make a full-sized plant by autumn. If more plants are needed, take cuttings in late spring from the new plants started from the freshly planted stolons; the stem cuttings root readily. Hardy chrysanthemums lose their vigour after one year of flowering, producing smaller and fewer blooms, so discard the clumps after removing the stolons and stem cuttings for new plants. Split up Rubellum and Korean chrysanthemums and replant every spring. Cut the stems back to ground level in December.

CIMICIFUGA
C. racemosa (black snakeroot); *C. simplex* (bugbane)

Bugbanes are notable not only for their ability to grow in shade but for their 60 cm (2 ft) spires of tiny flowers, and their impressive leaves, some as long as 60 cm (2 ft). *C. racemosa* grows 1.5 to 2.4 metres (5 to 8 ft) tall, and blooms in mid- and late summer. *C. simplex* grows 1 to 1.5 metres (3 to 5 ft) tall and blooms in autumn; a particularly fine, compact cultivar, is the pure white 'White Pearl' which flowers in September and October.

HOW TO GROW. Bugbanes do well in temperate climates in moist soil that has been well supplemented with moss peat or compost; the soil should be watered deeply in dry weather. Light shade is ideal, but the plants will tolerate both full sun and deep shade. Set new plants about 30 cm (12 in.) apart. Mulch in spring with 5 cm (2 in.) of compost or rotted manure. The plants should not be disturbed except for propagation purposes. New plants can be started by division of clumps in early spring.

CLEMATIS
C. heracleifolia var. *davidiana* (herbaceous clematis); *C. integrifolia*; *C. recta*

Although clematis is usually thought of as a climber, these three species grow no more than 1.2 metres (4 ft) tall. *C. heracleifolia* grows 1 to 1.2 metres (3 to 4 ft) tall and in late summer and early autumn bears clusters of fragrant 2.5 cm (1 in.) pale blue blossoms. *C. integrifolia* grows 45 to 60 cm (18 to 24 in.) tall and from early summer to midsummer bears a single 4 cm (1½ in.) pale blue flower on each stem. *C. recta* grows 1 to 1.2 metres (3 to 4 ft) tall and in early summer to midsummer is crowned with great clusters of fragrant white flowers; its 15 cm (6 in.) leaves are feather-shaped with five to nine leaflets.

HOW TO GROW. Clematis grows in full sun or light shade. It must have well-drained, slightly alkaline to neutral soil (pH 7.0 to 7.5) that has been well supplemented with moss peat or leaf-mould. Space plants 45 to 60 cm (18 to 24 in.) apart. Keep the soil cool and moist during the growing season by covering it with a 5 to 7.5 cm (2 to 3 in.) organic mulch of compost or moss peat. Do not cultivate around the plants, as the lower parts of the stems are easily damaged. Because clematis stems are weak, a short twiggy branch should be set in the ground next to each plant in the spring for support. New plants can be started from stem cuttings taken in spring and rooted in a cold frame. Clematis can remain undisturbed indefinitely.

CONOCLINIUM COELESTINUM See *Eupatorium*

CONVALLARIA
C. majalis (lily of the valley)

Lilies of the valley are popular spring-blooming perennials with arching 15 to 20 cm (6 to 8 in.) stems carrying five to eight richly scented waxy white, pendent, bell-shaped flowers. The smooth oval-oblong leaves grow in pairs. Cultivars with pink flowers, double flowers, and gold striped leaves are available. A popular large flowered white cultivar called 'Fortin's Giant' is often used for forced blooms.

HOW TO GROW. Lilies of the valley are shade lovers and excellent for wild gardens and shrubberies. They are less happy in hot, dry regions. The roots must be cool and the soil should contain plenty of leaf-mould or rotted compost. Plant lilies of the valley 8 to 10 cm (3 to 4 in.) apart. Propagate by division of the crowns in autumn or early spring.

CONVOLVULUS
C. mauritanicus (ground morning-glory)

The ground morning-glory is a handsome, trailing evergreen plant that is especially suited to the hot, sunny, dry gardens of southern Europe; from late spring to late autumn it bears 2.5 cm (1 in.) blue-purple flowers above grey-green foliage.

HOW TO GROW. Ground morning-glories grow in frost-free regions, in full sun. They need very well-drained, even gravelly, soil. Space plants about 1 metre (3 ft) apart and avoid overwatering, especially in winter. When plants get straggly, cut them back to the ground in spring. In cool regions they are not hardy and should be overwintered in pots in a frost-free place. New plants can be started from clumps divided in spring, from seeds sown in autumn to blossom the following summer or from stem cuttings made in late summer for flowers the next spring. Divide clumps after two or three years of flowering.

COREOPSIS
C. auriculata; *C. grandiflora* (tickseed); *C. verticillata*

The yellow flowers of coreopsis are borne on slender wiry stems and bloom abundantly throughout the summer. *C. auriculata*, grows 30 to 90 cm (1 to 3 ft) tall and has 5 cm (2 in.) yellow daisy-like flowers with brown bands at the centres. It is very free growing, as is an improved cultivar 'Astolat Variety'. *C. grandiflora*, the most popular species, grows 60 to 90 cm (2 to 3 ft) tall and has 5 to 7.5 cm (2 to 3 in.) blossoms; two fine cultivars are 'Sunburst', with several rows of petals, and 'Mayfield Giant', with blossoms over 7.5 cm (3 in.) across. *C. verticillata* makes a stocky little bush with bright green, finely divided, needle-like leaves, and myriads of 2.5 cm (1 in.) starry, yellow flowers. It grows 30 to 45 cm (1 to 1½ ft) tall and has a deep gold form 'Grandiflora'.

HOW TO GROW. Coreopsis will grow in a sunny site in any soil, but it must be well-drained, especially during the winter dormant period. Place plants about 30 cm (12 in.) apart. New plants may be started easily from seeds or clump divisions in spring. Divide clumps after two or three years of flowering.

CORONILLA
C. varia (crown vetch)

Crown vetch, which grows 30 to 30 cm (1 to 2 ft) tall, bears small clusters of 12 mm (½ in.) wide pink-and-white flowers from early to late summer; the cultivar 'Penngift' produces mostly pink flowers. Crown vetch is a tough, aggressively

LILY OF THE VALLEY
Convallaria majalis

GROUND MORNING-GLORY
Convolvulus mauritanicus

TICKSEED
Coreopsis grandiflora

CROWN VETCH
Coronilla varia

PAMPAS GRASS
Cortaderia selloana

YELLOW CORYDALIS
Corydalis lutea

spreading plant that will crowd out its neighbours in a show garden, but is well suited to a sunny bank, where it will take care of itself indefinitely. Its deep, tenacious roots and thick, fern-like leaves provide excellent erosion control where it is used as ground cover.

HOW TO GROW. Crown vetch grows in almost any soil if the position is sunny. Space plants about 90 cm (3 ft) apart. To propagate named cultivars, dig up and divide the clumps in spring or autumn.

CORTADERIA
C. selloana, also called *C. argentea, Gynerium argenteum* (pampas grass)

Pampas grass, native to Argentina, is widely grown in warm-climate gardens both for its huge mounds of tough sawtooth-edged leaves and for its spectacular 30 to 90 cm (1 to 3 ft) flower plumes, which appear in late summer and autumn. Plants usually grow 2.4 to 3 metres (8 to 10 ft) tall, but may become twice that height. Pampas grass therefore serves well in the rear of a shrub border or alone as a specimen plant. Its feathery plumes, the best of which are borne on female plants, range from silvery-white to pink and may be dried for winter bouquets if cut before heavy autumn rains.

HOW TO GROW. Pampas grass flourishes in temperate and hot areas, in any soil, wet or dry, provided the position is sunny. To be sure of the best flowers, ask the nurseryman for female plants. Set them at least 1.8 metres (6 ft) apart. Pampas grass seldom needs division, but can be divided for propagation purposes.

CORYDALIS
C. lutea (yellow corydalis)

Yellow corydalis grows 30 to 38 cm (12 to 15 in.) tall and its grey-green, fern-like foliage is attractive from spring until autumn. The 18 mm ($\frac{3}{4}$ in.) flowers are borne above the leaves from spring until midsummer and sometimes later. The species often grows wild in cracks of old walls where drainage is excellent.

HOW TO GROW. Yellow corydalis does best in light shade, but will tolerate both full sun and deep shade. Excellent drainage is vital. Set plants 20 to 25 cm (8 to 10 in.) apart. New plants can be started by dividing and replanting clumps in early spring, but the plants often seed themselves so prolifically as to become a nuisance. Keep them in check by repeatedly removing self-sown seedlings.

D
DELPHINIUM
D. elatum, also called *D.x cultorum* (candle delphinium); *D. belladonna* hybrids; *D. grandiflorum*, also called *D. chinense* (bouquet larkspur, Chinese delphinium); *D. zalil.* (All also called larkspur and delphinium)

The spire-like flowers of delphiniums—usually blue, lavender, purple or white, but sometimes pink, red or yellow—make a spectacular sight in the garden and provide some of the best cut flowers. The plants vary in height from 30 to 180 cm (1 to 6 ft); the tall growing types are breathtaking but fragile; the medium-sized strains are more popular not only because they seldom require staking but also because their stalks are a better length for flower arrangement. Delphiniums bloom abundantly in early summer and flower again in autumn if the flowers are removed before seed pods develop. To produce a second crop, cut the stems just below the flowers; when the new growth at the base of the plants is about 15 cm (6 in.) tall, remove the original stems to the ground (*drawings, page 54*). The new stalks will bear flowers smaller than the summer ones but no less colourful in about two and a half months—usually in early autumn.

Although seen today only in botanic gardens, *D. elatum*, a European species bearing blue flowers with brownish centres, has become the parent of a prodigious race of hybrids. These have been derived from crosses with *D. grandiflorum* and other species and fall into two main groups: the large-flowered or Elatum hybrids and the smaller Belladonna hybrids.

The Elatum hybrids, sometimes called candle delphiniums because of their stately upright habit, grow 1.5 to 2 metres (5 to 7 ft) in height. The erect central stems are clothed for almost half their length with tightly packed 5 to 7.5 cm (2 to 3 in.) flowers and also bear several short-stemmed spikes lower down on the stems. The colour range is impressive, including all shades of blue, purple, and white, also pinks, yellows and reds; many have contrasting eyes or "bees" of other shades, usually white or black. Recommended strains are Pacific Hybrids, and Blackmore and Langdon Hybrids.

The Belladonna hybrids are smaller, 90 to 120 cm (3 to 4 ft) tall, with branching stems loosely clothed with spurred flowers, mostly in shades of blue although there is a remarkable pink cultivar called 'Pink Sensation'. Other good sorts are 'Blue Bees', bright blue; 'Lamartine', deep violet-blue; and 'Moerheimii', white.

The Chinese delphinium is ideal for small gardens or for the front of borders because the plants become only 30 to 45 cm (12 to 18 in.) tall. This species has 2.5 cm (1 in.) flowers in shades of blue and white. Recommended cultivars are 'Azure Fairy', sky blue; 'Blue Butterfly', deep blue; and 'Cambridge Blue', medium blue. *D. zalil* is a lemon-yellow species from Persia, where its 4 cm (1½ in.) flowers are used to make a dye for silk. It grows only 30 to 45 cm (12 to 18 in.) tall, but its weak stems need staking.

HOW TO GROW. Delphiniums grow as perennials in cool or temperate areas and in warmer areas where the nights are cool. They do best in full sun and a well-drained soil that has been enriched with compost, well-rotted manure or leaf-mould. In areas where the summers are long and hot, delphiniums should be treated as hardy annuals; sow the seeds early in autumn to flower the following year. Plant perennial delphiniums 30 to 60 cm (12 to 24 in.) apart, depending on size, and set the crown, 2.5 to 5 cm (1 to 2 in.) beneath the surface of the soil. Seeds sown in early summer will bloom the following year. Delphiniums lose their vigour after two or three years and should be replaced by young plants.

DIANTHUS

D.x allwoodii (Allwood's pink); *D. barbatus* (sweet william); *D. caryophyllus* (border carnation); *D. plumarius* (pink)

Pinks and carnations are perennials noted for their clove-like fragrance, whereas the sweet scented sweet williams are usually grown as biennials. All are prized for their long blooming seasons and long-lasting cut flowers. Their foliage, which grows in dense grass-like tufts, is evergreen.

Allwood's pinks, which grow 30 to 45 cm (12 to 18 in.) high, are superb hybrids that combine the hardiness and free-flowering of the border pink with the large blossoms of the carnation. The flowers, about 5 cm (2 in.) across, are red, pink, white or a combination of these colours; they provide a lavish display in spring and continue to bear some blooms into early autumn. Sweet william is covered

CANDLE DELPHINIUM
Delphinium elatum hybrid

CHINESE DELPHINIUM
Delphinium grandiflorum

ALLWOOD'S PINK
Dianthus x allwoodii

SWEET WILLIAM
Dianthus barbatus

in mid to late spring with massive flat-topped flower heads 7.5 to 12.5 cm (3 to 5 in.) across that are densely packed with single or double flowers in red, pink, white or combinations of those colours. In general, sweet williams grow about 45 to 60 cm (1½ to 2 ft) tall; there are cultivars that do not exceed 15 cm (6 in.); but their blossoms are easily spattered by mud and their stems are too short for cutting. Some strains of sweet william will blossom the first year from seeds sown early in the spring, but they do not have the fine flowers of other types. The border carnation, 45 to 60 cm (1½ to 2 ft) tall, belongs to the same species as the greenhouse carnation, but is better suited to cold winters outdoors. Its 5 cm (2 in.) double flowers come in white, yellow, orange, pink, red and lavender, and open from early summer to autumn. The border pink grows 30 to 38 cm (12 to 15 in.) tall and bears 4 cm (1½ in.) single, double or fringed blossoms in pink, rose, purple and white in late spring; the double white 'Mrs. Sinkins' belongs here.

HOW TO GROW. Border carnations grow as perennials in cool areas, but Allwood's pinks and border pinks are hardy perennials in both cool and temperate regions. All should be treated as biennials in warmer areas, where summers are hot. Sweet williams grow as biennials in temperate regions. All need full sun and do best in a well-drained, light sandy soil; all of them like lime. Plant *Dianthus* species 30 to 45 cm (12 to 18 in.) apart. The crown, or top of the root structure, must be level with the surface of the soil; never bury any part of the stems. The plants should not be mulched; their tender root tops and trailing stems require good air circulation at all times and must be kept as free from moisture as possible. New plants can be started from seeds sown in spring or early summer to flower the following year or from stem cuttings (pipings) rooted in pure sand in the summer; such plants are best moved to the garden in the autumn. Pinks and carnations usually lose their vigour after their second flowering and should be replaced. Sweet williams must be grown from seeds each year for new plants the following year; pull up and discard plants after they flower.

DICENTRA, also called DIELYTRA
D. eximia (fringed bleeding heart); *D. formosa*; *D. spectabilis* (bleeding heart)

D. spectabilis, the bleeding heart, grows 75 to 150 cm (2½ to 5 ft) tall and blossoms in mid to late spring. Its arching stems, dripping with 2.5 cm (1 in.) heart-shaped deep pink flowers, are clothed with graceful, deeply divided blue-green leaves. There is also a white form; both kinds can be forced for early flowers. By midsummer this Chinese species shrivels away and disappears until the following spring. Other, less well-known species and hybrids outshine it, blooming longer and offering a variety of colours. All these plants have fern-like foliage and grow only about 30 to 38 cm (12 to 15 in.) high. One is the fringed bleeding heart, native to eastern North America. From mid-spring to late autumn it bears 12 mm (½ in.) rose-pink flowers. *D. formosa*, native to shady woodlands of the Pacific Coast, bears pale rosy lavender blooms in spring; an excellent white-flowered cultivar called 'Sweet Heart' blossoms from spring to autumn. Hybrids bred by crossing bleeding hearts are even more spectacular and produce a great abundance of 18 mm (¾ in.) flowers from late spring to midsummer and again in the autumn, with a scattering of flowers in between. 'Bountiful' is a particularly good form with fuchsia-red flowers twice the size of the type on 60 cm (2 ft) stems; 'Adrian Bloom' is a good crimson; 'Alba' is white. All grow best in light shade, but *D. spectabilis* and its hybrids will also tolerate full sun if the soil is moist.

FRINGED BLEEDING HEART
Dicentra eximia

BLEEDING HEART
Dicentra spectabilis

HOW TO GROW. Bleeding hearts do best in well-drained soil generously supplemented with moss peat or leaf-mould. Plant the smaller kinds 38 to 45 cm (15 to 18 in.) apart, the larger ones about 75 cm (2½ ft) apart. New plants can be obtained by division during the dormant season, root cuttings in early spring, or seeds sown in boxes in early spring and kept in a cold frame to germinate. To prevent overcrowding, divide the clumps in spring after three or four years of flowering; handle the roots carefully as they are extremely brittle.

DICTAMNUS
D. albus, also called *D. fraxinella* (gas plant, fraxinella, dittany, burning bush)

The gas plant is named for the volatile oil produced in the upper parts of the stems, particularly near the old inflorescences. This can be ignited on a hot, still day without injuring the plant. But fireworks are not the main attraction of the gas plant. Its shiny, leathery, dark green leaves, which smell like lemon peel when rubbed, form a handsome 60 cm (2 ft) mound. In summer, spikes of 4 to 5 cm (1½ to 2 in.) pinkish-purple or snow-white flowers rise 25 to 30 cm (10 to 12 in.) above the foliage. Mature gas plants—four to five years old—bloom most lavishly, and will flourish indefinitely. *D. albus* var. *caucasicus* has larger flowers and 'Purpureus' is a pink, red-striped cultivar. The seed pods are attractive in dried arrangements.

HOW TO GROW. Gas plants grow in full sun or light shade, in a well-drained soil enriched with compost. Set plants 1 to 1.2 metres (3 to 4 ft) apart. New plants can be started from seeds sown in spring to blossom in about three or four years. Gas plants grow best if left undisturbed.

DIELYTRA See *Dicentra*

DIERAMA
D. pulcherrimum; *D. pendulum* (wand flower, angel's fishing rod)

The wand flower is a charming South African perennial with a congested, bulbous rootstock, prized for its 1.8 metre (6 ft) long arching sprays hung with deep rosy-red, tubular flowers and 'Purpurea' is a pink, red-striped cultivar considered to be a stronger growing form of *D. pendulum*. Various named cultivars are available of which 'Port Wine', purple; 'Album', white; 'Heron', wine-red; 'Windhover', rosy pink; and 'Skylark', deep violet, are recommended. The long, grass-like leaves grow in tufts.

HOW TO GROW. Wand flowers are hardy in all but very cold areas, where they have to be protected or lifted and stored in sand for the winter. They require well-drained soil in a hot, sunny position, except in very warm areas where they thrive in part shade. Corms should be planted in autumn or spring 60 cm (2 ft) apart. Propagation is by seed, or named cultivars by offsets taken from adult plants in autumn.

DIGITALIS
D. ferruginea, also called *D. aurea* (rusty foxglove); *D. grandiflora*, also called *D. ambigua* (yellow foxglove); *D.x mertonensis*; *D. purpurea* (common foxglove)

The genus name *Digitalis* is familiar because the leaves of common foxglove provide the heart stimulant called by that name. The plant's spire-like stems are clothed with white, yellow, pink, rose, purple or rusty-red flowers, each 2.5 to 7.5 cm (1 to 3 in.) speckle-throated flower shaped like

GAS PLANT
Dictamnus albus 'Purpureus'

WAND FLOWER
Dierama pendulum

Illustration by Dorothy Bovey

113

FOXGLOVE
Digitalis purpurea Shirley Hybrids

CAUCASIAN LEOPARD'S BANE
Doronicum plantagineum 'Miss Mason'

the finger of a glove. Foxgloves bloom mainly in early summer; but if the first stems are cut off below the seed pods before the seeds mature, more flowers often appear in midsummer. Foxgloves are native to western Europe, but have become naturalized in many parts of the world, including New Zealand, the United States, North Africa and even in the Colombian Andes. Most are biennials, but some species and hybrids are perennials.

The rusty foxglove is usually grown as a biennial or a short-lived perennial; 1.2 to 1.8 metres (4 to 6 ft) tall, it has rusty-red flowers. The yellow foxglove, also a biennial or short-lived perennial, grows 60 to 90 cm (2 to 3 ft) tall, and has honey-coloured flowers blotched with brown. *D.x mertonensis*, a perennial that grows about 1 metre (3 ft) tall, has deep red flowers. The common foxglove, a biennial, grows 1.2 to 1.5 metres (4 to 5 ft) tall, and has rosy-purple or white flowers. It has been bred, however, to provide cultivars of many distinctive characteristics. The Shirley Hybrids include many pastel shades, the 'Gloxiniaflora' strain produces an abundance of wide-flaring flowers that all open simultaneously, and a 1 metre (3 ft) strain called 'Foxy', comes into blossom so quickly—about five months after seeds are sown in the spring—that it can be grown as an annual. But the most striking strain is Excelsior Hybrids; its flowers are borne on all sides of the spike, rather than on one side as on other foxgloves, and face outwards rather than downwards.

HOW TO GROW. Foxgloves thrive in full sun or light shade, but in hot areas should be kept in part to full shade. They do best in moist, well-drained soil. Plant foxgloves 38 to 45 cm (15 to 18 in.) apart. Perennial foxgloves can be propagated by dividing and replanting clumps in early spring or autumn, but are more commonly grown from seeds. Sow the seeds in mid- to late spring to get flowers the following summer.

DORONICUM
D. caucasicum, also called *D. orientale* (Caucasian leopard's bane); *D. pardalianches*; *D. plantagineum* 'Excelsium', also called *D.* 'Harpur Crewe' (leopard's bane)

Most spring flowers are short, but leopard's bane shoots up 45 to 150 cm (1½ to 5 ft), flaunting bright yellow daisy-like flowers 5 to 10 cm (2 to 4 in.) across. Usually borne singly on stems, the flowers are excellent for cutting. Their height is accentuated by ground-hugging leaves that deteriorate by midsummer and may disappear entirely. To avoid an unkempt or bare appearance, set leopard's bane beside plants whose leaves will provide a mask during summer and autumn. The Caucasian leopard's bane grows about 45 cm (1½ ft) tall; most cultivars have flowers about 5 cm (2 in.) across. Recommended are the cultivars of *D. plantagineum*, like 'Excelsium' ('Harpur Crewe'), with golden-yellow flowers up to 7.5 cm (3 in.) across on 90 to 120 cm (3 to 4 ft) stems; 'Miss Mason', bright yellow on 45 cm (1½ ft) stems; and *D. caucasicum* 'Magnificum', which bears blossoms slightly larger than usual. *D. pardalianches* bears its flowers in clusters on 60 to 90 cm (2 to 3 ft) stems.

HOW TO GROW. Leopard's banes do best in moist, well-drained soil and light shade, but will tolerate full sun in areas where summers are cool. Mulch plants with chunky moss peat or compost to conserve moisture around the roots, which are generally shallow, as well as to control weeds. Set plants about 30 cm (12 in.) apart. New plants can be grown from seeds sown in spring to flower the following year. Propagate named cultivars by dividing clumps during the dormant season. Divide clumps when they become overcrowded—usually after two or three years of flowering.

DRACOCEPHALUM

D. hemsleyanum (dragon's head); *D. sibiricum*, also called *Nepeta macrantha*

The dragon's head is an erect perennial with branched and leafy 45 cm (1½ ft) stems, terminating in loose spikes of purplish-blue, sage-like flowers in early summer. Each of these is from 2.5 to 4 cm (1 to 1½ in.) in length and the stalkless leaves are oblong. *D. sibiricum* resembles a giant catmint (see *Nepeta*, page 134) and is a fine, robust summer-flowering plant for the front of the border, with 60 to 120 cm (2 to 4 ft) stems having spikes of mauve flowers and silvery-grey foliage.

HOW TO GROW. Both these plants resent winter damp and waterlogged positions. In temperate climates they are best grown in raised beds; in warmer areas they can be grown almost anywhere, but in very cold regions they should be overwintered under cover as cuttings taken in late summer. They can also be propagated by division.

DRACOCEPHALUM VIRGINIANUM See *Physostegia*

E

ECHINACEA

E. purpurea, also called *Rudbeckia purpurea* (purple cone-flower)

The garden cultivars of coneflower are drought-resistant 90 cm (3 ft) perennials that bear long-lasting bright-coloured 7.5 to 10 cm (3 to 4 in.) blossoms shaped like sun-flowers during late summer and early autumn. A cultivar called 'The King', has crimson flowers with mahogany-red domed centres; 'Bright Star' has rosy-red flowers with maroon centres; 'Robert Bloom' has purple flowers with orange centres; and 'White Lustre', also called 'White King', has white blossoms with bronze centres. All have bold rough leaves 5 to 20 cm (2 to 8 in.) in length.

HOW TO GROW. Coneflowers do best in full sun, but tolerate light shade. They require soil that is never soggy, especially during winter. Plant coneflowers 45 to 60 cm (18 to 24 in.) apart. New plants can be started from root cuttings or clump divisions in spring or autumn. To prevent overcrowding, divide clumps after three or four years of flowering.

ECHINOPS

E. ritro 'Taplow Blue' (globe thistle)

This eye-catching 1 to 1.2 metre (3 to 4 ft) plant bears striking 5 to 7.5 cm (2 to 3 in.) flower heads high above its distinctive foliage from midsummer to early autumn. The deeply lobed leaves, up to 30 cm (12 in.) long, are shiny dark green above and woolly white beneath, and are tipped with spines. Globe thistles make excellent cut flowers, and hold their blue to purple colour when dried for winter arrangements, if picked just as the flowers open.

HOW TO GROW. Globe thistles grow in sunny positions, in well-drained soil; they will tolerate very dry soil. Plant globe thistles 45 to 60 cm (18 to 24 in.) apart. New plants may be started from clump divisions or root cuttings taken in early spring to flower the same season. To prevent overcrowding, divide the clumps after three or four years of flowering.

EPIMEDIUM

E. grandiflorum, also called *E. macranthum*; *E. pinnatum*, also called *E. colchicum*; *E.x rubrum*, also called *E. alpinum rubrum*; *E.x versicolor* 'Sulphureum', also called *E. sul-*

DRAGON'S HEAD
Dracocephalum hemsleyanum

PURPLE CONEFLOWER
Echinacea purpurea 'The King'

GLOBE THISTLE
Echinops ritro 'Taplow Blue'

Illustration by Dorothy Bovey

115

phureum; *E.x youngianum*, also called *E. niveum*. (All called barrenwort)

Most gardeners value epimediums for their delicate-looking but leathery-textured leaves, made up of 5 to 7.5 cm (2 to 3 in.) heart-shaped leaflets and borne on wiry stems about 20 to 30 cm (8 to 12 in.) tall. In early spring the foliage is light green interlaced with pink veins; by midsummer it is glossy deep green; in autumn it turns reddish-bronze. The masses of 12 mm ($\frac{1}{2}$ in.) blossoms, often multicoloured, appear above the foliage in late spring to early summer and are excellent for cutting. The flowers of *E. grandiflorum* may be deep rose, yellow, violet or white; *E. pinnatum*, bright yellow with purplish-brown markings; *E.x rubrum*, a mixture of red and yellow; *E.x versicolor* ('Sulphureum'), pale yellow; and *E.x youngianum*, white, or in the cultivar 'Roseum', pink or pale violet.

HOW TO GROW. Epimediums grow in cool or temperate areas in light shade and moist soil supplemented with compost, moss peat or leaf-mould. Set plants 20 to 25 cm (8 to 10 in.) apart. Clumps may be divided for new plants in autumn or early spring, or can be left undisturbed.

EREMURUS
E. robustus; *E. olgae*; *E. elwesii*; *E. stenophyllus bungei* (foxtail lilies)

Foxtail lilies are striking plants of noble stature with long, strap-shaped leaves that remain close to the ground and massive 60 to 300 cm (2 to 10 ft) spikes of closely packed flowers in pastel shades of white, cream, pink or yellow in early summer to midsummer. *E. robustus*, the tallest, has 2.5 to 3 metre (8 to 10 ft) stems; *E. elwesii* bears fragrant pink flowers with yellow stems, and grows to 2 metres (6 ft); *E. stenophyllus bungei*, 1.2 to 1.5 metres (4 to 5 ft) tall, has bright yellow flowers; and a race known as 'Shelford Hybrids' produces 60 to 90 cm (2 to 3 ft) spikes of pink, buff, white and orange blossoms on 1.8 metre (6 ft) stems.

HOW TO GROW. Foxtail lilies are disappointing when grown in unsuitable conditions. The roots are shaped like an octopus and are fleshy, brittle and easily damaged. Foxtail lilies dislike extremes of temperature. They also resent standing in the wet and so should be planted 15 cm (6 in.) deep, standing on sharp sand and surrounded by sand in the planting hole. Give them full sun, but in a position where they miss the early morning sun. Mulch the roots annually with moss peat or leaf-mould and cover the crowns in spring as a protection against late frosts. Propagation is by seeds which take five to six years to reach flowering size.

ERIGERON
E. speciosus hybrids (fleabane)

These bushy 45 to 75 cm ($1\frac{1}{2}$ to $2\frac{1}{2}$ ft) plants produce 5 cm (2 in.) yellow-centred blossoms, usually in shades of pink to purple, in summer. Typical cultivars are 'Foerster's Liebling' and 'Pink Jewel', both bright pink; and 'Wuppertal', rich violet. Fleabanes are excellent as cut flowers.

HOW TO GROW. Fleabanes do best in full sun in relatively moist, but well-drained sandy soil. Set plants about 30 cm (12 in.) apart. Plants are best propagated by dividing clumps in spring. To prevent overcrowding, divide clumps after two or three years of flowering.

ERYNGIUM
E. amethystinum; *E. giganteum*; *E.x oliverianum* (sea holly)

The sea holly, a European wild flower that grows on sand dunes, has spiny leaves that look like holly foliage.

BARRENWORT
Epimedium x *youngianum* 'Roseum'

FOXTAIL LILY
Eremurus robustus

Illustration by Dorothy Bovey

FLEABANE
Erigeron speciosus hybrid

E. amethystinum is a bushy plant 45 to 60 cm (1½ to 2 ft) tall, its many-branched stems tipped from midsummer to early autumn with 12 mm (½ in.) blue flowers that have spiny ruffs. Even the upper parts of the stems are bluish. *E.x oliverianum* grows 90 to 120 cm (3 to 4 ft) tall. *E. giganteum* grows 90 to 120 cm (3 to 4 ft) tall and is silvery-blue in all its parts—stems, leaves and flower heads. It blooms from midsummer to early autumn and once established renews itself about the garden from self-sown seedlings. The old plant dies after flowering, so must be treated as a biennial. Sea holly makes an excellent cut flower and, if picked when fully open, will hold its colour when dried.

HOW TO GROW. Sea holly does best in full sun and dry sandy soil. Set plants 30 to 45 cm (12 to 18 in.) apart. New plants can be started from seeds sown in spring or root cuttings taken in autumn or early spring for flowers the following year. The clumps spread slowly and can remain undisturbed indefinitely.

ERYSIMUM See *Cheiranthus*

EUPATORIUM

E. coelestinum, also called *Conoclinium coelestinum* (mist-flower)

Mist-flowers come from the United States and in late summer bear 7.5 to 10 cm (3 to 4 in.) flat-topped clusters of blue blossoms that look like shaving brushes, on 45 to 90 cm (1½ to 3 ft) stems. The hairy, heart-shaped leaves have serrated edges. Mist-flowers are excellent for cutting.

HOW TO GROW. Mist-flowers grow in well-drained garden soil; they do best in full sun, but will tolerate light shade. Plant them 45 to 60 cm (1½ to 2 ft) apart. The roots are shallow, so mulch the plants with chunky moss peat or compost to conserve moisture around the roots as well as to control weeds. New plants can be started from clump divisions in spring, from seeds sown in spring or from stem cuttings taken in spring. Clumps spread rapidly and should be dug up and divided after a year or two of flowering.

EUPHORBIA

E. characias; *E. cyparissias* (cypress spurge); *E. epithymoides*, also called *E. polychroma* (cushion spurge)

Like their relatives the poinsettias, spurges have milky sap and petal-like leaves called bracts that appear to be blossoms; the true flowers are set in the centres of the bracts. *E. characias* grows to a height of 90 to 120 cm (3 to 4 ft), and is very spectacular with masses of tightly packed, glaucous green, oblong leaves along its length. These remain evergreen in a mild winter or position, and in early summer expand to huge terminal heads of sulphur-yellow flowers. In the sub-species *wulfenii*, these are about 22 cm (9 in.) long on 120 cm (4 ft) stems. The stems of cypress spurge are set with 2.5 to 5 cm (1 to 2 in.) greyish-green, needle-like leaves; dense heads of 12 m (½ in.) yellow bracts appear on the tops of the 30 cm (12 in.) stems in late spring and early summer. Cushion spurge grows 30 cm (12 in.) tall and spreads to 60 cm (24 in.) wide. In late spring and early summer, the tops of the plants are covered with clusters of bright yellow 2.5 cm (1 in.) bracts; their leaves also turn red in the autumn.

HOW TO GROW. Cypress and cushion spurges grow in cool or temperate areas. *E. characias* and its sub-species *wulfenii* are less hardy and so should be given a sheltered position, as against a wall, in cold, exposed areas. All do best in full sun and well-drained soil. Plant spurges 45 to 60 cm (18 to 24 in.) apart. New plants of *E. characias* and

SEA HOLLY
Eryngium x *oliverianum*

MIST-FLOWER
Eupatorium coelestinum

E. epithymoides are best grown from seeds sown in spring for flowers the following year. Cypress spurge can be propagated by clump division in the spring; otherwise, plants can remain undisturbed indefinitely.

F

FELICIA

F. amelloides, also called *Agathaea coelestis* (blue daisy, blue marguerite, Kingfisher daisy)

A perennial in warm regions, the blue daisy forms a thick 15 cm (6 in.) mound of 2.5 cm (1 in.) leaves, from which rise 30 to 60 cm (12 to 24 in.) stalks bearing 4 cm (1½ in.) blossoms; the cultivar 'Santa Anita' has flowers as large as 7.5 cm (3 in.) across.

HOW TO GROW. Blue daisies grow as perennials in full sun in warm, sheltered areas where the soil is well-drained; in all other areas blue daisies are grown as annuals and if seeds are sown periodically from February until September, flowering plants may be had all the year around. The late kinds are useful for winter flowering under glass. Pinch out the leading and side-shoots when the plants are quite small to make compact plants with plenty of flowers. Set plants 15 to 30 cm (6 to 12 in.) apart. New plants can be started from clump divisions in spring or from stem cuttings taken at any time.

FILIPENDULA

F. hexapetala, also called *F. vulgaris* (dropwort); *F. kamtschatica*; *F. rubra* (queen of the prairie); *F. ulmaria*, also called *Spiraea ulmaria* (meadowsweet, queen of the meadow)

Meadowsweets are topped by tiny flowers in clusters up to 30 cm (12 in.) across. The dropwort and its heavily petalled double form, *F. hexapetala* 'Flore Pleno', grows 60 cm (2 ft) tall, and has long fern-like leaves from which slender flower stems arise in late spring. The other, taller species have large, coarse, palm-shaped or deeply lobed leaves. The 1 to 3 metre (3 to 10 ft) *F. kamtschatica* has white flowers in early summer; the 1.8 metre (6 ft) *F. rubra*, has fragrant pale pink flowers in late spring and early summer, and its form, sold as *F. venusta magnifica*, is a truly magnificent plant up to 1.5 metres (5 ft) tall with huge heads of peach-pink to carmine flowers, according to their age; the 1.2 metre (4 ft) *F. ulmaria* has fragrant white flowers in late spring and early summer. The last has several cultivars, including one with double flowers, 'Flore Pleno'; one with golden foliage, 'Aurea'; and 'Variegata' with green and cream leaf variegations.

HOW TO GROW. Meadowsweets grow in cool and temperate parts in full sun or light shade. All do best in very wet soil, but dropworts also tolerate dry soil. Plant dropworts about 30 cm (12 in.) apart, other species 60 to 90 cm (2 to 3 ft) apart. Propagate named cultivars by dividing clumps in spring: start other types from seeds sown in autumn for flowers in two years. All types can remain undisturbed indefinitely.

G

GAILLARDIA

G. aristata, also called *G. grandiflora* (blanket flower, gaillardia)

Blanket flowers bear bright 5 to 10 cm (2 to 4 in.) blossoms continuously from early summer until frost. The flowers, which are excellent for cutting, are held on slender stems above mounds of hairy foliage. Among the many fine cultivars are 'Sun Dance', about 20 cm (8 in.) tall, with red,

CUSHION SPURGE
Euphorbia epithymoides

BLUE DAISY
Felicia amelloides

DROPWORT
Filipendula hexapetala
'Flore Pleno'

BLANKET FLOWER
Gaillardia aristata

yellow-tipped petals; 'Mandarin', 90 cm (3 ft) tall, wine-red flowers; 'Goblin', brilliant flame-orange; 'Dazzler', bronze-yellow; and 'Sun God', yellow, all 60 cm (2 ft) tall.

HOW TO GROW. Blanket flowers do best in full sun and well-drained soil. In heavy clay soil the leaves grow at the expense of the flowers, and the plants are also likely to die in winter. Plant blanket flowers 25 to 30 cm (10 to 12 in.) apart. New plants can be started from seeds sown early in spring to blossom the same year; propagate named cultivars from clumps divided and replanted in spring or from root cuttings taken in spring to bloom the same year. The clumps should be dug up and divided in spring, usually after two or three years of flowering.

GALIUM

G. odoratum, also called *Asperula odorata* (sweet woodruff)

Sweet woodruff, often used in rock gardens and as ground cover in shady areas, bears an abundance of tiny, fragrant, white flowers in late spring and early summer that are excellent for cutting; the dense mound of foliage 15 to 20 cm (6 to 8 in.) high is attractive all summer.

HOW TO GROW. Sweet woodruff does best in light shade and moist, acid soil (pH 4.5 to 5.5) liberally supplemented with leaf-mould or moss peat. Set plants 25 to 30 cm (10 to 12 in.) apart. New plants can be started from clump divisions in early autumn or spring.

GAZANIA

G. longiscapa (gazania, treasure flower)

In temperate or warm climates, gazanias often blossom all year, although the greatest display appears during the height of summer. They grow 15 to 30 cm (6 to 12 in.) tall, and have daisy-like blossoms up to 10 cm (4 in.) across: the colours range from creamy white through yellow to blazing orange and from lavender and pink to deep bronzy red. They usually appear in sharply contrasting concentric rings. The foliage is evergreen, narrow and grass-like with pale undersides. Many of the cultivars are of hybrid origin and not hardy in cooler climates. They are, however, easily preserved from cuttings made from side-shoots in late summer. Root these in pots of sandy soil and overwinter in a frost-free place.

HOW TO GROW. Gazanias grow as perennials in warm regions and as annuals in cooler areas, in full sun and well-drained soil. Set plants about 30 cm (12 in.) apart. New plants can be started from clump divisions or from seeds sown in early spring to flower the same year.

GENTIANA

G. asclepiadea (willow gentian); *G. septemfida*. (Both called gentian)

Blue is the usual colour of gentian flowers, but some cultivars have white or yellow blossoms. The willow gentian grows 30 to 45 cm (12 to 18 in.) tall and has slender stems clothed with prominently veined 5 to 7.5 cm (2 to 3 in.) leaves. During late summer, the upper 15 to 20 cm (6 to 8 in.) of each stem are studded with dark blue, tubular flowers. *G. septemfida*, which blossoms at the same time as willow gentian, grows only 20 to 30 cm (8 to 12 in.) tall. It has 2.5 cm (1 in.) white-throated, deep blue flowers.

HOW TO GROW. Gentians grow in cool or temperate regions and do best in light shade. They need a moist, acid soil (pH 5.0 to 6.5) liberally supplemented with moss peat or leaf-mould. Plant gentians 30 to 45 cm (12 to 18 in.) apart. New plants are best started from seeds sown in autumn for flowers the following year.

SWEET WOODRUFF
Galium odoratum

Illustration by Dorothy Bovey

GAZANIA
Gazania longiscapa hybrids

GENTIAN
Gentiana septemfida

CRANE'S-BILL
Geranium grandiflorum

BARBERTON DAISY
Gerbera jamesonii

SCARLET AVENS
Geum chiloense 'Fire Opal'

GERANIUM

G. endressii; *G. grandiflorum*, now more correctly *G. meeboldii*; *G. ibericum* (Iberian crane's-bill); *G. sanguineum* (bloody crane's-bill); *G. psilostemon*, also called *G. armenum* (Armenian crane's-bill); *G.x* 'Johnson's Blue'. (All called crane's-bill)

Crane's-bills are related to the common geranium (*Pelargonium*), but belong to a different genus. They bear 2.5 to 5 cm (1 to 2 in.) flowers almost all summer and form attractive mounds of dark, usually deeply lobed, foliage. Two fine 45 cm (18 in.) cultivars of *G. endressii* are 'Rose Clair', salmon-rose and 'Wargrave Pink', deep pink; both bloom from early summer to autumn. *G. grandiflorum*, 38 to 45 cm (15 to 18 in.) tall, produces red-veined, blue flowers from late spring until frost. Iberian crane's-bill, 30 to 45 cm (12 to 18 in.) tall, has purple flowers in early summer to midsummer. Most types of bloody crane's-bill have purplish-red flowers and grow about 30 cm (12 in.) tall, but spread to about twice that in diameter; a pink-flowered variety, *G. sanguineum* var. *lancastriense*, grows 10 to 15 cm (4 to 6 in.) tall with a spread of 45 cm (18 in.). The Armenian crane's-bill has brilliant magenta flowers with black centres and grows to 90 cm (3 ft), while the hybrid *G.x* 'Johnson's Blue' has cup-shaped, clear blue flowers on branching 45 cm (18 in.) stems.

HOW TO GROW. *G. endressii* and *G. ibericum* grow in cool and temperate regions. *G. grandiflorum*, *G. sanguineum* and *G. psilostemon* will also grow in warm areas. All do best in a sheltered, sunny site and grow in almost any garden soil. Plant crane's-bills about 30 cm (12 in.) apart. New plants of named cultivars are best started from stem cuttings taken in summer; the species types can be grown from seeds sown in spring or autumn. All will flower the following year. Clumps do best undisturbed.

GERBERA

G. jamesonii (gerbera daisy, Barberton daisy, Transvaal daisy)

In the gardens of mild-climate areas gerbera daisies offer a continuous display of blossoms from spring to late autumn. Their long-lasting 10 to 12.5 cm (4 to 5 in.) blossoms are borne on leafless 30 to 45 cm (12 to 18 in.) stems, and their colours range from white through cream, yellow, orange, pink, salmon and rose to red. The flowers may be singles, with one ring of petals, or heavily petalled doubles. They make excellent cut flowers. The 20 to 30 cm (8 to 12 in.) leaves are shallowly lobed, dark green above and woolly white beneath, and rise directly from the ground.

HOW TO GROW. Gerberas need warm, sheltered spots, such as under a south-facing wall. Elsewhere, grow in a frost-free greenhouse in pots or soil borders. They need full sun and good but well-drained soil; some gardeners grow them in sand regularly watered with liquid manure. Plant gerbera daisies 30 to 38 cm (12 to 15 in.) apart, setting the crown, or top of the root structure, level with the surface of the soil. New plants may be started from divisions of clumps in spring. Clumps should be divided when they become overcrowded, usually after three or four years of flowering.

GEUM

G.x borisii; *G. chiloense*, also known as *G. quellyon* and *G. coccineum* (scarlet avens). (Both also called geum)

The handsome 5 to 7.5 cm (2 to 3 in.) flowers of geums, which are available as semi-doubles (more than one row of petals) and doubles (heavily overlapping petals), resemble roses, and the genus is in fact a member of the rose family.

Geums bloom all summer with occasional flowers until frost if faded blooms are removed before they produce seeds. Colours include many shades of yellow, orange and red. Most flower stems grow 45 to 60 cm (18 to 24 in.) tall, from clumps of dark green, finely divided foliage. *G.x borisii* has vivid orange-scarlet flowers. There are many excellent cultivars of scarlet avens, including 'Princess Juliana', semi-double, bronzy orange; 'Fire Opal', semi-double, scarlet; 'Lady Stratheden', semi-double, golden yellow; and 'Mrs. Bradshaw', double, scarlet.

HOW TO GROW. Geums grow well in rich, moist soil, but need good drainage, especially in winter. They do best in full sun, but tolerate light shade. Plant geums 25 to 30 cm (10 to 12 in.) apart. New plants are best started from clump divisions in spring, but the old favourites 'Mrs. Bradshaw' and 'Lady Stratheden' come true from seeds sown outside in early summer for flowers the following year.

GYNERIUM ARGENTEUM See *Cortaderia sellcana*

GYPSOPHILA

G.x monstrosa var. *bodgerii*, also known as *G. paniculata* 'Nana Plena'; *G. paniculata* (baby's-breath); *G. repens* (creeping baby's-breath). (All also called chalk plant)

The lacy stems and myriad blossoms of baby's-breath add airy grace to a summer border or bouquet. The hybrid *G.x monstrosa* var. *bodgerii* is a dwarf, compact plant 25 to 38 cm (10 to 15 in.) tall, with double white flowers in dense sprays. Two cultivars with pink flowers are 'Rosy Veil' (Rosenschleier) and 'Pink Star'. *G. paniculata* is the parent of several good baby's-breaths, including 'Bristol Fairy', double white; 'Flamingo', double pale pink; all grow about 90 cm (3 ft) tall. They flower in early summer, but will continue to produce stray blossoms until frost, provided the first stems are removed when they fade. If the flowers are picked when fully open and dried upside down in a shaded, airy place, they make excellent winter bouquets. *G. repens* 'Rosea' is a 15 cm (6 in.) type that bears pink flowers in mid- to late spring; its trailing stems may spread to a diameter of 45 to 60 cm (1½ to 2 ft).

HOW TO GROW. Baby's-breath does best in cool or temperate regions in full sun and well-drained, neutral or even slightly alkaline soil (pH 6.5 to 7.5). The common name chalk plant reflects its need for lime, which must be added if the soil is acid. Plant baby's-breath 45 to 60 cm (1½ to 2 ft) apart in early spring. In colder climates, protect baby's-breath over winter with a mulch of straw. Most of the plants grown commercially are cultivars grafted on to seedlings of *G. paniculata*. Grafted plants have a gnarled joint where the stem and root meet and this joint should be set about 2.5 cm (1 in.) below the soil level so that the graft can develop its own root system. They can also be propagated from soft cuttings in the spring.

H

HELENIUM

H. autumnale (sneezeweed)

Despite its common name, this delightful plant does not provoke sneezing. Modern cultivars of this North American wild flower bloom in late summer and early autumn, decorating the garden with great clusters of 5 cm (2 in.) daisy-like flowers in shades that range from yellow to mahogany. Recommended cultivars are 'Bruno', 90 to 105 cm (3 to 3½ ft) tall, deep reddish brown; 'Butterpat', 90 to 105 cm (3 to 3½ ft) tall, golden yellow; 'Chipperfield Orange', 1 to 1.2 metres (3½ to 4 ft) tall, gold; 'Baudirektor

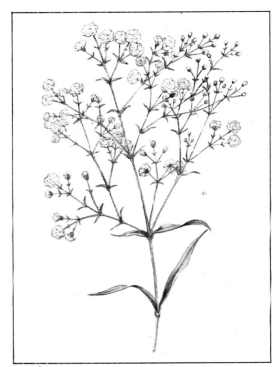

BABY'S-BREATH
Gypsophila paniculata 'Bristol Fairy'

SNEEZEWEED
Helenium autumnale

Linne', orange and mahogany red, 1.2 metres (4 ft) tall; 'Coppelia', similar colouring, but 90 to 105 cm (3 to 3½ ft) tall; 'Bressingham Gold', deep gold suffused with crimson and 90 cm (3 ft) tall; and 'Pumilum Magnificum', about 60 cm (2 ft) tall, soft yellow. The flowers of all cultivars are excellent for cutting.

HOW TO GROW. Sneezeweeds grow in almost any soil in full sun, but they do best if the site is moist. Set plants 30 to 45 cm (12 to 18 in.) apart. Pinch out the tips of the shoots in early summer to force additional branches and flowers. New plants can be started by dividing clumps during the dormant period.

HELIANTHUS

H. decapetalus var. *ligulosus*, also called 'Flore Pleno'; *H. decapetalus* var. *multiflorus* (double sunflower)

In its single-flowered form—with one ring of petals— this sunflower, and its double-flowered garden cultivars— those that have many overlapping petals—can be grown almost anywhere. In mid- to late summer they produce golden 10 cm (4 in.) dahlia-like blossoms. As these plants are about 120 cm (4 ft) tall, with coarse leaves, they should be set at the back of a border. 'Loddon Gold' and 'Capenock Star' are double and single respectively.

HOW TO GROW. Helianthus can be grown in almost any soil as long as the site is sunny. Plant them 45 to 60 cm (18 to 24 in.) apart. The plants spread rapidly; to prevent them from crowding other plants in a border, dig them up and divide them every other year in spring or autumn.

HELIOPSIS

H. helianthoides var. *scabra* (heliopsis, orange sunflower)

The garden cultivars of heliopsis grow about 90 cm (3 ft) tall, and bear double (heavily petalled) or semi-double yellow or orange flowers 7.5 to 10 cm (3 to 4 in.) across from midsummer to autumn. Recommended cultivars are 'Golden Greenheart', green-centred, golden-yellow flowers; 'Gold Plume' and 'Incomparabilis', both with orange-yellow flowers; and 'Light of Loddon', bright yellow flowers. Heliopsis is valuable at the back of a border for its bright colours and extended blooming season; its flowers, borne on long stems, are excellent for cutting, and can be dried for winter decoration.

HOW TO GROW. Heliopsis grows well in temperate regions in a sunny position, especially when the soil is enriched with compost or leaf-mould and there is ample moisture. Set plants about 60 cm (24 in.) apart. Heliopsis spreads by underground roots, and the clumps should be dug up and divided in either spring or autumn when they become overcrowded, usually every three or four years.

HELLEBORUS

H. niger (Christmas rose); *H. orientalis* (Lenten rose); *H. lividus* ssp. *corsicus* (Corsican hellebore)

Both Christmas and Lenten roses are 30 to 38 cm (12 to 15 in.) plants that, despite their names, are more closely related to buttercups than to roses. The Christmas rose produces 5 to 10 cm (2 to 4 in.) white blossoms with prominent yellow, pollen-bearing stamens. It blooms any time from early winter to late spring, depending upon the climate, and individual flowers last a month or more. The cultivar *H. niger* 'Potter's Wheel' has flowers up to 12 cm (5 in.) across. The flowers will last longer if protected by a temporary plastic-covered frame to keep off snow and ice. The blossoms of the Lenten rose, usually about 5 cm (2 in.) across, vary in colour from white to chocolate-brown

DOUBLE SUNFLOWER
Helianthus decapetalus
'Flore Pleno'

HELIOPSIS
Heliopsis helianthoides var. *scabra*
'Golden Greenheart'

CHRISTMAS ROSE
Helleborus niger

and purple and even green; they open between late winter
and mid-spring. The flowers of both species are suitable for
cutting; but before placing in water, the stem ends should
be seared with a match or candle flame. Both species have
leathery evergreen leaves; the roots of both are poisonous.
H. lividus ssp. *corsicus* is a splendid plant for shady positions; with clusters of 5 cm (2 in.) apple-green flowers full
of golden stamens on 60 to 90 cm (2 to 3 ft) stems. These
come in late winter and last for several months. The dark
green, spiny-edged leaves persist over winter.

HOW TO GROW. Christmas roses and Lenten roses
grow best in partial shade and a moist, neutral or slightly
alkaline (pH 7.0 to 8.0) soil that has been liberally supplemented with moss peat, leaf-mould or compost. When
well suited in moist soil and well-drained conditions,
H. lividus ssp. *corsicus* spreads naturally by means of self-
sown seedlings. In spring place the plants 30 to 38 cm (12 to
15 in.) apart, setting the crowns, or tops of the root structures, about 2.5 cm (1 in.) below the top of the soil. Each
spring apply a 2.5 cm (1 in.) mulch of compost or well-
rotted manure around the plants. New plants are best
grown from seeds sown in early autumn. They will flower
in three or four years. Do not divide clumps.

HEMEROCALLIS
H. hybrids (hybrid day lilies)

Day lilies used to be either yellow or orange, but today's
hybrids cover a spectrum from palest yellow through
orange to pink, red and dark mahogany. Day lilies known
as polychromes are a blend of related shades; bi-colour
and eyed day lilies combine different hues. There are now
so many cultivars, each blossoming at a different time,
that they can be planted to bloom successively from early
spring until frost. A wide range of heights is also available,
from miniatures that grow 38 to 45 cm (15 to 18 in.) tall,
to giants that reach 120 cm (4 ft) or more. Blossoms may be
less than 7 cm (3 in.) or more than 20 cm (8 in.) across and
may have a single ring of petals or a double row of overlapping petals. Although individual blossoms are short-
lived, day lilies are excellent for bouquets; cut whole stems
and remove the faded flowers as new buds open indoors.

HOW TO GROW. Day lilies will grow in almost any soil,
but do best in well-drained soil liberally enriched with
compost or leaf-mould. They flower more freely in full
sun, but will tolerate light shade; in hot areas, afternoon
shade is desirable. Plant day lilies 45 to 60 cm (1½ to 2 ft)
apart. Clumps should be divided for propagation in spring
or autumn, when they become overcrowded, usually every
four to six years of flowering.

HESPERIS
H. matronalis (sweet rocket, dame's violet)

Sweet rocket, a European native, grows so readily that
it will naturalize itself in shrubberies and wild gardens if
left undisturbed. In mixed garden borders, however, the
plants are unfortunate perennials, in as much as they exhaust the soil more rapidly than other plants and then die
off. They are therefore best treated as biennials. The
plants reach a height of 60 to 90 cm (2 to 3 ft) and from
mid-spring to midsummer bear large, loose clusters of
fragrant 18 mm (¾ in.) purple, lilac or white flowers. If
faded flowers are removed before they form seeds, the
plants may continue to blossom until early autumn.

HOW TO GROW. Sweet rockets grow in almost any
moist well-drained soil in full sun or light shade. Plant
them 38 to 45 cm (15 to 18 in.) apart. Plants can be started
from seeds sown in spring for flowers the following year.

DAY LILY
Hemerocallis hybrid

SWEET ROCKET
Hesperis matronalis

HEUCHERA
H. sanguinea (coral bells, alum root)

The name coral bells once described the colour as well as the shape of the blossoms of this graceful perennial, but today the colours range from pure white to fiery red. The foliage, bronze-coloured 2.5 to 5 cm (1 to 2 in.) heart-shaped leaves that remain on the plants the year round, provides a handsome background for the hundreds of tiny flowers that are borne on wiry 30 to 60 cm (12 to 24 in.) stems from late spring until early autumn. Recommended cultivars of coral bells are 'Freedom', rose pink; 'June Bride', white; 'Pluie de Feu', bright red; 'Red Spangles', rich crimson-scarlet and very free-flowering; 'Greenfinch', greenish-yellow; 'Oakington Jewel', coral-red; and 'Pearl Drops', which is almost pure white. Coral bells can be placed at the front of a border or used to line a path or accent a rock garden. They also make excellent cut flowers.

HOW TO GROW. Coral bells flower most profusely in full sun, but will tolerate light shade, especially in hot areas. As they have shallow roots, coral bells require moist, well-drained soil that has been liberally enriched with organic materials such as compost, moss peat or leaf-mould. Coral bells hybrids may be grown successfully from commercial seeds and will blossom when two years old. Set plants about 30 cm (12 in.) apart. New plants can be started from divisions of clumps in spring. The clumps should be divided every four or five years.

HIBISCUS
H. moscheutos, also called H. palustris (rose mallow)

Rose mallows, colourful relatives of the hollyhock, bear enormous red, white or pink flowers 15 to 30 cm (6 to 12 in.) in diameter from midsummer until frost. The wild rose mallow is native to swampy land in the United States, and has become naturalized in France. Garden cultivars may grow up to 2.5 metres (8 ft), but unless the soil is extremely moist in summer, mature plants seldom exceed 1.5 metres (5 ft). Southern Belle and Avalon Hybrids are recommended strains that can be grown from seeds.

HOW TO GROW. Rose mallows do best in full sun, but will tolerate light shade. Although they can grow in almost any soil, they prefer moist ground liberally supplemented with compost, leaf-mould or other organic material. Rose mallows should be spaced about 90 cm (3 ft) apart. If you are setting out growing plants, place the crowns, or tops of the root structures, about 10 cm (4 in.) beneath the soil. To start plants from seeds, sow in early spring; the new plants will produce only a few flowers the first year, but will come into full bloom in subsequent years. Propagation of named cultivars that are not sold in seed form requires professional skills. As rose mallow clumps do not spread underground, the plants can be allowed to remain undisturbed indefinitely.

HOSTA
H. crispula, also called H. fortunei marginata-alba; H. lancifolia; H. plantaginea; H. undulata; H. ventricosa; H. hybrids. (All called plantain lily)

Although plantain lilies, or hostas, produce attractive 2.5 to 4 cm (1 to 1½ in.) lily-like flowers atop slender leafless stems, they are valued more for the highly decorative foliage that they present from late spring until frost. H. crispula, 30 to 45 cm (1 to 1½ ft) tall, has dark green, long-pointed leaves with prominent white margins and pale purple flowers that open in midsummer. H. fortunei, 60 to 90 cm (2 to 3 ft) tall, has long-stalked, grey-green, prominently veined leaves and lilac flowers in summer; the

CORAL BELLS
Heuchera sanguinea
'Freedom'

ROSE MALLOW
Hibiscus moscheutos

PLANTAIN LILY
Hosta plantaginea

cultivar 'Albopicta', is distinguished by heavy leaf variegations of soft yellow when young, which become glaucous-green at flowering time. *H. lancifolia* has narrow, glossy green leaves, overlapping and forming mounds, and pale lilac flowers; there is a white-edged cultivar known as 'Thomas Hogg'. *H. plantaginea*, 30 to 45 cm (1 to 1½ ft), has white, scented flowers in late summer, and heart-shaped, glossy, yellow-green leaves; *H. undulata*, 30 cm (2 ft) tall, has mid-green leaves marked with central bands of white or silver; its light purple flowers open in midsummer. *H. ventricosa*, 90 cm (3 ft) tall, is a vigorous species with violet-mauve, funnel-shaped flowers in midsummer and ovate, glaucous leaves. Among the cultivars 'Honeybells', 60 cm (2 ft) tall, with deep mauve, scented flowers and green leaves; 'Royal Standard', 90 cm (3 ft), with white, fragrant blossoms and green leaves; and 'Tall Boy', 120 cm (4 ft), green-leaved with violet-mauve flowers, are outstanding. All bloom around midsummer.

HOW TO GROW. Plantain lilies thrive in moist soil liberally enriched with compost of leaf-mould. They do best in light shade, but will tolerate full sun or deep shade if the ground is moist, and are particularly happy near water. Space plants 30 to 60 cm (12 to 24 in.) apart, depending on the size of the species. New plants can be started by dividing clumps in early spring. Clumps may otherwise remain undisturbed indefinitely.

HYPERICUM
H.x moserianum (St John's wort)

The blossoms of this hybrid shrublet bring a lively note of colour to gardens from midsummer to early autumn. The five-petalled, rich yellow, cup-shaped blossoms, clustered at the ends of 60 to 90 cm (2 to 3 ft) stems, are about 5 cm (2 in.) across and have centres crowded with golden pollen-bearing stamens with red tips. The leaves retain their colour throughout the year in mild climates, but die down to the ground in cold winters.

HOW TO GROW. St John's wort can be grown in mild areas in full sun or light shade. It grows in almost any soil, but does best in a moist soil that has been well supplemented with moss peat or leaf-mould. Set plants 40 to 60 cm (16 to 24 in.) apart. The stems should be cut to ground level each year to force healthy new growth. New plants can be propagated from soft basal cuttings taken and rooted in summer and overwintered in a cold frame. They will flower the following year.

IBERIS
I. sempervirens (perennial candytuft)

This low-growing evergreen candytuft is almost completely covered with 5 cm (2 in.) clusters of tiny, dazzling white flowers from early spring to early summer. Plants grow 15 to 22 cm (6 to 9 in.) tall, and spread as much as 60 cm (2 ft) across. The narrow leaves, 2.5 to 5 cm (1 to 2 in.) long, are attractive throughout the year. Superior cultivars include 'Little Gem', 10 cm (4 in.), which flowers abundantly in spring, and 'Plena', with double flowers.

HOW TO GROW. Candytufts can be grown in full sun or light shade and well-drained garden soil. Set plants 30 to 38 cm (12 to 15 in.) apart. Shear off the old flower stems as soon as they stop blossoming to encourage the growth of fresh new stems. New plants can be started from seeds sown in early spring for flowers the following year, but named cultivars must be propagated from stem cuttings taken from non-flowering shoots in midsummer.

ST. JOHN'S WORT
Hypericum x moserianum

PERENNIAL CANDYTUFT
Iberis sempervirens

TALL BEARDED IRIS
Iris, bearded hybrids

JAPANESE IRIS
Iris, beardless hybrid

YELLOW FLAG IRIS
Iris pseudacorus

IRIS

I. hybrids (bearded iris, beardless iris, aril iris), *I. pseudacorus* (yellow flag iris); *I. kaempferi*; *I. laevigata*

There are more than 200 species of irises that grow wild (or did once) and thousands of hybrids, but all have two characteristics in common: sword-shaped leaves and a distinctive flower structure consisting of three, usually erect petals, called standards, and three outer petals or sepals, called falls, that hang down from the base of the blossom. Between each pair of standards and falls rise the flower's reproductive organs, often crowned with a colourful crest.

There are two broad categories of hybrid irises—bearded and beardless. On bearded irises, each of the falls is ornamented with a fuzzy, often brightly coloured, strip or beard. Bearded irises include the familiar standard bearded hybrids as well as the group of hybrids called aril irises, which are distinguished by their rounded flowers, veined petals and subdued colours. The colours of standard bearded irises range from snowy white through every conceivable shade, including yellow, orange, pink, red, blue, lavender, purple, brown and near black; the standards and falls are often of different colours. The height of standard bearded irises ranges from 7.5 to 100 cm (3 to 40 in.) or more, with flowers 4 to 20 cm (1½ to 8 in.) across.

Plant height, flower size and blooming season are the key factors in the classification of standard bearded irises: MINIATURE DWARF BEARDED IRISES, less than 25 cm (10 in.) tall, bear 4 to 5 cm (1½ to 2 in.) flowers in mid-spring. INTERMEDIATE BEARDED IRISES are 25 to 45 cm (10 to 18 in.) tall in the short group with flowers 7.5 to 12.5 cm (3 to 5 in.) across; and 45 to 70 cm (18 to 28 in.) tall in the taller group with flowers 10 to 12.5 cm (4 to 5 in.) across; intermediate bearded irises bloom slightly later in spring than miniature dwarf irises. TALL BEARDED IRISES are more than 70 cm (28 in.) tall, often 1.5 metres (5 ft) tall, and have 10 to 20 cm (4 to 8 in) flowers. The ARILLATE group includes Oncocyclus and Regelia irises, all very beautiful and in various colours such as white and tan, or smokey-grey, many with prominently veined petals of other colours. They are however, rather difficult to cultivate; they grow 60 to 90 cm (2 to 3 ft) tall, and from late spring to early summer bear 10 to 15 cm (4 to 6 in.) bearded flowers.

The beardless irises are divided into five sub-sections: Californicae, also known as Pacific Coast irises, come in various shades, but are dominantly blue with veining on the falls. They have broad, strap-shaped leaves and grow about 30 to 45 cm (1 to 1½ ft) tall. They are summer-flowering and usually dislike lime. Irises in the Hexagona group have six-ribbed seedpods. They include the Louisiana hybrids, 60 to 90 cm (2 to 3 ft) tall, with 7.5 to 10 cm (3 to 4 in.) flowers in cream to yellow and bronze, pink, red, blue, purple and near black. These blossom from mid-spring until early summer. The Laevigatae group contains various summer-flowering, moisture-loving irises like the aquatic *I. pseudacorus*, the yellow water flag; also *I. laevigata* and the Japanese irises, *I. kaempferi*. The latter have flat-topped blooms like parasols, 15 to 20 cm (6 to 8 in.) across, in a wide range of colours, usually mottled, striated or striped in other shades. The Sibiricae group has flat, grassy leaves and branched 45 to 90 cm (1½ to 3 ft) tall stems carrying several 7.5 to 10 cm (3 to 4 in.) flowers, mostly in blue shades, but also claret, white and violet. They are usually known as Siberian irises. The Spuria group has tough, fibrous rhizomes and variously coloured 6 to 9 cm (2½ to 3½ in.) flowers.

HOW TO GROW. All irises bloom best in full sun, but soil, moisture and climatic requirements vary with the types. All bearded irises like a well-drained soil. The Arillate group thrives in hot, dry regions and needs well drained, neutral soil. Both bearded irises and aril bearded irises grow from thick underground stems called rhizomes, that creep along just beneath the surface of the soil; plant both types from midsummer to early autumn, setting them 25 to 38 cm (10 to 15 in.) apart, with the tops of the rhizomes level with the surface of the soil. Both can be propagated by dividing the rhizomes. In warm, dry areas, to which they are best suited, aril bearded irises should be dug up after flowering and replanted annually; in areas with more rainfall than they prefer, they should be dug up early each summer after they have flowered and stored in dry sand until autumn. Standard bearded irises multiply rapidly and in the third or fourth flowering season, after flowering, the rhizomes should be dug up, divided and replanted.

Among the beardless irises, Louisiana irises grow in cool to temperate and hot areas, Japanese irises in temperate zones and Siberian irises in both cool and temperate areas. Spuria irises grow in cool, temperate or warm regions, although most cultivars blossom more freely in warm gardens. Spuria irises prefer neutral soil, but Louisiana, Japanese and Siberian irises require acid soil with a pH of 5.5 to 6.5; add sulphur if necessary to acidify the soil. Both Louisiana and Japanese irises thrive in moist but well-drained soil. Plant all of them 38 to 45 cm (15 to 18 in.) apart. Spuria irises usually require two or three years to become fully established and should remain undisturbed indefinitely. All of the other beardless hybrids can be propagated by dividing clumps in early autumn. Otherwise they can be left alone for as long as 8 or 10 years, when they may become overcrowded.

Yellow flag irises thrive on neglect as long as they have moist soil. Space plants 45 to 60 cm (18 to 24 in.) apart. Clumps can be left undisturbed indefinitely, or dug up for division to start new plants.

K

KIRENGESHOMA
K. palmata (yellow waxbells)

This Japanese plant is indispensable for late flowering, especially in shade; it grows luxuriantly in a north-facing border. It is a stately plant with 90 cm (3 ft) glaucous stems with purple suffusions, slender, palmately-lobed leaves and terminal clusters of 2.5 to 5 cm (1 to 2 in.), drooping, waxy yellow flowers.

HOW TO GROW. Yellow waxbells are hardy except in extremely cold or very hot and dry areas; they need moist soil enriched with peat or leaf-mould, and light to deep shade. They are usually increased from seeds or by dividing plants carefully in spring. Plant waxbells 60 to 75 cm (2 to 2½ ft) apart.

KNIPHOFIA
K. uvaria, also called K. alooides and Tritoma uvaria (red-hot poker, torch lily, tritoma)

The blossoms of red hot pokers are unusual, 30 cm (12 in.) lance-shaped spikes made up of about 5 cm (2 in.) tubular flowers. In the original species the flowers were yellow at the base, shading upwards to the fiery red tips from which the plant derives its name. Modern hybrids, however, are available in many colours from pure white to delicate shades of yellow and rosy red. Some bloom from early summer into autumn. Most cultivars grow 60 to 75 cm (2 to 2½ ft) tall, although some may reach 1.8 metres (6 ft). Their long narrow leaves resemble coarse grass, and their flowers are long-lasting.

YELLOW WAXBELLS
Kirengeshoma palmata

RED-HOT POKER
Kniphofia uvaria 'Springtime'

HOW TO GROW. Red-hot pokers can be grown in full sun and well-drained garden soil, but will not tolerate extreme cold. Plant them 45 to 60 cm (1½ to 2 ft) apart. In cool areas tie the leaves together over each clump in the autumn, and protect the plants with a winter mulch of straw or bracken. New plants can be started from seeds sown in early spring or from clump divisions in spring, but require two or three years to reach flowering size. Except for propagation purposes, red-hot pokers are best if left undisturbed indefinitely.

L

LATHYRUS
L. latifolius (perennial pea)

This hardy climber, 1.2 to 2.4 metres (4 to 8 ft) long, bears clusters of five to nine 4 cm (1½ in.) blossoms from early summer to early autumn, at the ends of 30 cm (12 in.) stems. The original species is a washed-out magenta, but cultivars come in pink, reddish-purple and pure white. They can be planted to climb on fences, trellis, or walls.

HOW TO GROW. Perennial peas grow in full sun and almost any well-drained soil. Space plants 45 to 60 cm (18 to 24 in.) apart. Remove faded flowers to extend the blooming season. Start new plants by sowing seeds in late autumn or early spring for blooms the following year.

LAVANDULA
L. officinalis, now more correctly *L. angustifolia*, but also known as *L. spica* and *L. vera* (lavender).

Lavender is an evergreen shrub over much of Europe, but nevertheless is often used in herbaceous borders on account of its fragrance and attractive flowers and foliage. The blossoms are borne in spikes of 12 mm (½ in.) blossoms, pale to mid- and deep blue or purple, that circle the plant's wiry stems in mid- to late summer. The silvery-grey leaves, shaped like blunt 2.5 cm (1 in.) needles, are highly aromatic; both flowers and foliage have long been used, after drying, for sweet-smelling sachets and pot pourris. True lavender is an excellent choice for the edges of paths and border; it also provides delightful cut flowers. Fine cultivars include 'Hidcote', deep purple with grey foliage, 30 cm (1 ft) tall; 'Munstead', 38 cm (15 in.) tall, compact-growing with short, violet flower stalks; *L. spica*, old English lavender, green leaves and lavender flowers on long spikes; and 'Twickle Purple', medium blue on 90 cm (3 ft) stems. There are also white and pink flowered forms.

HOW TO GROW. True lavender grows in full sun and well-drained soil. Space plants 38 to 45 cm (15 to 18 in.) apart. New plants can be raised from heel cuttings taken in midsummer and rooted in a cold frame. Here they should remain all winter and be planted out the following spring. Straggly plants can be cut hard back in early spring to encourage new shoots from near the base; lavenders should be lightly trimmed after flowering in late summer.

LIATRIS
L. pycnostachya (Kansas or cat-tail gay-feather); *L. scariosa*); *L. spicata* (blazing star, spike gay-feather). (All also called liatris)

The tiny fuzzy blossoms of most gay-feathers usually begin to open at the top of the plants' 45 cm (1½ ft) flower spikes rather than in the normal bottom-to-top sequence of other plants. The Kansas gay-feather grows 1.2 to 1.8 metres (4 to 6 ft) tall and bears rosy lavender or white flowers in late summer and early autumn. Two notable cultivars of *L. scariosa* blossom in early autumn: 'Sep-

PERENNIAL PEA
Lathyrus latifolius

LAVENDER
Lavandula officinalis 'Hidcote'

SPIKE GAY-FEATHER
Liatris spicata 'Silver Tips'

Illustration by Dorothy Bovey

tember Glory', with deep purple flowers, and 'White Spire', with pure white blossoms; both grow 1.5 to 1.8 metres (5 to 6 ft) tall. The spike gay-feather also boasts two fine cultivars: the 45 cm (1½ ft) 'Kobold', with deep rosy purple flowers, and the 90 cm (3 ft) 'Silver Tips', with lavender blossoms; both bloom in mid- to late summer.

HOW TO GROW. Gay-feathers grow in full sun or light shade. Soil must be well drained in winter in cool areas. Space plants 30 to 45 cm (12 to 18 in.) apart. Start new plants of named cultivars by clump division in spring; others can be grown from seeds sown in spring to bloom the second year. To prevent overcrowding, divide clumps after three or four years of flowering.

LIGULARIA

L. dentata also known as *Senecio clivorum* (golden groundsel); *L. przewalskii*, also known as *Senecio przewalskii*; *L. tangutica*, also known as *Senecio tanguticus*; *L. hodgsonii*

A family of coarse perennials allied to, and often confused with, *Senecio*. All have daisy-like flowers in late summer and early autumn, and appreciate moist growing conditions. For this reason, they are highly suitable for bog gardens or the margins of damp woodland. *L. dentata* has large heart-shaped leaves up to 30 cm (1 ft) across and sturdy, much-branched heads of large 5 to 8 cm (2 to 3 in.) orange-yellow flowers with brown centres. It grows 90 to 120 cm (3 to 4 ft) high and has several cultivars such as 'Othello', which has handsome, purplish leaves; and 'Greynog Gold', with rich golden flowers. *L. hodgsonii* has orange flowers and oval leaves, and grows 60 cm (2 ft) tall. *L. przewalskii* has the finest foliage, deeply cut and thin-textured on blackish stems, as well as masses of dainty yellow flowers.

HOW TO GROW. Ligularias are easy and accommodating plants, provided that the ground never dries out in summer. They cannot tolerate extremes of heat or cold; shade suits them best, particularly *L. przewalskii* which soon collapses in hot sun. Mulches of moist peat or compost are beneficial. Normally the plants need dividing every two or three years. This prevents them from becoming invasive and also provides new stock.

LIMONIUM

L. latifolium (sea lavender, statice)

The slender, many-branched flower stalks of sea lavender, 45 to 60 cm (1½ to 2 ft) tall, appear from mid- to late summer and are soon hidden beneath broad billows of tiny pink-to-lavender blossoms. Two lovely cultivars are the violet 'Violetta' and the lavender-mauve 'Blue Cloud'. Sea lavenders are excellent for borders; as they are very resistant to salt spray, they are unexcelled for seaside planting. They also make superb cut flowers and dried bouquets; cut sea lavenders when they are fully open and hang them upside down to dry in a shady, airy place.

HOW TO GROW. Sea lavenders grow well in full sun and well-drained soil. Space plants 45 to 60 cm (18 to 24 in.) apart. New plants can be started from seeds sown in early spring, or from root cuttings taken during the dormant winter period. Clumps should remain undisturbed.

LINUM

L. flavum (golden flax); *L. narbonense*; *L. perenne* (perennial flax)

Flaxes are noted for their never-failing supply of dainty 2.5 cm (1 in.) flowers from early summer to early autumn if

Illustration by Dorothy Bovey

GOLDEN GROUNDSEL
Ligularia dentata

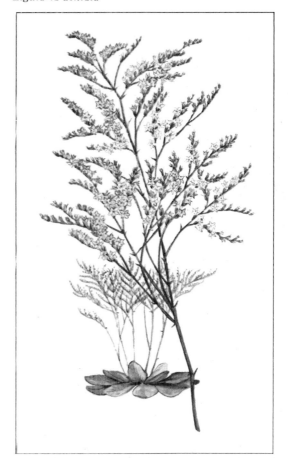

SEA LAVENDER
Limonium latifolium

PERENNIAL FLAX
Linum perenne

BIG BLUE LILY-TURF
Liriope platyphylla

HONESTY
Lunaria annua

the blossoms, which last only a day, are removed after they fade. Most types of golden flax grow 30 cm (12 in.) or more in height, but there is a 15 cm (6 in.) cultivar, *L. flavum* 'Compactum'; all bear bright yellow flowers and blossom in midsummer. *L. narbonense*, generally about 60 cm (2 ft) tall, bears blue flowers with white centres from late spring to midsummer; an abundantly flowering cultivar, 'Heavenly Blue', grows just above 30 cm (12 in.) tall. The 25 cm (10 in.) perennial flax flowers from early summer to midsummer; most are pale blue but *L. perenne* 'Album' is a fine white-flowered cultivar. All types have 5 cm (2 in.), needle-like, blue-green leaves that make the plants attractive even when not flowering. Flaxes have a spread equal to their height and are especially useful at the front of a border or in rock gardens.

HOW TO GROW. Perennial flax, *L. flavum* and *L. narbonense* do best in full sun and well-drained soil. Space plants 30 to 45 cm (12 to 18 in.) apart. New plants can be started from cuttings taken from non-flowering stems in spring to bloom the following year, or from seeds sown in spring or summer to bloom the next summer. Do not divide flax as the species are short-lived.

LIRIOPE
L. platyphylla also called *L. muscari* (big blue lily-turf), *L. spicata* (creeping lily-turf)

Lily-turf is of special interest to gardeners in favoured areas, where its foliage remains green in most seasons. The big blue lily-turf, 30 to 45 cm (12 to 18 in.) tall, forms clumps of grass-like leaves up to 60 cm (2 ft), from which rise 15 to 30 cm (6 to 12 in.) spikes of tiny flowers. The flowers bloom from midsummer to autumn and are followed by tiny black berries. Most types have purple flowers and dark green leaves, but several cultivars are available with white or lavender flowers, and white- or yellow-striped leaves. Creeping lily-turf, often used as ground cover, spreads by underground runners and grows up to 30 cm (12 in.) tall. It has long grass-like leaves, slender 15 to 20 cm (6 to 8 in.) spikes of pale lilac or white flowers that bloom in late summer, and blue-black berries. The flowers of both species, although short-stemmed, are good for cutting.

HOW TO GROW. Lily-turf will grow in almost any soil, but dislikes extreme cold. It does best in light shade, but tolerates a wide range of light conditions, growing very slowly in deep shade and withstanding sun (except in the hottest areas) if the soil is sufficiently moist. Space plants about 30 cm (12 in.) apart. Cut off old leaves in the spring to encourage the growth of new foliage. New plants can be started from clumps divided and replanted in early spring, but the clumps can remain undisturbed indefinitely.

LUNARIA
L. annua, also called *L. biennis* (honesty, satin flower, moonwort)

Honesty—a biennial sometimes grown as an annual—is best known for the flat translucent centres of its seed pods, which are widely used in dried arrangements; however, its many clusters of sweet-scented, lilac to purple, pink or white blossoms make it splendid in the garden, too. The flowers bloom in late spring and early summer, followed by the round or oval 2.5 cm (1 in.) pods in early autumn. Honesty grows up to 90 cm (3 ft) tall, and has large, coarsely toothed leaves. To dry the seed pods for winter bouquets, gather them as soon as they start to turn brown (they often rot during wet weather if allowed to ripen on the plants). Rub off the outer parts of the pods to expose the central discs. The cultivar 'Variegata', with crimson flowers and heavily cream-splashed leaves, is outstanding and comes true from seed.

HOW TO GROW. Honesty grows well in full sun or light shade in almost any well-drained soil. Space plants 30 to 38 cm (12 to 15 in.) apart. Honesty generally multiplies in the garden by sowing its own seeds, often coming up year after year without further care. It can be grown from seeds sown in midsummer to bloom the following spring; if treated as an annual and sown in early spring, the plants flower later in the spring, but never become as large and colourful as those grown as biennials.

LUPINUS
L. polyphyllus 'Russell Hybrid' (Russell Hybrid lupin)

Russell Hybrid lupins provide some of the grandest flowers of the gardening year. Their blue, white, yellow, red or pink blossoms, up to 2 cm ($\frac{3}{4}$ in.) across, are tightly set along 60 cm (2 ft) or more of their 1 to 1.5 metres (3 to 5 ft) stems; they bloom from mid-spring to midsummer. The handsome foliage is deeply divided.

HOW TO GROW. Russell Hybrid lupins can be grown in nearly all regions except very hot and dry ones. Lupins do best in full sun or part shade and a well-drained, neutral or slightly acid soil. Space plants 45 cm (18 in.) apart. In spring and autumn dust bone-meal lightly around the plants to encourage the development of blossoms in mid-summer. Propagate from seeds sown in spring or summer to flower the next year. Avoid seeds from home-grown plants with blue in them (the dominant colour), otherwise they will all revert in time to this shade. Plants can also be grown from 10 to 15 cm (4 to 6 in.) stem cuttings taken in early spring with a tiny piece of the top of the root structure, or crown, attached; they will flower the following year. Clumps can remain undisturbed for three or four years, then they should be replaced.

LYCHNIS
L. chalcedonica (Maltese cross); *L. coronaria*, also called *Agrostemma coronaria* (rose campion); *L. viscaria*, also called *Viscaria viscosa* and *Viscaria vulgaris* (German catchfly)

These *Lychnis* species differ greatly from one another. The Maltese cross bears 4 cm (1$\frac{1}{2}$ in.) clusters of scarlet blossoms shaped like small Maltese crosses atop 60 to 90 cm (2 to 3 ft) stems in summer. The 60 cm (2 ft) rose campion, mainly a biennial, has woolly, whitish leaves; its angular stems bear 2.5 cm (1 in.) bright rose-purple or white flowers in summer. The German catchfly bears abundant clusters of 2 cm ($\frac{3}{4}$ in.) deep carmine blossoms from early summer to midsummer; a many-petalled double cultivar, 'Splendens Plena', is excellent for cutting.

HOW TO GROW. All three species do best in full sun, but grow in any well-drained soil; good drainage is essential in cold areas. Set plants 30 to 38 cm (12 to 15 in.) apart. Maltese cross and rose campion, a poor perennial, are best grown from seeds in spring or autumn to bloom in one or two years. Propagate by dividing clumps in early spring after three or four years of flowering.

LYTHRUM
L. salicaria (purple loosestrife, lythrum)

The wild form of purple loosestrife is 1.5 to 1.8 metres (5 to 6 ft) tall, but a number of fine cultivars are short enough to be suitable for gardens. Their 2.5 cm (1 in.) blossoms are borne on slender spikes more than 30 cm

LUPIN
Lupinus polyphyllus 'Russell Hybrid'   MALTESE CROSS
Lychnis chalcedonica

PURPLE LOOSESTRIFE
Lythrum salicaria 'Morden's Pink'

131

PLUME POPPY
Macleaya cordata

HOLLYHOCK MALLOW
Malva alcea 'Fastigiata'

HIMALAYAN BLUE POPPY
Meconopsis betonicifolia

(12 in.) tall, rising high above dark green, willow-like leaves in summer and early autumn. Among the best are 'Happy', dark pink and up to 45 cm (18 in.) tall; 'Morden's Pink', rose pink and about 90 cm (3 ft) tall; 'Robert', rose red and up to 60 cm (2 ft) tall, with scarlet foliage in the autumn; 'Lady Sackville', bright rosy-pink, 1.4 metres (4½ ft) tall; 'The Beacon', rosy-crimson, 1 metre (3½ ft) tall; and 'Brightness', rosy-pink and 90 cm (3 ft) high. All are highly effective in a border and in moist, sunny semi-wild settings.

HOW TO GROW. Purple loosestrifes do best in full sun, but tolerate light shade and grow in any damp soil. Space plants 38 to 45 cm (15 to 18 in.) apart. New plants may be propagated by dividing and replanting clumps in spring or autumn after three years of flowering.

M

MACLEAYA

M. cordata, also called *Bocconia cordata* (plume poppy)

The imposing plume poppy, 1.8 to 2.4 metre (6 to 8 ft) tall has buff-pink 30 cm (12 in.) flower clusters, opening from bronze buds in mid- to late summer. The flowers have no petals, but numerous pollen-bearing stamens rise over the upper 60 to 90 cm (2 to 3 ft) of the stems to produce an airy effect; seed pods are similar in appearance to the blossoms and continue the plume-like appearance into autumn. Heart-shaped, deeply lobed leaves are grey-green above and nearly white underneath; they range in size from 30 cm (12 in.) across at ground level to 2.5 to 7.5 cm (1 to 3 in.) at the base of the flower stalks. Plume poppies are best set by themselves where their quickly spreading roots cannot encroach on other plants. The flowers are good for cutting and can be dried for winter use.

HOW TO GROW. Plume poppies grow in sun or light shade and almost any soil, but do best in moist soil that has been well-supplemented with moss peat or leaf-mould. Space plants 90 to 120 cm (3 to 4 ft) apart. Plants can be started from clump divisions, root cuttings or seeds sown in spring; all will bloom the next year. To prevent over-crowding, divide clumps after three or four years.

MALVA

M. alcea (hollyhock mallow)

Hollyhock mallows bear masses of bright pink blossoms from midsummer to late autumn. *M. alcea* 'Fastigata' crowds its 5 cm (2 in.) flowers at the top of 90 to 120 cm (3 to 4 ft) stems, above downy palm-shaped leaves.

HOW TO GROW. Hollyhock mallows do well in full sun or light shade, and almost any soil, and can tolerate hot, sunny positions. Space plants 30 cm (12 in.) apart. New plants can be started from clump divisions, from cuttings taken in spring or summer, or from seeds sown in summer to bloom the following year. The clumps can remain undisturbed indefinitely.

MATRICARIA EXIMIA See *Chrysanthemum*

MECONOPSIS

M. betonicifolia, also called *M. baileyi* (Himalayan blue poppy); *M. cambrica* (Welsh poppy)

Meconopsis species are related to true poppies (*page 136*). The Himalayan blue poppy, native to western China and Tibet, grows 60 to 150 cm (2 to 5 ft) tall and in early and mid-summer bears clusters of glistening, sky-blue, gold-centred flowers about 5 cm (2 in.) across. The Welsh poppy, from Western Europe, grows 30 to 45 cm (12 to 18 in.) tall and in summer produces smaller yellow or orange flowers; some cultivars bear heavily petalled double blossoms.

HOW TO GROW. Himalayan blue and Welsh poppies grow in moist areas of temperate and cool regions. They do best in light shade and need an acid soil (pH 5.5 to 6.5) that has been well-supplemented with leaf-mould or moss peat. Good drainage, important the year round, is vital in winter. Space plants 30 to 38 cm (12 to 15 in.) apart. Himalayan blue poppies must be grown from seeds sown immediately after gathering. They should not be allowed to blossom until their third year, and any flower buds that develop before that time should be picked off; if young plants are allowed to blossom they soon die. Most Welsh poppies can be grown from seeds sown in spring or summer to blossom the next year or from clumps divided in early spring to bloom the same year; the heavily petalled double types can be grown only from clump divisions.

MIRABILIS
M. jalapa (four-o'clock plant, marvel-of-Peru)

Four-o'clock plants are appropriately named; their blossoms open in late afternoon, scenting the air with a delightful fragrance before closing the next morning. The plants grow up to 60 cm (2 ft) tall and blossom continuously from midsummer to early autumn. The 2.5 cm (1 in.) trumpet-shaped flowers come in white, pink, red, yellow and violet, and more than one colour may appear on the same plant. The dense leaves are shiny green, sometimes sticky and 5 to 15 cm (2 to 6 in.) long.

HOW TO GROW. Four-o'clock plants may be grown as perennials in warm regions, in full sun and well-drained soil that has been well supplemented with organic material such as compost or leaf-mould. Set plants 45 to 60 cm (18 to 24 in.) apart. New plants may be started from seeds sown in spring to blossom by midsummer. In cool and temperate regions four-o'clock plants are widely grown as annuals; but they can survive the winters if they are dug up in autumn and stored in a frost-free place. In warm areas, perennial four-o'clock plants should remain undisturbed.

MONARDA
M. didyma (bergamot, bee balm, Oswego tea)

Bergamots, which exude a delightful mint fragrance, bear slender tubular flowers in 5 to 7.5 cm (2 to 3 in.) whorls from early summer to midsummer and sometimes later. The plants, up to 90 cm (3 ft) tall, have rough hairy leaves. The easy-to-grow cultivars include 'Adam', bright red; 'Cambridge Scarlet', crimson; 'Croftway Pink' and 'Melisa', rose pink; and 'Mahogany', dark red.

HOW TO GROW. Bergamots grow in full sun or light shade in temperate areas; they do best in moist soil that has been well supplemented with organic material such as moss peat or leaf-mould. Space plants 30 to 38 cm (12 to 15 in.) apart. To prolong flowering, remove faded blooms before they produce seeds. New plants can be started from clump divisions during the dormant period. Divide clumps after every three or four years of flowering.

MYOSOTIS
M. alpestris, also called *M. rupicola* (alpine forget-me-not); *M. palustris* (water forget-me-not); *M. sylvatica* (woodland forget-me-not)

These tiny, sky-blue, yellow-centred flowers are among the first cheery signs of spring. Pink and white cultivars are also available. The alpine forget-me-not grows about

FOUR-O'CLOCK PLANT
Mirabilis jalapa

BERGAMOT
Monarda didyma 'Adam'

FORGET-ME-NOT
Myosotis palustris

Illustration by Dorothy Bovey

CATMINT
Nepeta x *faassenii*

BLUE CUP FLOWER
Nierembergia hippomanica var. *violacea*

15 cm (6 in.) tall, the water type about 30 cm (12 in.). Two recommended cultivars are 'Mermaid', with deep blue flowers and stout stems. and 'Semperflorens', a variable but more compact type. All bloom from late spring onwards, at first freely and then spasmodically until frost. The woodland forget-me-not grows 30 cm (1 ft) tall, with fragrant blue flowers.

HOW TO GROW. Forget-me-nots thrive in light shade and moist soil supplemented with moss peat or other organic material. Set plants 22 to 30 cm (9 to 12 in.) apart. Alpine and woodland types are generally treated as biennials and are started from seeds sown outdoors in summer to bloom in spring. To grow them as annuals, sow seeds indoors very early in spring to bloom in late spring or early summer. Water forget-me-nots should be started from clumps divided in late summer or from stem cuttings taken in summer to bloom the next year. Divide clumps after three or four years of flowering.

N

NEPETA
N.x faassenii, also, but erroneously called *N. mussinii* (catmint)

Catmint grows 30 to 45 cm (12 to 18 in.) tall, forming soft mounds of mint-scented, crinkled, grey-green leaves about 2.5 cm (1 in.) long. From late spring until midsummer it is covered with clusters of tiny lavender flowers that have a pungent fragrance.

HOW TO GROW. Catmint grows in full sun in almost any well-drained soil. Space plants 30 to 38 cm (12 to 15 in.) apart. To encourage occasional blooms until frost, cut the flower stalks back to the foliage mound after the first flowers have faded. In autumn cover the plants in exposed places with a winter mulch such as bracken or evergreen branches; leave old stalks on the plants as added protection. Start new plants from stem cuttings taken in summer to bloom the following year. Plants may remain undisturbed indefinitely.

NEPETA MACRANTHA See *Dracocephalum*

NIEREMBERGIA
N. hippomanica var. *violacea*, also called *N. caerulea* (blue cup flower); *N. frutescens*; *N. repens*, also called *N. rivularis*

Cup flowers, being native to South America, are usually treated as annuals in cool or temperate areas, but as perennials in warmer regions. They are beautiful little plants for edging purposes or for providing low drifts of colour throughout summer in mixed borders—although heavy summer rains can mar their fragile beauty. *N. hippomanica* grows 15 to 30 cm (6 to 12 in.) tall, with small narrow leaves and open sprays of pale lavender, yellow-throated flowers about 3 cm ($1\frac{1}{4}$ in.) across. *N. frutescens* has 2.5 cm (1 in.) pale blue or white flowers. *N. repens*, with white flowers, is a mat-forming plant for the rock garden. Cultivars with larger and deep-coloured blooms exist.

HOW TO GROW. Cup flowers grow in moist but well-drained soil; they do best in light shade, but can stand full sun in places that remain relatively cool. Set plants 15 to 30 cm (6 to 12 in.) apart. To encourage continuous bloom and force new growth for the following year, pick off old flowers in autumn and cut foliage and stems almost to the ground. In cool regions they are best treated as annuals and grown from seeds sown indoors in early spring; they should be transplanted to the garden in early summer for blooming the same year. New plants of *N. repens* can be grown from clump divisions or from 10 cm (4 in.) stem cuttings. Divide clumps in spring after three or four years of flowering. *N. hippomanica* and *N. frutescens* can remain undisturbed until they lose vigour.

O

OENOTHERA
O. missouriensis (Ozark sundrops); *O. tetragona*, also called *O. fruticosa* var. *youngii* (Young's sundrops)

Sundrops are related to evening primroses and are sometimes mistakenly called by that name; however, evening primroses open at night and sundrops blossom during the day. Ozark sundrops are sprawling plants that eventually become 25 to 30 cm (9 to 12 in.) high; they bear 10 to 12.5 cm (4 to 5 in.) cup-shaped, golden-yellow flowers throughout the summer and have slender, willow-like leaves 2.5 to 7.5 cm (1 to 3 in.) long. *O. tetragona* grows about 60 cm (2 ft) tall and produces 4 cm (1½ in.) flowers throughout the summer; their leaves are 7.5 to 15 cm (3 to 6 in.) long. Two fine cultivars are 'Yellow River', about 60 cm (2 ft) tall, with 5 cm (2 in.) lemon-yellow flowers, and 'Fyrvaerkeri', ('Fireworks'), which grows 30 cm (12 in.) tall, and bears many 5 cm (2 in.) golden-yellow flowers.

HOW TO GROW Sundrops grow in full sun and well-drained soil; excellent drainage is especially important during winter to prevent rotting. Space plants 30 to 38 cm (12 to 15 in.) apart. Divide clumps for propagation or when they become overcrowded.

P

PAEONIA
P. lactiflora, also called *P. albiflora* (Chinese peony); *P. officinalis* (common peony); *P. tenuifolia* (fern-leaved peony)

To most gardeners the term peony means plants from the Chinese species, native to parts of China, Siberia and Japan. Mature Chinese peony plants reach 60 to 120 cm (2 to 4 ft) in height and spread, and in late spring and early summer produce flowers that may be as much as 25 cm (10 in.) across. The blossoms are classified as single flowered (or anemone) and double. Single flowers have one row of five or more petals with a central mass of golden, pollen-bearing stamens; anemone-flowered cultivars have two or more rows of petals and centres made up of feathery petal-like structures called staminodes. Double flowers, with so many petals that the centres are nearly or wholly concealed, are the most popular, but require staking. All range from snowy white through pale yellow to many shades of pink and red.

Although there are superb new cultivars of Chinese peonies, many of the best are long-time classics: 'Festiva Maxima', a white cultivar made its debut in 1851; 'Walter Faxon', a handsome pink, in 1904; and the deep red 'Philippe Rivoire', in 1911.

The common peony, *P. officinalis*, a wild flower from France to Albania, has been grown in gardens since ancient times. The wild form is rarely obtainable. Instead the double garden cultivars with white, rosy-red or crimson flowers are commonly planted. Unlike the Chinese peonies, these have an unpleasant scent. They grow 60 to 90 cm (2 to 3 ft) tall and blossom in spring, a week or two ahead of Chinese peonies.

The fern-leaved peony has dark crimson, single or double flowers about 7.5 cm (3 in.) across and blooms in spring with common peonies. Native to eastern Europe, it grows about 45 cm (1½ ft) tall and its fern-like foliage is orna-

SUNDROPS
Oenothera tetragona 'Yellow River'

CHINESE PEONY
Paeonia lactiflora 'Philippe Rivoire'

ICELAND POPPY
Papaver nudicaule

mental throughout the summer. For indoor arrangements, cut the flowers as soon as the buds open, leaving at least three leaves on each stem.

HOW TO GROW. Peonies do best in cold climates, even surviving temperatures well below freezing. They can be grown in temperate and other areas where nights are cool. They flourish in well-drained soil and are best planted in positions which miss the early morning sun; for example, in a west-facing border. This prevents emerging buds from being killed by a quick thaw after night frost. The planting hole should be about 60 cm (2 ft) in diameter and 45 cm (1½ ft) deep, and the soil liberally supplemented with moss peat, well-rotted manure or compost. For each plant, mix a double handful of bone-meal with the soil. Plant peonies in early autumn, and set the roots so that the tops of the buds are no more than 5 cm (2 in.) below the surface of the soil. In heavy clay soil plant them 2.5 cm (1 in.) deep. Shallow planting will not hurt them; it encourages flower production. Mulch light soils annually in early spring with well-rotted manure or compost and occasionally sprinkle a little bone-meal around established plants in autumn. Peonies usually take three to five years to obtain mature size; there may be no blossoms the first year and only a few the second season. Once planted, peonies can be left to grow undisturbed indefinitely. Propagation of new plants by any method is difficult for the amateur gardener; purchase new divisions of named cultivars.

PAPAVER
P. nudicaule, also called *P. croceum* (Iceland poppy); *P. orientale* (Oriental poppy)

The flowers of both these species are eye-catching—Iceland poppies because of their abundance and Oriental poppies because of their size and brilliance. At close hand, the blossoms of both species seem to be made of silky tissue; most come in single-flowered form, with four or six petals, and in semi-double form, with up to a dozen petals. They make delightful bouquets if the flowers are cut just as the buds begin to open. Sear the stem ends immediately with a match or candle flame, and place the flowers in warm water.

The Iceland poppy (best treated as a biennial or annual) has soft grey-green foliage growing in low clumps from which sprout wiry stems up to 60 cm (2 ft) tall. The sweet-scented 5 to 10 cm (2 to 4 in.) flowers come in many shades of red, pink, orange and yellow as well as white. 'Champagne Bubbles', with flowers of the same colours, is an especially fine strain. In most areas the blossoms appear from late spring until frost, but in hot climates they bloom in early spring. The flowers are dramatic when massed in large groups.

The common types of Oriental poppies are a flamboyant orange-red, but newer cultivars are available in a range of colours from white through delicate shades of pink to deep red. Many cultivars have a black blotch at the base of each petal; all are studded in the centres with a boss of black, pollen-bearing stamens. The blossoms are 15 cm (6 in.) across and are borne on hairy-leaved stems 75 to 120 cm (2½ to 4 ft) tall. Especially recommended cultivars are 'Barr's White', white with black spots; 'Mrs. Perry', soft salmon-pink; 'Marcus Perry', bright orange-scarlet with very large flowers; and 'Salmon Glow', double salmon-orange. Oriental poppies blossom in early summer, and their foliage dies down and disappears in mid- to late summer. In autumn Oriental poppies send up fresh leaves that last through winter.

HOW TO GROW. Both species do best in full sun and very well-drained soil. Iceland poppies grow in temperate regions and must be started from seeds. Space Iceland poppies 20 to 25 cm (8 to 10 in.) apart.

Oriental poppies are perennials in cool and temperate regions and in warmer areas where the nights are cool. Space the plants 37 to 45 cm (15 to 18 in.) apart. New plants can be started from 10 to 15 cm (4 to 6 in.) root cuttings of dormant plants taken in the winter; they usually flower when two years old. Set the tops of the root cuttings 7.5 cm (3 in.) below the surface of the soil.

PENSTEMON

P. hartwegii (beard-tongue)

P. hartwegii is a Mexican species with dark green foliage and spikes of blood-red, tubular flowers; it is rare in cultivation, but noteworthy as the parent of an important race of garden hybrids—*P.*x *hybridus*, also known as *P.*x *gloxinioides*. These are not reliably hardy in cool climates and, accordingly, are usually grown as bedding plants. Recommended cultivars, all with an average height of 60 cm (2 ft) and 5 cm (2 in.) long flowers borne in loose spikes in midsummer: 'Garnet', deep red; 'Schonholzeri', also known as 'Firebird', rich scarlet; 'Myddleton Gem', light crimson; and 'Pink Endurance', clear pink.

HOW TO GROW. Perennial penstemons will grow in temperate and warm regions, but are extremely sensitive to winter moisture and do best in raised beds. In gardens where the drainage is not excellent, they should be overwintered in a frame as cuttings rooted at the end of the summer. Penstemons will grow in full sun or light shade, and need acid soil (pH 5.5 to 6.5) that has been liberally enriched with compost or leaf-mould. Set plants 30 to 45 cm (12 to 18 in.) apart. In cooler areas, but not in very cold regions, penstemons may be treated like other perennials, but should be protected with a mulch of straw or leaves if necessary. Seed-grown types can also be grown in these parts as annuals if started indoors in midwinter for flowers 12 to 14 weeks later. In warm climates, new plants of seed-grown types should be started in summer to flower the following spring.

PHLOMIS

P. fruticosa (Jerusalem sage); P. samia

Although *P. fruticosa* is a shrubby evergreen plant in mild climates, it is included with perennials as it is normally grown amongst other perennials in herbaceous borders. It grows 90 cm (3 ft) or so tall with a branching habit and oval, wedge-shaped leaves, grey-green and velvety to the touch; it puts forth whorls of 2.5 cm (1 in.) long, yellow, nettle-like flowers on the upper stems in midsummer. *P. samia* with green sage-like leaves bears creamy-yellow flowers in early summer; it is a true herbaceous perennial, dying down in autumn.

HOW TO GROW. Both species appreciate sun and well-drained soil and do not tolerate a very cold climate. *P. fruticosa* stands clipping and should be cut when necessary to keep it shapely. Cut *P. samia* to the ground annually in autumn. Propagate by division in autumn or spring in the case of *P. samia*, and *P. fruticosa* from late summer cuttings rooted in peat and sand in a frame or propagating case.

PHLOX

P. divaricata, also called P. canadensis (Canada phlox); P. paniculata (garden phlox); P. subulata (moss phlox)

Phloxes are widely grown perennials for good reasons. They bear spectacular flowers, many of which are fragrant,

BEARD-TONGUE
Penstemon x *hybridus* 'Firebird'

JERUSALEM SAGE
Phlomis fruticosa

and they are easy to grow.

The 30 cm (12 in.) tall Canada phlox and its cultivar, *P. divaricata* var. 'Laphamii', are lovely in late spring. The soft blue or white flowers, less than 2.5 cm (1 in.) across, are borne in loose clusters. Canada phlox is most often used at the front of a border, but also grows untended in lightly shaded, wooded areas. If faded flowers are removed, the plant produces foliage that is attractive all summer.

The 60 to 120 cm (2 to 4 ft) garden phlox is the backbone of late summer gardens, as cultivars are available to bloom almost any time from midsummer to early autumn. They bear huge clusters of sweetly scented, disc-shaped flowers, each 2.5 cm (1 in.) or more across, in colours ranging from snowy white through every shade of pink to red and from pale blue to deep purple. Many cultivars have conspicuous central eyes of contrasting colours. Individual clusters on a single stem are often 30 to 35 cm (12 to 14 in.) tall and 15 to 25 cm (6 to 10 in.) or more across, but the flowers fade quickly when cut. Removing faded flower heads, however, encourages a second flowering.

A favourite for rock gardens, moss phlox begins the gardener's year in early spring with clouds of vivid colour made up of thousands of flowers clothing the tops of 10 to 12 cm (4 to 5 in.) high plants. The flowers on newer cultivars may be 2.5 cm (1 in.) across and are available in white as well as many shades of pink, red, blue and lavender. Moss phlox has evergreen foliage of closely-set, tiny, needle-like leaves. After the flowers fade, the tops of the plants should be sheared back about halfway; the plants then produce fresh foliage and may blossom again in the autumn.

HOW TO GROW. All the phloxes described can be grown in warm regions, but they do best where it is cool or temperate. Garden phloxes grow in full sun or light shade, in a moist soil, rich in compost or leaf-mould. Space the plants about 45 cm (18 in.) apart. In spring when young shoots are 10 to 15 cm (4 to 6 in.) tall, thin each clump to four or five shoots spaced 10 to 15 cm (4 to 6 in.) apart to get the largest possible flower clusters (*drawings, page 55*). New plants of garden phlox can be grown from 5 cm (2 in.) root cuttings taken in autumn to flower in two years.

Canada phlox does best in light shade in moist soil, rich in organic matter, but will grow in full sun if there is sufficient moisture. Set plants 20 to 30 cm (8 to 12 in.) apart. New plants may be grown from stem cuttings taken in summer to flower the following year or by dividing clumps after the plants have had two years of flowering.

Moss phlox needs full sun and well-drained soil. Set plants 20 to 30 cm (8 to 12 in.) apart. New plants can be started easily from stem cuttings taken in summer to flower the next year.

PHORMIUM
P. tenax (New Zealand flax)

The sword-shaped leaves of New Zealand flax, which grow in massive clumps 1.2 to 2.4 metres (4 to 8 ft) high, dominate many gardens, especially in mild-coastal areas. The leaves of several cultivars are dramatically coloured. Most are shades of purplish red, although one type, the variegated New Zealand flax, has prominent ivory-white stripes. In early summer and midsummer the plants extend zigzag stems with 2.5 to 5 cm (1 to 2 in.) mahogany or yellow flowers about 60 cm (2 ft) above the tops of the leaves. New Zealand flax is tough enough to withstand heat, wind and seaside conditions. Because of its bold lines, New Zealand flax is most often used in gardens as an accent plant.

HOW TO GROW. New Zealand flax can be grown in warm to temperate regions, even though its foliage may be damaged during the winter. (Injured leaves should be

CANADA PHLOX
Phlox divaricata var. 'Laphamii'

NEW ZEALAND FLAX
Phormium tenax 'Rubrum'

cut away; new ones will replace them in the spring.) It is also possible to grow New Zealand flax as a summer plant in cool regions; the plants should be lifted and potted in autumn and stored in a frost-free place for the winter. The plant grows in full sun and almost any soil, wet or dry. Start new plants from division of clumps in early spring before new growth starts. Clumps usually need dividing after four or five years to prevent overcrowding.

PHYSALIS
P. alkekengi; *P. franchetii* (both called Chinese lantern plant, bladder cherry)

These plants are valued for their inflated, orange-red, seed coverings resembling miniature Chinese lanterns. The plants should be set apart, for they tend to spread and overwhelm other garden plants. They grow 30 to 45 cm (12 to 18 in.) tall; *P. franchetii*, being the tallest, bears 5 to 7.5 cm (2 to 3 in.) leaves that obscure tiny white flowers in summer. Inside each 5 cm (2 in.) long lantern is an edible, but insipid-tasting, scarlet berry. For winter arrangements, pick the stems in autumn just as the lanterns turn colour, remove the leaves and hang the stems upside down to dry in a shady, airy place.

HOW TO GROW. Chinese lantern plants grow in almost any soil in full sun or light shade. Set the plants about 60 cm (2 ft) apart. New plants can be grown from seeds sown in spring, from root cuttings taken in autumn or spring, or from clump divisions in autumn or spring; all will produce lanterns during the first growing season. Plants can remain undisturbed indefinitely.

PHYSOSTEGIA
P. virginiana, also called *Dracocephalum virginianum* (obedient plant)

The flowers of obedient plants, which resemble those of snapdragons, open during late summer and early autumn. The plants grow 60 to 120 cm (2 to 4 ft) tall and have dark green, willow-like leaves 7.5 to 12.5 cm (3 to 5 in.) long. The flower spikes, 20 to 25 cm (8 to 10 in.) long, are made up of four widely-spaced, vertical rows of small flowers. Among recommended cultivars 'Vivid' grows 60 cm (2 ft) tall and has pale pink flowers; 'Summer Spire' grows 90 to 120 cm (3 to 4 ft) tall and has pale pink flowers; and 'Summer Snow' grows about 60 cm (2 ft) tall and has translucent white flowers. A peculiarity of all physostegias is that if individual flowers are pushed around the stem, they stay as placed—hence the name 'obedient plant'.

HOW TO GROW. Obedient plants can be grown in sun or shade and in almost any soil, wet or dry, but mulch or water them in dry weather to prevent the roots from drying out. Set plants 60 cm (2 ft) apart. New plants can be started from divisions of clumps in autumn or spring. To prevent overcrowding, dig up and divide clumps every second year of flowering.

PLATYCODON
P. grandiflorum (balloon flower, Chinese bellflower)

Balloon flowers get their name from the way each bud swells before its starry petals unfold to a salver-shaped flower. The plants bear 5 to 7.5 cm (2 to 3 in.) blossoms on stems 60 to 90 cm (2 to 3 ft) tall. The flowers bloom throughout the summer and come in blue, pale pink or white. *P. grandiflorum*, 'Mariesii', grows 45 cm (18 in.) tall and comes only in blue and white. The flowers are excellent for cutting, but their stems should be seared with a match or candle flame before being placed in water.

CHINESE LANTERN
Physalis alkekengi

OBEDIENT PLANT
Physostegia virginiana 'Vivid'

BALLOON FLOWER
Platycodon grandiflorum 'Mariesii'

JACOB'S-LADDER
Polemonium coeruleum

SOLOMON'S SEAL
Polygonatum x *hybridum*

HOW TO GROW. Balloon flowers will grow in most areas except for hot, dry positions in a Mediterranean-type climate. They thrive in full sun or light shade in well-drained garden soil. Set plants 30 to 45 cm (12 to 18 in.) apart. Be careful in spring when cultivating the area where you have planted balloon flowers; they do not sprout until other plants have begun to grow, and it is easy to dig them up inadvertently. New plants can be started from seeds sown in spring or summer, but take two or three years to flower. The clumps do not spread and should remain undisturbed.

PLUMBAGO LARPENTAE See *Ceratostigma*

POLEMONIUM
P. coeruleum (Jacob's-ladder, Greek valerian); *P. reptans*; *P.*x *richardsonii*

Jacob's-ladders are among the first perennials to produce new growth in spring, sending up mounds of feathery apple-green leaves that are topped from late spring to midsummer with soft clusters of dainty, cup-shaped blossoms 2.5 cm (1 in.) or less across. Jacob's-ladder, with sky-blue flowers, and its pure white cultivar, *P. coeruleum* 'album', grows 60 to 75 cm (2 to 2½ ft) tall. *P. reptans*, a sprawling plant, reaches a height of only 15 to 20 cm (6 to 8 in.) and has blue or white flowers. *P.*x *richardsonii*, a hybrid of *P. coeruleum*, bears sky-blue flowers on 22.5 cm (9 in.) stems in early summer.

HOW TO GROW. Jacob's-ladders grow in cool and temperate regions and do best in light shade and moist but well-drained soil that has been supplemented with compost, moss peat or leaf-mould. They may also be grown in full sun if additional moisture is provided. Space plants 45 cm (18 in.) apart. Cut faded flower stems back as soon as flowering is over. New plants can be grown from clump divisions during the dormant season.

POLYGONATUM
*P.*x *hybridum*, also called *P. multiflorum* (Solomon's seal); *P. commutatum*; *P. roseum*

Solomon's seals are useful for shady beds and borders and make good cut flowers in early summer. They grow well with ferns, foxgloves, lilies of the valley and other woodland plants. The long, tubular flower bells are borne in small pendulous clusters beneath the arching stems. The leaves are oval and usually arranged in opposite pairs.

*P.*x *hybridum* is the correct name for the plants commonly sold as *P. multiflorum* and is really a hybrid between that species (a native of Europe, but rare in Britain) and the sweetly scented *P. odoratum*, also called *P. officinale*. It grows to about 1.5 metres (5 ft) in height and has white 2.5 cm (1 in.) flowers; double and variegated forms exist. *P. commutatum* is a giant species—up to 2 metres (7 ft) tall—from the United States, with white 2.5 cm (1 in.) flowers. *P. roseum* grows to 60 cm (2 ft) and has small, soft pink flowers.

HOW TO GROW. Solomon's seals grow in temperate areas but cannot tolerate extreme cold; they need moist but well-drained soil. They grow well in shade and also in the sun if the roots are shaded. Mulching the soil with moist peat or leaf-mould encourages strong growth. Propagate by division in early autumn or in spring. Seeds can be sown as soon as ripe in a cold frame outdoors. They take three to four years to flower. Sawfly larvae sometimes damage the leaves; spray with derris to control.

Illustration by Dorothy Bovey

POLYGONUM

P. reynoutria, now more correctly *Reynoutria japonica* (Japanese fleece flower)

The Japanese fleece flower grows 60 cm (2 ft) tall and bears great numbers of tiny pink flowers that open from red buds in late summer and autumn; its 2.5 cm (1 in.) heart-shaped leaves turn brilliant red in autumn and are followed by brick-red fruits. The plant is easy to grow; because its roots spread rapidly underground, it makes good ground cover, but should not be used where the roots may encroach on other plants.

HOW TO GROW. Japanese fleece flowers thrive in sun or part shade and almost any soil; they will not grow in very hot and dry regions. Space plants 45 to 60 cm (18 to 24 in.) apart. Shear the plants to the ground early each spring to encourage fresh, vigorous growth. Propagate by division of clumps in autumn or spring. Old plants can remain undisturbed indefinitely.

POTENTILLA

P. hybrids (cinquefoil)

The herbaceous cinquefoils are useful front-of-the-border plants for summer flowering. They are easily grown, long blooming and colourful, with strawberry-like grey-green leaves and loose sprays, up to 60 cm (2 ft) wide, of single or double saucer-shaped flowers. Most of the cultivated kinds are hybrids from *P. atrosanguinea* and *P. nepalensis*. They include 'Gibson's Scarlet', with single, brilliant scarlet flowers, 30 cm (12 in.) tall; 'Wm. Rollison', semi-double, orange-red, 45 cm (18 in.) tall; 'Yellow Queen', semi-double yellow flowers and silvery leaves, 30 cm (12 in.) tall; and 'Miss Willmott', rosy-pink with deep pink centres, 60 cm (2 ft) tall.

HOW TO GROW. The herbaceous potentillas are suitable for any good garden soil in full sun, except in extremely cold or very hot, dry regions. Water freely in dry weather and keep the roots cool with mulches of peat or compost. Propagate from cuttings rooted in spring in equal parts sand and compost under glass.

PRIMULA

P. auricula (common auricula); *P. beesiana*; *P.x bullesiana*; *P. bulleyana*; *P. cockburniana*; *P. cortusoides*; *P. denticulata* (Himalayan primrose, drumstick primrose); *P. elatior*; *P. japonica* (Japanese primrose); *P. juliae*; *P. vulgaris elatior* (polyanthus primrose); *P. rosea*; *P. sieboldii*; *P. veris*, also called *P. officinalis* (cowslip); *P. vulgaris*, also called *P. acaulis* (English or true primrose)

Of the more than 500 kinds of primroses, the species and hybrids recommended here are among the easiest to grow and among the most beautiful. They present a procession of handsome blossoms that usually appear in 5 to 15 cm (2 to 6 in.) clusters. The flowers bloom from early to late spring.

The sweet-scented auriculas bear their clusters of 2.5 cm (1 in.) single (one ring of petals) or heavily-petalled double blossoms atop 15 to 20 cm (6 to 8 in.) stems in mid-spring; the flowers range in colour from creamy-white through grey, rose, copper, chestnut-red and reddish purple to deep blue, and appear above thick, leathery, evergreen leaves. Four types that bear their flowers in candelabra-like tiers from mid-spring to early summer are *P. beesiana* 45 to 60 cm (1½ to 2 ft) tall, with rosy-lilac, yellow-eyed flowers; *P. bulleyana* about 75 cm (2½ ft) tall, with golden-yellow flowers; the Bullesiana hybrids derived from crosses between the two preceeding which grow 60 cm

JAPANESE FLEECE FLOWER
Polygonum reynoutria

CINQUEFOIL
Potentilla hybrid.

HIMALAYAN PRIMROSE
Primula denticulata

JAPANESE PRIMROSE
Primula japonica

POLYANTHUS PRIMROSE
Primula vulgaris elatior

(2 ft) tall and come in shades of cream, rose, mauve, rust-red, wine-red and purple; and *P. cockburniana*, about 45 cm (1½ ft) tall, with coppery-scarlet flowers.

P. cortusoides bears clusters of bright, rosy-pink flowers on 20 to 25 cm (8 to 10 in.) stems in mid-spring, sometimes with two tiers of flowers on a stem. The Himalayan primrose bears 12 mm (½ in.), soft lilac flowers in 5 cm (2 in.), ball-like clusters atop 20 to 30 cm (8 to 12 in.) stems in early spring and has foliage covered with a whitish-yellow powder; the flowers of the cultivar *P. denticulata* 'Cachemiriana', the Kashmir primrose, are purple with yellow centres. *P. elatior* has evergreen leaves and produces large clusters of pale yellow blossoms on 20 cm (8 in.) stems in mid-spring. The Japanese primrose, one of the most popular of the candelabra types, grows about 60 cm (2 ft) tall and bears white, pink, rose, deep crimson or terra-cotta blossoms from late spring to early summer. *P. juliae* produces wine-red flowers, but its hybrid called 'Juliana', is available in white, cream, yellow, pink, red and deep purple; the plants grow about 7.5 cm (3 in.) tall and blossom so profusely in mid-spring that their evergreen foliage becomes hidden.

The polyanthus primrose, the most familiar of all, grows 20 to 30 cm (8 to 12 in.) tall and in mid-spring bears immense clusters of single or double flowers. A hybrid with evergreen foliage, it comes in an amazing colour range, with seedlings often showing up in striped or blended combinations of white, grey, ivory, yellow, pink, lavender, salmon, burnt-orange, copper, bronze, brown, blue and purple.

P. rosea sends up its flowering stems before its leaves appear in mid-spring; the plants grow 20 to 25 cm (8 to 10 in.) tall and have clusters of rose-pink flowers. Cultivars of *P. sieboldii* come in white, pink, rose, crimson and purple; the flowers are borne in clusters on 20 to 25 cm (8 to 10 in.) stems in mid-spring above crinkled, scallop-edged leaves that die away in late summer and reappear the following spring. *P. veris* is the European cowslip and about 20 cm (8 in.) tall; it blooms in mid-spring and is normally cream to yellow, but selections are also available in copper-red and purple, as well as in a double yellow form known as hose-in-hose in which one cup-like flower is set within another. The delightfully fragrant English primrose, so often mentioned by Elizabethan poets, blooms singly on 15 cm (6 in.) stems in mid-spring and has evergreen leaves. One of the parents of the polyanthus primrose, it is normally a soft "primrose" yellow in colour, but also comes in pink, red, apricot, amber, blue and purple, and in heavily petalled double as well as single forms. There are other hose-in-hose cultivars as well as "Jack-in-the-Green's" which have their flowers framed by a leafy collar of green bracts.

HOW TO GROW. When William Wordsworth wrote, "A primrose by a river's brim", he was noting a situation that all primroses find congenial. All the kinds mentioned do well in temperate regions provided they always have a cool, moist root run and protection from hot summer sun. None should be allowed to become dry at any time, and some—notably, *P. beesiana*; *P.* x *bullesiana*; *P. rosea*; *P. japonica*, and *P. sieboldii*—need more than ordinary amounts of moisture and thrive in boggy situations, such as beside a pond or brook. All grow best in part shade and an acid soil well supplemented with organic matter such as leaf-mould or compost.

Space plants 15 to 30 cm (6 to 12 in.) apart. New plants of named cultivars and most double forms (but not strains of polyanthus primroses) can be propagated only by dividing clumps immediately after the plants have flowered. *P. denticulata* can be increased by means of root cuttings. All other primroses are most easily grown from seeds. The seeds should be sown as soon as they are ripe, as they rapidly lose their vitality. Sow them in pans or boxes of seed compost. Place these in a cold frame and cover with glass or sheets of plastic to preserve humidity. After germination, remove the covering, but keep the seedlings moist and lightly shaded—one day's hot sun can kill the lot. Prick off seedlings into boxes of leafy, sandy compost, or into a shaded bed outdoors. Plant in their flowering positions in late summer or the following spring.

PULMONARIA
P. angustifolia (blue or cowslip lungwort); *P. saccharata* (Bethlehem sage)

Blue lungwort and Bethlehem sage are excellent for shady gardens and provide a display of colours in spring with their drooping clusters of trumpet-shaped, 12 mm (½ in.) flowers. The flowers of the blue lungwort open pink and then turn bright blue, but some cultivars have constant colours: 'Alba', with white flowers, and 'Munstead Blue', a rich gentian-blue shade. The plants grow 20 to 30 cm (8 to 12 in.) tall and have 10 to 15 cm (4 to 6 in.) leaves. Bethlehem sage blooms from late spring to early summer; it grows about 30 cm (12 in.) tall and has white-spotted 7.5 to 15 cm (3 to 6 in.) leaves.

HOW TO GROW. Blue lungworts and Bethlehem sage grow well in most areas except in hot, dry Mediterranean-type climates. They need shade and moist soil well supplemented with organic material such as moss peat, compost or leaf-mould. Space plants about 25 cm (10 in.) apart. New plants can be grown from seeds sown in early spring, or from clumps divided in spring or autumn. Water such divisions well to enable them to develop a root system before cold or hot weather.

PYRETHRUM See *Chrysanthemum*

R
REYNOUTRIA JAPONICA See *Polygonum*

ROMNEYA
R. coulteri (California tree poppy, matilija poppy)

The fragrant flowers of the California tree poppy are distinctive: they are 7.5 to 15 cm (3 to 6 in.) across and have golden centres surrounded by six snow-white petals that resemble crumpled silk. They bloom from mid- to late summer, one on each of the short branches that cover the 1.2 to 2.4 metre (4 to 8 ft) plants. Although they are rather short-lived, lasting only two to four days, they make handsome bouquets; pick them just before the buds open and sear the ends with a match before putting them in water.

HOW TO GROW. California tree poppies do best in warm regions where rainfall is scant in the summer, but they can also be grown in cool and temperate regions if given excellent drainage and covered with a frame light or thick winter mulch. They require full sun and flower most freely in dry infertile soil. They are best planted by themselves because their underground roots spread rapidly and can encroach on other plants. Space plants 90 to 120 cm (3 to 4 ft) apart. Cut plants back to about 15 cm (6 in.) from the ground in early autumn to encourage fresh growth the following year. New plants should be grown from suckers arising some distance from established plants, not too close as they resent root disturbance, or from seeds sown in spring. They require two or three years to reach flowering size.

BLUE LUNGWORT
Pulmonaria angustifolia

MATILIJA POPPY
Romneya coulteri

143

RUDBECKIA

R. fulgida (orange coneflower); *R. hirta* 'Gloriosa' (gloriosa daisy); *R. laciniata* (cut-leaved coneflower)

Rudbeckia coneflowers are often confused with coneflowers in the genus *Echinacea* (page 115). The distinguishing characteristic of *Rudbeckia* coneflowers is their colour, always a shade of yellow with a dark centre; *Echinacea* coneflowers come in other colours. Outstanding, easy-to-grow cultivars of the orange coneflower are 'Goldquelle', a 75 cm (2½ ft) plant that bears lemon-yellow, heavily petalled, double flowers 7.5 cm (3 in.) or more across in late summer and early autumn, and 'Goldsturm', which grows 60 cm (2 ft) tall and bears up to 12.5 cm (5 in.) golden-yellow flowers from midsummer to mid-autumn. The gloriosa daisy, a handsome 75 cm (2½ ft) hybrid that bears 12.5 to 17.5 cm (5 to 7 in.) daisy-like flowers all summer long in many shades of yellow, orange and mahogany, all with dark brown centres; the flowers come in single form with one ring of petals, or heavily petalled doubles. An excellent descendant of the old-fashioned cut-leaved coneflower is the 1.2 to 1.5 metre (4 to 5 ft) cultivar 'Golden Globe', whose heavily petalled 7.5 cm (3 in.) bright yellow blossoms appear in late summer and early autumn.

HOW TO GROW. Coneflowers thrive in well-drained soil and full sun, but tolerate light shade. Space plants 30 to 38 cm (12 to 15 in.) apart. Gloriosa daisies should be grown only from seeds sown in early spring; plants will blossom the first year and live for many years, multiplying in the garden by dropping their own seeds. Propagate all other types by clump divisions during the dormant season. Divide clumps every other year of flowering.

RUDBECKIA PURPUREA See *Echinacea*

S

SALVIA

S. azurea (blue sage) and its variety *pitcheri*; *S. haematodes*, now more correctly *S. pratensis* var. *haematodes*; *S.x superba*, also called *S. virgata* vat. *nemorosa*. (All also called salvia)

Most perennial sages have blue or violet flowers, distinguishing them from the popular annual, scarlet sage. The blue sage grows 90 to 120 cm (3 to 4 ft) tall and sends out slender spikes of 12 mm (½ in.) sky-blue flowers in late summer and early autumn; its form *pitcheri* is similar, but a richer blue. *S. haematodes* grows to 90 cm (3 ft) and is a short-lived but much-branched plant with grey-green corrugated leaves and a profusion of light blue flowers from early summer to early autumn. *S.x superba*, of garden origin, is the most dependable and useful, coming up year after year with 60 to 90 cm (2 to 3 ft) branching stems, carrying many rich purple-blue flowers, each about 2 cm (¾ in.) long. It blooms from midsummer to early autumn. Its cultivar 'East Friesland' has dark violet flowers and grows 45 cm (1½ ft) tall.

HOW TO GROW. Sages will grow in all except extremely cold regions, although the blue sage will grow there, too. They do best in full sun and very well-drained soil. Space plants 38 to 45 cm (15 to 18 in.) apart. To propagate *S.x superba* the roots can be divided during the dormant season, a method also possible with *S. haematodes*. However, it is more readily increased from seeds, as is the blue sage. Clumps should remain undisturbed indefinitely.

SANTOLINA

S. chamaecyparissus, also called *S. incana* (lavender

CONEFLOWER
Rudbeckia fulgida 'Goldsturm'

SALVIA
Salvia haematodes

LAVENDER COTTON
Santolina chamaecyparissus

cotton); *S. virens* (green lavender cotton)

The lavender cottons are really evergreen shrubs, but dwarf enough to be used in flower borders as a foil for bright colours. They have woody stems and fern-like, aromatic, silvery-grey foliage If left unpruned, lavender cotton may grow 60 cm (2 ft) tall and 90 cm (3 ft) across. Most gardeners never see the 2 cm (¾ in.) button-like, yellow flowers that bloom from early summer to mid-summer, because they shear the plants back occasionally to stimulate growth of fresh new foliage. *S. virens* is similar to *S. chamaecyprissus*, but has green thread-like leaves instead of silver.

HOW TO GROW. Lavender cottons grow as perennials in cool, temperate or warm regions. They need full sun, but will thrive in almost any soil. Set plants 45 to 60 cm (18 to 24 in.) apart. Old plants should be cut to a height of 15 cm (6 in.) in the spring to encourage new growth. New plants can be started from heel cuttings taken in summer. Clumps can remain undisturbed indefinitely.

SAPONARIA

S. officinalis (soapwort, bouncing Bet)

The soapwort is a European plant which takes its name from the fact that the chopped leaves form a soapy lather in water and are used for various washing purposes, such as cleaning tapestries. It grows 30 to 90 cm (1 to 3 ft) tall, with smooth, pale-green, opposite, lanceolate leaves and sprays of large, single, pink, salver-shaped flowers in late summer. In cultivation the species is superseded by various double cultivars such as the white 'Alba-plena', pink 'Roseo-plena', and red 'Rubra-plena', all with 2.5 to 4 cm (1 to 1½ in.) flowers.

HOW TO GROW. An easy plant for sun or light shade and ordinary garden soil. The plants may need keeping in check as they spread by means of underground runners and the taller cultivars may need twiggy sticks for support. Runners can be used for propagation purposes. Cut established plants to ground level in the autumn.

SCABIOSA

S. caucasica (pincushion flower)

Prominent dark grey, pollen-bearing stamens that stand out like pins from the centre of the pincushion flower give the plant its name. The 60 to 75 cm (2 to 2½ ft) stems bear 7.5 cm (3 in.) blossoms from summer to early autumn, and even later if faded flowers are removed. In addition to the light blue of the basic species, mauve, lavender, violet, blue and white cultivars are available.

HOW TO GROW. Pincushion flowers do best in full sun and need soil that is moist during the growing season and extremely well-drained in winter. All make excellent cut flowers. Plant pincushion flowers 30 to 38 cm (12 to 15 in.) apart. New plants can be grown from clump divisions or from seeds sown in summer for blooms the next year.

SEDUM

S. spectabile (showy stonecrop, also called live-forever, sedum)

The showy stonecrop grows about 45 cm (18 in.) tall, and from late summer to late autumn bears 7.5 to 10 cm (3 to 4 in.) clusters of tiny ivory, pink or red flowers at the ends of its stems. Its thick leaves die to the ground each year, but the plant is noted for its strength; it is tolerant of drought and is pest-free. Several excellent cultivars are available, including 'Brilliant', raspberry-red; 'Carmine', rose red; 'Meteor', deep carmine red; and 'Star Dust',

SOAPWORT
Saponaria officinalis

Illustration by Dorothy Bovey

PINCUSHION FLOWER
Scabiosa caucasica

STONECROP
Sedum spectabile 'Meteor'

PRAIRIE MALLOW
Sidalcea malvaeflora hybrid

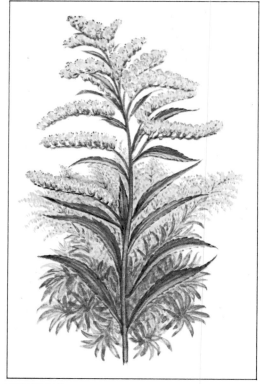

GOLDEN ROD
Solidago x *hybrida* 'Goldenmosa'

ivory. The showy stonecrop is suitable for borders as well as rock gardens.

HOW TO GROW. The showy stonecrop grows well in full sun or light shade in almost any soil, preferably well-drained. Set plants 45 to 60 cm (18 to 24 in.) apart. New plants can be started from stem cuttings taken in summer to bloom the next year or by clump divisions in the spring. Except for propagation purposes, leave clumps undisturbed indefinitely.

SENECIO See *Ligularia*

SIDALCEA
S. malvaeflora hybrids (prairie mallow)

Prairie mallows grow 45 to 120 cm (1½ to 4 ft) tall, and have a great many branching spikes, covered in mid- to late summer with 2.5 to 4 cm (1 to 1½ in.) cup-shaped flowers ranging from blush-pink to crimson. The leaves of the prairie mallows are palmate in shape, often scalloped or deeply lobed. One excellent cultivar is 'Rose Queen', whose colour reflects its name.

HOW TO GROW. Prairie mallows grow well in full sun and well-drained soil. Strains of hybrid prairie mallows such as 'Rose Queen' must be started from seeds sown in summer to bloom the next year. Once established, named cultivars can be multiplied in spring by dividing clumps, which develop quite rapidly and usually need to be dug up and divided every three or four years.

SOLIDAGO
*S.*x *hybrida* (golden rod)

Golden rods have become increasingly popular since the late H. Walkden, a British plantsman, raised a dwarf range of hybrids. These well-known perennials have 25 to 30 cm (10 to 12 in.) yellow flower heads composed of many tiny blossoms, and combine especially well in borders with lavender and purple Michaelmas daisies. Some begin to blossom in midsummer, others later, and last through autumn. Among the best cultivars of hybrid golden rods are 'Goldenmosa', which has fluffy, yellow flowers in late summer and grows up to 90 cm (3 ft) tall; 'Leraft', which has bright golden-yellow flowers in late summer, and is 75 cm (2½ ft) tall; 'Goldstrahl', also known as 'Peter Pan', which has bright canary-yellow flowers in early autumn and grows up to 90 cm (3 ft) tall.

HOW TO GROW. Golden rods grow in full sun or very light shade and thrive in almost any soil. Set plants 45 cm (18 in.) apart. New plants of named cultivars should be started by clump divisions during the dormant season; clumps should be divided when they become overcrowded.

x SOLIDASTER
x *S. luteus*, also called x *S. hybridus* and *Aster hybridus luteus* (solidaster)

In 1909 a nurseryman in Lyons, France, achieved the unusual feat of crossing an aster and a golden rod, plants from two separate genera. The resulting hybrid, named x *Solidaster*—from *Solidago* (golden rod) and *Aster*—inherited its golden-yellow colour from its golden rod parent and its masses of 12 mm (½ in.) star-like flowers from the aster side of the family. Its flowers blossom from midsummer to early autumn; the plant grows 45 to 60 cm (1½ to 2 ft) high and may billow to spread twice that width.

HOW TO GROW. Solidasters do best in well-drained soil and full sun, but will tolerate light shade. Set plants

38 to 45 cm (15 to 18 in.) apart. New plants can be started by dividing and replanting clumps in spring or autumn.

SPIRAEA See *Aruncus, Filipendula*

STACHYS
S. grandiflora, also called *S. macrantha* and *Betonica grandiflora* (big betony); *S. olympica*, also called *S. lanata* lamb's tongue, donkey's ears)

Big betony, which may grow as tall as 90 cm (3 ft), bears spikes of 2.5 cm (1 in.) deep violet flowers in early and mid-summer. The flowers, good for cutting, are arranged in closely set whorls along the spikes. The wrinkled, hairy leaves of this species are heart-shaped and have scalloped edges. Lamb's tongue is most notable for its silvery-white, tongue-shaped leaves, which are 10 to 15 cm (4 to 6 in.) long. This species grows 30 to 45 cm (12 to 18 in.) tall and begins to bear spikes of small pinkish-purple flowers in early summer; they will bloom until frost if faded flowers are removed. The foliage is highly ornamental, and the most useful form is the non-flowering cultivar 'Silver Carpet'.

HOW TO GROW. Both species do best in full sun and very well-drained soil. Space plants 30 to 45 cm (12 to 18 in.) apart. New plants may be obtained by sowing seeds in early spring for flowering the following year or by dividing clumps in early spring or early autumn. Divide clumps after two or three years of flowering.

STOKESIA
S. laevis, also called *S. cyanea* (Stokes' aster)

The Stokes' aster grows 30 to 45 cm (12 to 18 in.) tall, and bears a continuous crop of 7.5 to 10 cm (3 to 4 in.) aster-like flowers from midsummer until autumn; its shiny leaves are 5 to 20 cm (2 to 8 in.) long. In addition to the popular blue cultivar, there are types with white, pink, purple and pale yellow blossoms. All are excellent for cutting.

HOW TO GROW. Stokes' asters do best in full sun and need very well-drained soil, particularly in dry regions. Set plants 30 to 38 cm (12 to 15 in.) apart. New plants can be started from divisions of clumps, or from seeds sown in spring to flower the next year; these, however, will give varied results.

THALICTRUM
T. aquilegifolium (columbine meadow rue); *T. diptero-carpum* (Yunnan meadow rue); *T. rocquebrunianum*; *T. flavum* ssp. *glaucum*, also known as *T. speciosissimum* (dusty meadow rue)

The lacy, fern-like foliage of meadow rues enhances the cloud-like clusters of tiny blossoms that shroud the plants' tops. Most species grow 90 to 120 cm (3 to 4 ft) tall, and are effective at the back of a border, or in a shady corner.

Columbine meadow rue, 75 to 90 cm (2½ to 3 ft) tall, sends up huge clusters of lavender, white or rose-pink flowers from late spring to early summer. An excellent cultivar is 'Purple Mist', whose flowers are a rich rosy purple. Yunnan meadow rue grows up to 1.5 metres (5 ft) tall and in late summer and early autumn bears enormous clusters of lavender flowers. There is a handsome double form called 'Hewitt's Double', with intricately branched, cob-web-like stems spangled with deep mauve, double florets like tiny balls. *T. rocquebrunianum* grows to 120 cm (4 ft) with fern-like leaves and loose panicles of rose-lavender flowers with yellow stamens from mid- to late summer. The

SOLIDASTER
x *Solidaster luteus*

BIG BETONY
Stachys grandiflora

LAMB'S TONGUE
Stachys olympica

STOKE'S ASTER
Stokesia laevis

MEADOW RUE
Thalictrum rocquebrunianum

CAROLINA THERMOPSIS
Thermopsis caroliniana

SPIDERWORT
Tradescantia virginiana

dusty meadow rue bears clusters of fragrant, fuzzy yellow flowers in midsummer and has bluish-green leaves.

HOW TO GROW. *T. rocquebrunianum* will grow in most regions, but the other species are not successful in extreme cold. They do best in moist soil enriched with compost or leaf-mould. Meadow rues thrive in very light shade, but tolerate full sun if the soil is moist. Excellent drainage in winter is vital in cool regions, including Britain; a light winter mulch such as leaves or straw is advisable. Plant meadow rues 38 to 45 cm (15 to 18 in.) apart. They can be started from the current season's seeds, sown in summer or autumn to bloom two years later. Clumps may be divided in spring for propagation or left undisturbed indefinitely.

THERMOPSIS
T. caroliniana (Carolina thermopsis)

This north American perennial bears pea-shaped, yellow blossoms in 25 to 30 cm (10 to 12 in.) spikes in summer, atop broadly spreading plants that grow 90 to 120 cm (3 to 4 ft) tall. The flowers, which are good for cutting, combine well with blue delphiniums, which flower at the same time.

HOW TO GROW. This thermopsis does best in fertile well-drained soil and full sun, although it can tolerate light shade. Set plants 90 to 120 cm (3 to 4 ft) apart. Propagate new plants from fresh seeds, sown in summer to bloom two years later; they do not transplant well except when young. Leave clumps undisturbed indefinitely.

TRADESCANTIA
T. virginiana (spiderwort)

Modern cultivars of spiderwort grow about 45 cm (18 in.) tall, and bear 4 to 7.5 cm (1½ to 3 in.) flowers in shades of violet-blue, pink and red, as well as white. Although individual flowers live only one day, new ones continue to open from early summer to autumn. They have narrow, smooth, rather floppy, strap-shaped leaves and three-petalled flowers with handsome feathered stamens. Good named cultivars are 'Osprey', one of the best, with large white flowers and blue stamens; 'Purewell Giant', carmine-purple; 'Blue Stone', deep blue; 'Rubra', purplish red; and 'Iris Prichard', white with bright blue stamens.

HOW TO GROW. Spiderworts grow in almost any soil, but do best in moist soil and light shade. Set plants 30 to 38 cm (12 to 15 in.) apart. Clumps of named cultivars can be divided for propagation in spring after three or four years of flowering. New plants can also be grown from seeds sown in spring or summer to flower the following year; their colour, however, is unpredictable.

TRITOMA UVARIA See *Kniphofia*

TROLLIUS
T. europaeus hybrids (globe flower); *T. chinensis*, also called *T. ledebourii*

Globe flowers, relatives of the buttercup, bear yellow-to-orange flowers about 5 to 10 cm (2 to 4 in.) across and bloom from late spring to late summer if flowers are removed as they fade. They grow 30 to 60 cm (1 to 2 ft) tall and have deeply cut leaves; the flower stems of some cultivars reach 90 cm (3 ft) in moist rich soil. Hybrid globe flowers are the best for garden purposes, but will thrive only in soil that does not dry out in summer. Worthwhile cultivars include 'Alabaster', pale primrose-yellow; 'Canary Bird', large lemon-yellow; 'Bee's Orange', orange-gold; 'Goldquelle', globular, rich orange; and 'Salamander', fiery orange. *T. chinensis* is distinct with prominent deep orange stamens rising above the 5 to 6 cm (2 to 2½ in.) bowl-shaped, orange flowers; it grows 90 cm (3 ft) tall.

HOW TO GROW. Globe flowers thrive in full sun or light shade. They are suited to moist soil—even the wet ground beside a pool—but the soil must be liberally supplemented with moss peat, leaf-mould, compost or rotted manure. Plant globe flowers 25 to 30 cm (10 to 12 in.) apart. New plants can be started by clump division in early autumn or from seeds sown as soon as they are ripe.

VALERIANA
V. officinalis (common valerian, all-heal plant)

Not to be confused with *Centranthus*, the red valerian, which has brighter flowers *V. officinalis* is the all-heal plant, long esteemed for its medicinal properties. It has masses of tiny pale-pink or white flowers in close 10 cm (4 in.) heads on 90 to 120 cm (3 to 4 ft) stems in summer. The segments of its pinnate leaves are arranged in pairs. Cats are very fond of the powdered roots, which, were once laid among clothes "to perfume them".

HOW TO GROW. Common valerian grows in sun or shade in almost any soil, and even tolerates very moist conditions. Space plants 38 to 45 cm (15 to 18 in.) apart. New plants can be started from clump divisions during the dormant season, or from seeds sown in summer to flower the following year.

VERATRUM
V. album; *V. nigrum*; *V. viride* (all known as false helle-bore, helleborine)

Veratrums are robust, erect perennials with striking foliage and handsome terminal clusters of small star-shaped flowers in midsummer. The leaves are arranged in threes round the stem. They are hairy beneath and strongly veined or pleated. All have stout, black, poison-ous roots. The main differences lie in the heights of the flower clusters and the colour of the blooms. *V. album* grows 90 to 120 cm (3 to 4 ft) tall and has 30 cm (12 in.) sprays of white flowers which are greenish outside; *V. nigrum*, 60 to 120 cm (2 to 4 ft) tall, has blackish-purple florets in 90 cm (3 ft) spikes; and *V. viride*, 1 to 2 metres (3 to 6 ft) tall, has 22 to 30 cm (9 to 12 in.) flower sprays in a striking shade of green.

HOW TO GROW. All the veratrums require a moist position in light shade. They grow in all parts except extremely cold areas. Propagate by division of the roots in spring.

VERBASCUM
V. hybridum (hybrid mullein)

Hybrid mulleins are stately many-branched plants with large fuzzy-grey leaves that grow in low clumps. The 90 to 120 cm (3 to 4 ft) stems are laden with 2.5 cm (1 in.) pink, white, yellow, amber or lavender flowers from midsummer to early autumn. Fine cultivars are 'Pink Domino', with rosy-pink flowers, and 'Cotswold Gem', with purple-centred, yellow flowers.

HOW TO GROW. Mulleins will grow in full sun and almost any well-drained soil; excellent drainage is vital in cool areas. Plant mulleins 30 to 38 cm (12 to 15 in.) apart. As plants sometimes die after blossoming, start new plants each year for replacements. Propagate named cultivars from root cuttings taken in early spring. New plants can also be grown from seeds sown in spring or

GLOBE FLOWER
Trollius chinensis

COMMON VALERIAN
Valeriana officinalis

Illustration by Dorothy Bovey

FALSE HELLEBORE
Veratrum album

HYBRID MULLEIN
Verbascum hybrids

SPEEDWELL
Veronica spicata 'Minuet'

VIOLA
Viola x *williamsii*

PANSY
Viola x *wittrockiana*

early summer to blossom the next year; their colour, however, is variable.

VERONICA

V. incana; *V. longifolia*; *V. spicata*; *V. teucrium*, also called *V. latifolia*. (All called speedwell)

Speedwells are highly valued as long-blooming plants that grow 30 to 45 cm (12 to 18 in.) tall and bear colourful 15 to 20 cm (6 to 8 in.) spikes of tiny flowers. *V. incana* has silvery leaves and light blue flowers in early summer and midsummer; notable cultivars are 'Saraband', violet-blue, and 'Rosea', with pink flowers. A good form of *V. longifolia* is 'Foerster's Blue', rich blue on 60 cm (2 ft) stems from midsummer until autumn; another cultivar called 'Icicle', has white flowers. Three excellent 45 cm (18 in.) cultivars of *V. spicata* blossom all summer: 'Barcarolle', deep pink; 'Minuet', medium pink; and 'Pavane', rose-pink. 'Crater Lake Blue', is a superb deep blue cultivar of *V. teucrium*.

HOW TO GROW. Speedwells need full sun and well-drained soil. Set plants 30 to 38 cm (12 to 15 in.) apart. Start named cultivars from stem cuttings in spring and summer for flowering the next year. Divide clumps after every three or four years of flowering.

VIOLA

V. odorata (sweet violet); *V.*x *williamsii* (viola, tufted pansy); *V.*x *wittrockiana*, also called *V. tricolor* var. *hortensis*, *V. tricolor* var. *maxima*; *V. tricolor* (both called pansy)

Sweet violets grow about 20 cm (8 in.) tall in the cultivars and from mid- to late spring produce 18 mm (¾ in.) pink, white or purple flowers, some single, with one ring of petals, some heavily petalled doubles. The familiar pansy grows about 20 cm (8 in.) tall, and has 5 to 7.5 cm (2 to 3 in.) flowers in many shades and combinations of yellow, pink, dark red, brown, blue, purple and white. Although a true perennial, the pansy weakens with the arrival of hot weather and is treated as a biennial. Plants blossom profusely from early spring to midsummer. Viola flowers are similar to pansies, but are usually smaller and generally come in solid shades of blue, purple, yellow and red, as well as white. Violas blossom from early spring until frost in cool or temperate regions, from winter until midsummer in warmer regions.

HOW TO GROW. Violas and pansies grow in most areas; sweet violets are the same, although not successful in cold regions. All do best in light shade and moist soil liberally enriched with compost or leaf-mould. Set plants 20 cm (8 in.) apart. Propagate sweet violets by clump division in the dormant season; single-flowered cultivars can also be grown from seeds in summer to blossom the following year. Pansies are easily grown from seeds in cool or temperate regions; sow the seeds outdoors in midsummer in light shade, then transplant them to a sunny nursery bed until the following spring. To protect the evergreen leaves over winter in cold and exposed places, grow the plants in a cold frame; this also induces early flowering. In southern hot areas, sow pansy seeds in late summer; the plants will grow through the autumn and blossom during winter and spring. Many types of violas can be started from seeds in the same manner as pansies, but named cultivars must be propagated from stem cuttings or clump divisions in early spring for flowers the same season, or in early autumn for flowers the following year.

VISCARIA See *Lychnis*

Appendix

Characteristics of 162 perennials and biennials

	FLOWER COLOUR					FLOWER SIZE			FLOWER TYPES			FLOWERING SEASONS				PLANT HEIGHT			NOTED FOR		LIGHT		SOIL	
	White	Yellow to orange	Pink to red	Blue to purple	Multicolour	Under 2.5 cm (1 in.)	2.5 to 7.5 cm (1 to 3 in.)	Over 7.5 cm (3 in.)	One per stem	Spikes/Plumes	Clusters	Spring	Summer	Autumn	Winter	Under 60 cm (2 ft)	60 to 90 cm (2 to 3 ft)	Over 1 metre (3 ft)	Fragrance	Distinctive foliage	Sun	Partial shade	Well-drained	Moist to wet
ACANTHUS MOLLIS (bear's-breeches)	●		●				●			●			●					●		●	●	●		●
ACHILLEA FILIPENDULINA (fern-leaved yarrow)		●				●					●		●	●			●			●	●		●	
ACHILLEA MILLEFOLIUM 'FIRE KING' (common yarrow)		●				●					●		●	●		●				●	●	●	●	
ACONITUM HENRYI 'SPARK'S VARIETY' (monkshood)			●				●	●		●			●	●			●		●		●	●	●	●
ACTAEA (baneberry)	●					●		●		●			●		●						●	●		●
ADONIS VERNALIS (spring adonis)		●				●		●	●			●				●				●	●	●	●	
ALCHEMILLA MOLLIS (lady's mantle)		●			●						●		●			●				●	●	●	●	●
ALTHAEA ROSEA (hollyhock)		●	●				●		●				●					●		●	●		●	
ALSTROEMERIA LIGTU				●		●				●			●				●				●		●	
ANAPHALIS YEDOËNSIS (Japanese pearl everlasting)	●					●					●		●	●		●				●	●	●	●	
ANCHUSA AZUREA (Italian bugloss)				●		●					●		●					●			●		●	
ANEMONE X HYBRIDA (Japanese anemone)	●		●				●		●				●	●			●				●	●		●
ANTHEMIS TINCTORIA (ox-eye chamomile)		●					●		●				●				●			●	●		●	
AQUILEGIA X HYBRIDA (columbine)	●	●	●	●	●		●		●				●				●				●	●	●	
ARMERIA ARENARIA (sea pink)		●				●				●	●	●	●			●				●	●		●	
ARTEMISIA LUDOVICIANA 'SILVER QUEEN' (wormwood)	●			●					●		●		●				●			●	●		●	●
ARUNCUS DIOICUS (goats beard)	●					●		●		●			●					●			●	●		●
ASCLEPIAS TUBEROSA (butterfly weed)		●				●					●		●	●		●			●		●		●	
ASTER X FRIKARTII (aster)			●			●		●			●		●	●	●	●					●	●	●	
ASTER NOVI-BELGII (Michaelmas daisy)	●		●	●	●		●		●				●	●			●				●	●	●	
ASTILBE X ARENDSII (astilbe)	●		●				●	●		●			●			●				●	●	●		●
ASTRANTIA (masterwort)	●		●			●			●				●			●				●	●	●		●
BAPTISIA AUSTRALIS (false indigo)			●				●		●			●	●				●				●	●	●	
BELLIS PERENNIS (English daisy)	●		●			●		●	●			●	●			●					●	●	●	
BERGENIA CORDIFOLIA (bergenia)	●		●				●		●	●			●			●				●	●	●	●	
BOLTONIA ASTEROIDES (white boltonia)	●		●	●		●		●			●		●	●				●			●		●	
BRUNNERA MACROPHYLLA (Siberian bugloss)			●		●			●		●	●									●		●		
CALLIRHOË (poppy mallow)			●				●	●	●				●			●					●	●	●	
CAMPANULA MEDIUM (Canterbury bell)	●		●	●			●			●			●	●			●				●	●	●	
CAMPANULA PERSICIFOLIA (peach-leaved bellflower)	●		●				●			●			●					●			●	●	●	
CASSIA MARILANDICA (wild senna)		●					●			●		●					●				●	●	●	
CATANANCHE CAERULEA (Cupid's-dart)	●		●				●	●			●		●	●		●				●	●		●	
CENTAUREA MONTANA (mountain knapweed)			●				●	●	●				●			●					●	●	●	
CENTAUREA RUTIFOLIA (dusty miller)		●		●	●	●					●		●			●				●	●		●	
CENTRANTHUS RUBER (red valerian)	●	●					●			●			●	●			●				●	●	●	
CEPHALARIA (giant yellow scabious)		●					●			●			●					●			●	●	●	
CERATOSTIGMA PLUMBAGINOIDES (leadwort)			●	●		●					●		●	●		●				●	●	●	●	
CHEIRANTHUS CHEIRI (English wallflower)	●	●	●	●	●		●			●		●	●			●			●		●	●	●	
CHELONE LYONII (pink turtle-head)			●				●			●				●			●					●		●
CHRYSANTHEMUM COCCINEUM (pyrethrum)	●		●				●		●				●	●			●				●	●	●	
CHRYSANTHEMUM MAXIMUM (Shasta daisy)	●					●		●	●				●	●			●				●	●	●	
CHRYSANTHEMUM X HORTORUM (hardy chrysanthemum)	●	●	●		●	●	●	●	●					●			●				●	●	●	
CIMICIFUGA SIMPLEX (bugbane)	●					●			●				●				●		●	●	●	●		●

Unless cultivar names are given, the information above includes the colours and sizes of all recommended cultivars of the species listed.

	FLOWER COLOUR					FLOWER SIZE			FLOWER TYPES			FLOWERING SEASONS				PLANT HEIGHT			NOTED FOR		LIGHT		SOIL	
	White	Yellow to orange	Pink to red	Blue to purple	Multicolour	Under 2.5 cm (1 in.)	2.5 to 7.5 cm (1 to 3 in.)	Over 7.5 cm (3 in.)	One per stem	Spikes/Plumes	Clusters	Spring	Summer	Autumn	Winter	Under 60 cm (2 ft)	60 to 90 cm (2 to 3 ft)	Over 1 metre (3 ft)	Fragrance	Distinctive foliage	Sun	Partial shade	Well-drained	Moist to wet
CLEMATIS HERACLEIFOLIA DAVIDIANA (herbaceous clematis)			●			●					●		●	●			●	●			●	●	●	●
CONVALLARIA (lily-of-the-valley)	●		●			●				●	●	●				●			●			●		●
CONVOLVULUS MAURITANICUS (ground morning-glory)			●			●		●			●	●	●	●		●					●		●	
COREOPSIS GRANDIFLORA		●				●		●					●				●				●		●	
CORONILLA VARIA (crown vetch)	●		●				●				●		●	●		●					●		●	
CORTADERIA SELLOANA (pampas grass)	●		●				●		●				●	●				●		●	●		●	
CORYDALIS LUTEA (yellow corydalis)		●			●		●			●		●	●			●				●	●	●	●	
DELPHINIUM ELATUM HYBRIDS	●	●	●	●			●			●			●					●			●		●	
DELPHINIUM BELLADONNA HYBRIDS	●		●	●			●			●			●				●				●		●	
DELPHINIUM GRANDIFLORUM (Chinese delphinium)	●		●			●		●					●			●					●		●	
DIANTHUS X ALLWOODII (Allwood's pink)	●		●		●		●	●					●			●			●		●		●	
DIANTHUS BARBATUS (sweet William)	●		●		●		●			●	●		●			●			●		●		●	
DIANTHUS CARYOPHYLLUS (border carnation)	●	●				●						●	●	●		●			●		●		●	
DICENTRA EXIMIA (fringed bleeding heart)		●			●			●			●	●	●	●		●				●	●	●		●
DICENTRA SPECTABILIS (bleeding heart)	●		●			●				●		●					●			●	●	●		●
DIERAMA PULCHERRIMUM (wand flower)		●	●			●							●					●		●	●		●	
DICTAMNUS ALBUS (gas plant)	●		●			●			●				●				●		●	●	●		●	
DIGITALIS PURPUREA (foxglove)	●	●	●	●			●			●			●					●			●	●	●	
DORONICUM CAUCASICUM (Caucasian leopard's bane)		●				●		●				●				●					●	●	●	
DRACOCEPHALUM HEMSLEYANUM (dragon's head)			●			●				●			●			●					●	●	●	
ECHINACEA PURPUREA (purple coneflower)	●		●	●			●		●				●	●			●				●		●	
ECHINOPS 'TAPLOW BLUE' (globe thistle)				●			●		●				●	●				●		●	●		●	
EPIMEDIUM (barrenwort)	●	●	●	●	●	●	●				●	●				●				●		●		●
EREMURUS STENOPHYLLUS BUNGEI (foxtail lilies)	●	●	●					●		●		●						●			●		●	
ERIGERON SPECIOSUS HYBRIDS (fleabane)			●	●		●		●					●			●					●		●	
ERYNGIUM X OLIVERIANUM (sea holly)			●	●		●							●	●			●			●	●	●	●	
EUPATORIUM COELESTINUM (mist flower)			●					●			●		●	●		●					●	●	●	
EUPHORBIA EPITHYMOIDES (cushion spurge)		●				●			●	●	●	●				●					●	●	●	
FELICIA AMELLOIDES (blue daisy)			●			●		●				●	●	●	●	●					●		●	
FILIPENDULA HEXAPETALA (dropwort)	●					●			●	●			●			●			●	●	●	●		●
GAILLARDIA ARISTATA (blanket flower)		●	●		●		●	●					●	●		●	●				●		●	
GALIUM ODORATUM (sweet woodruff)	●				●						●	●	●			●			●	●		●		●
GAZANIA LONGISCAPA HYBRIDS (gazania)	●	●	●		●		●	●				●	●	●	●	●				●	●		●	
GENTIANA SEPTEMFIDA (gentian)				●		●		●					●			●					●		●	
GERANIUM GRANDIFLORUM (crane's-bill)				●		●		●				●	●			●				●	●	●	●	
GERBERA JAMESONII (Barberton daisy)	●	●	●				●	●	●			●	●	●		●					●		●	
GEUM CHILOENSE (scarlet avens)		●	●			●		●					●			●					●	●	●	●
GYPSOPHILA PANICULATA (baby's-breath)	●		●			●			●			●	●				●		●		●		●	
HELENIUM AUTUMNALE (sneezeweed)		●	●			●							●	●			●	●			●		●	
HELIANTHUS DECAPETALUS 'FLORE PLENO' (double sunflower)		●					●	●					●	●				●			●		●	
HELIOPSIS HELIANTHOIDES var. SCABRA (heliopsis)		●					●	●					●	●		●					●			●
HELLEBORUS NIGER (Christmas rose)	●						●		●						●	●				●		●		●
HEMEROCALLIS HYBRIDS (day lily)		●	●		●		●	●	●			●	●	●		●	●			●	●	●	●	

Unless cultivar names are given, the information above includes the colours and sizes of all recommended cultivars of the species listed.

Species	White	Yellow to orange	Pink to red	Blue to purple	Multicolour	Under 2.5 cm (1 in.)	2.5 to 7.5 cm (1 to 3 in.)	Over 7.5 cm (3 in.)	One per stem	Spikes/Plumes	Clusters	Spring	Summer	Autumn	Winter	Under 60 cm (2 ft)	60 to 90 cm (2 to 3 ft)	Over 1 metre (3 ft)	Fragrance	Distinctive foliage	Sun	Partial shade	Well-drained	Moist to wet
HESPERIS MATRONALIS (sweet rocket)	●			●	●		●				●	●	●				●		●		●	●	●	●
HEUCHERA SANGUINEA (coral bells)	●	●	●		●					●	●	●	●	●		●				●	●	●	●	●
HIBISCUS MOSCHEUTOS (rose mallow)	●		●				●	●			●	●	●				●				●	●	●	●
HOSTA PLANTAGINEA (plantain lily)	●					●		●		●			●			●			●	●	●	●	●	●
HYPERICUM X MOSERIANUM (St. John's wort)		●				●			●				●	●		●				●	●	●	●	●
IBERIS SEMPERVIRENS (candytuft)	●					●			●	●	●	●				●				●	●	●	●	
IRIS, BEARDED HYBRIDS (tall bearded iris)	●	●	●	●	●		●	●	●			●	●	●		●	●		●		●	●	●	
IRIS, BEARD-LESS HYBRID (Japanese iris)	●	●	●	●	●		●	●	●				●	●			●	●			●	●	●	●
IRIS PSEUDACORUS (yellow flag iris)		●					●		●				●				●	●			●	●		●
IRIS SIBIRICA (Siberian iris)	●		●	●			●		●				●				●				●	●		●
KIRENGESHOMA PALMATA (yellow waxbells)		●					●			●				●			●				●	●		●
KNIPHOFIA UVARIA (red-hot poker)	●	●	●		●			●	●				●	●		●				●		●	●	
LATHYRUS LATIFOLIUS (perennial pea)	●		●	●			●			●			●	●				●			●	●	●	
LAVANDULA OFFICINALIS (lavender)	●		●	●		●			●				●	●		●	●		●	●	●	●	●	
LIATRIS SPICATA (spike gay-feather)			●	●			●			●			●			●	●				●	●	●	
LIGULARIA DENTATA (golden groundsel)		●		●		●				●			●	●			●			●		●		●
LIMONIUM LATIFOLIUM (sea lavender)		●	●			●				●			●			●					●	●	●	
LINUM PERENNE (perennial flax)	●		●			●	●			●			●	●		●					●	●	●	
LIRIOPE PLATYPHYLLA (big blue lily-turf)	●		●			●	●			●			●	●		●				●	●	●		●
LUNARIA ANNUA (honesty)	●		●	●			●			●	●	●				●			●	●	●	●	●	
LUPINUS 'RUSSELL HYBRID' (lupin)	●	●	●	●	●		●			●			●	●			●		●		●	●	●	
LYCHNIS CHALCEDONICA (Maltese cross)			●			●			●		●	●				●				●		●	●	
LYCHNIS VISCARIA (German catchfly)			●			●			●		●	●			●					●		●	●	
LYTHRUM SALICARIA (purple loosestrife)			●			●				●			●	●			●				●	●		●
MACLEAYA CORDATA (plume poppy)			●				●			●			●				●			●	●	●		
MALVA ALCEA 'FASTIGIATA' (hollyhock mallow)			●				●		●				●	●			●				●	●		
MECONOPSIS BETONICIFOLIA (Himalayan blue poppy)				●			●		●				●				●	●				●		●
MIRABILIS JALAPA (four-o'clock plant)	●	●	●	●	●		●				●	●	●			●			●		●	●	●	
MONARDA DIDYMA (bergamot)			●				●			●			●	●			●		●	●	●	●		●
MYOSOTIS PALUSTRIS (forget-me-not)	●		●	●			●			●	●	●	●	●	●	●					●	●		●
NEPETA X FAASSENII (catmint)			●	●		●				●	●	●	●			●			●	●	●	●	●	
NIEREMBERGIA HIPPOMANICA var. VIOLACEA (cup flower)			●	●		●				●			●	●		●					●	●	●	●
OENOTHERA TETRAGONA (sundrops)		●				●		●					●			●					●	●	●	
PAEONIA LACTIFLORA (Chinese peony)	●	●	●				●	●	●			●	●			●	●		●	●	●	●	●	
PAPAVER NUDICAULE (Iceland poppy)	●	●	●				●	●	●		●	●				●				●		●	●	
PAPAVER ORIENTALE (Oriental poppy)	●		●				●	●	●				●				●	●		●	●	●	●	
PENSTEMON HARTWEGII (penstemon)			●			●			●				●				●				●	●	●	
PHLOMIS FRUTICOSA (Jerusalem sage)		●				●			●				●				●			●	●	●	●	
PHLOX DIVARICATA (Canada phlox)	●		●			●			●	●	●				●					●	●	●	
PHLOX PANICULATA (garden phlox)	●		●	●	●		●			●			●				●	●	●		●	●		●
PHORMIUM TENAX (New Zealand flax)		●	●			●		●		●			●				●	●		●	●	●		
PHYSALIS ALKEKENGI (Chinese lantern)	●			●		●			●			●	●			●				●	●	●	●	
PHYSOSTEGIA VIRGINIANA (obedient plant)	●		●			●		●		●			●	●		●	●				●	●		

Unless cultivar names are given, the information above includes the colours and sizes of all recommended cultivars of the species listed.

	FLOWER COLOUR					FLOWER SIZE			FLOWER TYPES			FLOWERING SEASONS				PLANT HEIGHT			NOTED FOR		LIGHT		SOIL	
	White	Yellow to orange	Pink to red	Blue to purple	Multicolour	Under 2.5 cm (1 in.)	2.5 to 7.5 cm (1 to 3 in.)	Over 7.5 cm (3 in.)	One per stem	Spikes/Plumes	Clusters	Spring	Summer	Autumn	Winter	Under 60 cm (2 ft)	60 to 90 cm (2 to 3 ft)	Over 1 metre (3 ft)	Fragrance	Distinctive foliage	Sun	Partial shade	Well-drained	Moist to wet
PLATYCODON GRANDIFLORUM (balloon flower)	●		●	●			●				●		●			●					●	●	●	
POLEMONIUM COERULEUM (Jacob's-ladder)	●		●				●		●	●	●		●			●				●	●	●	●	●
POLYGONATUM X HYBRIDUM (Solomon's seal)	●				●				●		●	●					●			●		●	●	●
POLYGONUM 'REYNOUTRIA' (Japanese fleece flower)		●				●		●			●		●	●	●					●	●	●		
POTENTILLA X HYBRIDA (cinquefoil)		●	●				●		●				●			●				●	●			
PRIMULA DENTICULATA (Himalayan primrose)			●			●			●	●		●				●					●			●
PRIMULA JAPONICA (Japanese primrose)	●	●	●	●			●		●			●	●				●				●			●
PRIMULA POLYANTHA (polyanthus primrose)	●	●	●	●	●	●			●			●				●				●		●		●
PULMONARIA ANGUSTIFOLIA (blue lungwort)	●		●			●			●			●				●				●		●		●
ROMNEYA COULTERI (California tree poppy)	●						●	●	●				●					●	●	●	●		●	
RUDBECKIA FULGIDA (orange coneflower)		●				●		●	●				●	●		●					●	●	●	
SALVIA HAEMATODES (salvia)			●				●		●	●			●	●		●				●	●	●	●	
SALVIA AZUREA var. PITCHERII (blue sage)			●					●		●			●	●			●				●	●	●	
SANTOLINA CHAMAECYPARISSUS (cotton lavender)		●			●		●		●				●			●			●	●	●		●	
SAPONARIA OFFICINALIS (soapwort)	●		●			●		●			●		●			●					●	●		
SCABIOSA CAUCASICA (pincushion flower)	●		●			●		●	●				●	●		●					●			●
SEDUM SPECTABILE (stonecrop)	●		●				●			●	●		●	●	●						●	●	●	
SIDALCEA HYBRIDS (prairie mallow)			●				●	●		●			●			●	●	●		●	●	●		
SOLIDAGO X HYBRIDA (golden rod)		●					●			●	●		●	●		●					●	●		
X SOLIDASTER LUTEUS (solidaster)		●					●			●	●		●	●		●					●	●	●	
STACHYS GRANDIFLORA (big betony)			●				●	●		●			●			●				●	●	●	●	
STACHYS OLYMPICA (lamb's tongue)			●			●				●			●	●		●				●	●	●	●	
STOKESIA LAEVIS (Stokes' aster)	●	●	●	●			●	●			●		●	●		●				●		●		
THALICTRUM ROCQUEBRUNIANUM (meadow rue)			●				●			●			●				●		●	●	●	●	●	●
THERMOPSIS CAROLINIANA (Carolina thermopsis)		●					●	●		●			●				●			●	●	●	●	
TRADESCANTIA VIRGINIANA (spiderwort)	●		●	●		●			●				●			●					●	●		●
TROLLIUS CHINENSIS (globe flower)		●					●	●	●		●	●					●			●	●	●		●
VALERIANA OFFICINALIS (common valerian)	●		●			●				●	●		●				●	●	●	●	●	●		●
VERATRUM ALBUM (false hellebore)	●					●				●	●		●				●		●	●	●			●
VERBASCUM HYBRIDS (hybrid mullein)	●	●	●				●			●			●	●			●			●		●		
VERONICA SPICATA (speedwell)		●				●		●		●			●			●				●		●		
VIOLA X WILLIAMSII (viola)	●	●	●	●	●		●				●	●	●	●	●	●					●			●
VIOLA X WITTROCKIANA (pansy)	●	●	●	●	●		●		●			●	●		●	●					●			●

Unless cultivar names are given, the information above includes the colours and sizes of all recommended cultivars of the species listed.

Picture credits

The sources for the illustrations that appear in this book are shown below. Credits for the pictures from left to right are separated by semicolons, from top to bottom by dashes. Cover—Evelyn Hofer. 4—Keith Martin courtesy James Underwood Crockett; Clem Harris. 6—"Picking Chrysanthemums by Night" by Susuki Harunobu, Nellie P. Carter collection, courtesy Museum of Fine Arts, Boston. 10—Private collection.11,12,13—Illustrations from Jane Loudon, "Ornamental Perennials", 1843; photos Eileen Tweedy. 16, 17—Gene Daniels from Black Star. 19—Drawings by Matt Greene. 23—Humphrey Sutton. 24, 25—Evelyn Hofer. 26—James Underwood Crockett. 27—Evelyn Hofer except top Peter Hunt. 28, 29—Evelyn Hofer. 30—Harry Smith Collection except right Evelyn Hofer. 31—Evelyn Hofer except centre Gottlieb Hampfler. 32, 33—Jerome Eaton. 34, 35—Humphrey Sutton 36, 37, 38—Evelyn Hofer. 40, 44, 46, 48, 50, 52, 53, 55—Drawings by Matt Greene. 56—Drawings by Rebecca Merrilees and Anna Pugh. 57, 58—Drawings by Davis Meltzer. 59—Drawings by Davis Meltzer and Anna Pugh. 60—Drawings by Matt Greene. 65—Laurie Lewis. 66—Patrick Thurston—Philip Dowell; Jasmine Taylor. 67—Michael Warren. 68, 69—Patrick Thurston. 70—Jasmine Taylor. 71—Michael Warren except centre Harry Smith Collection—Harry Smith Collection except centre Michael Warren. 72—Philip Dowell. 73—Harry Smith Collection. 74, 75—Philip Dowell except right Patrick Thurston. 76, 77—Philip Dowell. 78—Humphrey Sutton. 81, 82, 84, 86, 87—Drawings by Matt Greene. 90 to 151—Illustrations by Alianora Rosse except where otherwise indicated next to illustration.

Acknowledgements

The editors would like to extend special thanks to the sub-editor Mrs. Lizzie Boyd, Kingston-on-Thames, England. They also wish to thank the following: Fumie Adachi, Japan Society, New York City; Agricultural Extension Service, Texas A&M University, College Station, Texas; Agricultural Extension Service, University of Florida, Institute of Food and Agricultural Sciences, Gainesville, Fla.; Bees Nursery Ltd., Chester, England; Mr. and Mrs. Robert B. Branstead, Bethesda, Md.; Miss Audrey Brookes, Wisley Garden (R.H.S.), England; Brother Charles, Mission Gardens, Techny, Ill.; A. F. De Werth, Floriculture Section, Texas A&M University, College Station, Texas; Mrs. William Dines, President American Primrose Society, Redmond, Wash.; Jerome A. Eaton, Director, Old Westbury Gardens, Old Westbury, N.Y.; Professor Charles C. Fischer, Department of Floriculture and Ornamental Horticulture, Cornell University, Ithaca, N.Y.; Fred Galle, Director of Horticulture, Callaway Gardens, Pine Mountain, Ga.; Miss Elizabeth Goodman, London, England; Mr. and Mrs. Reuben Guzman, Danville, Calif.; Jim Hicks, London, England; Mrs. William Hoffman, Bar Harbor, Me.; Keiso Ishizu, Sunnyslope Gardens, San Gabriel, Calif.; Kelways Nurseries, Langport, England; Ted King, King's Chrysanthemums, Hayward, Calif.; Norman Kolpas, London, England; Dr. Leslie Laking, Director, Royal Botanical Gardens, Hamilton, Ontario; Donald Leaver, Bromley, England; Miss Lornie Leete-Hodge, Devizes, England; Larry Leuthold, Extension Horticulturist, Cooperative Extension Service, Kansas State University, Manhattan, Kansas; Mildred D. McCormick, Bar Harbor, Me.; Russell Miller, London, England; Mrs. Samuel Eliot Morison, Northeast Harbor, Me.; Dr. Neil G. Odenwald, Louisiana Cooperative Extension Service, Louisiana State University A&M College, University Station, La.; Robert Schreiner, Schreiner's Gardens, Salem, Ore.; Dr. Thomas J. Sheehan, Department of Ornamental Horticulture, University of Florida, Gainesville, Fla.; Mr. and Mrs. Frank P. Sheppard, East Hampton, N.Y.; George H. Spalding, Botanical Information Consultant, Los Angeles State and County Arboretum, Los Angeles, Calif.; Mr. and Mrs. Walter H. Stryker, Forge Village, Mass.; Alex J. Summers, President, American Hosta Society, Roslyn, N.Y.; Theodore S. Swanson, Swanson's Land of Flowers, Seattle, Wash.; Mr. and Mrs. R. Amory Thorndike, Bar Harbor, Me.; Andre Viette, Martin Viette Nurseries, East Norwich, N.Y.; Mrs. Troy R. Westmeyer, President, Society for Japanese Irises, Stamford, Conn.; Roy T. Whitesel, Silver Spring, Md.; Wayne C. Whitney, Department of Horticulture and Forestry, University of Nebraska, Lincoln, Neb.

Bibliography

*Berrall, Julia S., *The Garden, An Illustrated History.* The Viking Press, 1966.

*Brooklyn Botanic Garden, *Handbook on Propagation.* Brooklyn Botanic Garden, 1970.

Coats, Alice M., *Flowers and Their Histories.* A. and C. Black, 1968.

Collingridge Books, *Pictorial Gardening.* The Hamlyn Publishing Group, Ltd., 1969.

*Cumming, Roderick W., *The Chrysanthemum Book.* D. Van Nostrand Company, Inc., 1964.

*Cumming, Roderick W. and Robert E. Lee, *Contemporary Perennials.* The Macmillan Company, 1960.

*Free, Montague, *All About the Perennial Garden.* The American Garden Guild and Doubleday and Company, Inc., 1955.

*Free, Montague, *Plant Propagation in Pictures.* Doubleday and Company, Inc., 1961.

*Hottes, Alfred C., *A Little Book of Perennials.* A. T. De La Mare Company, 1923.

*Jekyll, Gertrude, *On Gardening.* Charles Scribner's Sons, 1964.

Lanning, Roper, *Hardy Herbaceous Plants.* Penguin Books, 1960.

*Nehrling, Arno and Irene, *The Picture Book of Perennials.* Hearthside Press, Inc., 1964.

*Pettingill, Amos, *The White-Flower-Farm Garden Book.* Alfred A. Knopf, 1971.

Pirone, Pascal P., *Diseases and Pests of Ornamental Plants.* Constable, 1960.

Robinson, William, *The English Flower Garden.* Charles Scribner's Sons, 1933.

*Rodale, J. I. and Staff, *Encyclopedia of Gardening.* Rodale Books, Inc. 1959.

*Shurtleff, Malcolm C., *How to Control Plant Diseases in Home and Garden.* Iowa State University Press, 1966.

Sitwell, Sacheverell, *Old Fashioned Flowers.* Charles Scribner's Sons, 1939.

*Sunset Books, *Organic Gardening.* Lane Books, 1971.

*Sunset Books, *Sunset Western Garden Book.* Lane Magazine and Book Company, 1967.

*Westcott, Cynthia, *The Gardener's Bug Book.* Doubleday and Company, Inc., 1964.

*Wyman, Donald, *Wyman's Gardening Encyclopedia.* The Macmillan Company, 1971.

Zander, *Handworterbuch der Pflanzennamen.* Verlag Eugen Ulmer, 1972.

denotes U.S. publication only.

Index

Numerals in italics indicate an
illustration of the subject mentioned.

Filmsetting by C. E. Dawkins (Typesetters) Ltd., London, SE1 1UN.
Printed in England by Petty & Sons Ltd., Leeds.
Bound by Hazell Watson & Viney Ltd., Aylesbury, Bucks.